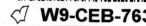
W9-CEB-763

SAN AUGUSTINE PUBLIC LIBRARY
Corazon Aquino : the story of a
B AQU

103289

019353

B
AQU   Komisar, Lucy
       Corazon Aquino; The Story
       of a Revolution

TO RENEW THIS BOOK
CALL 275-5367

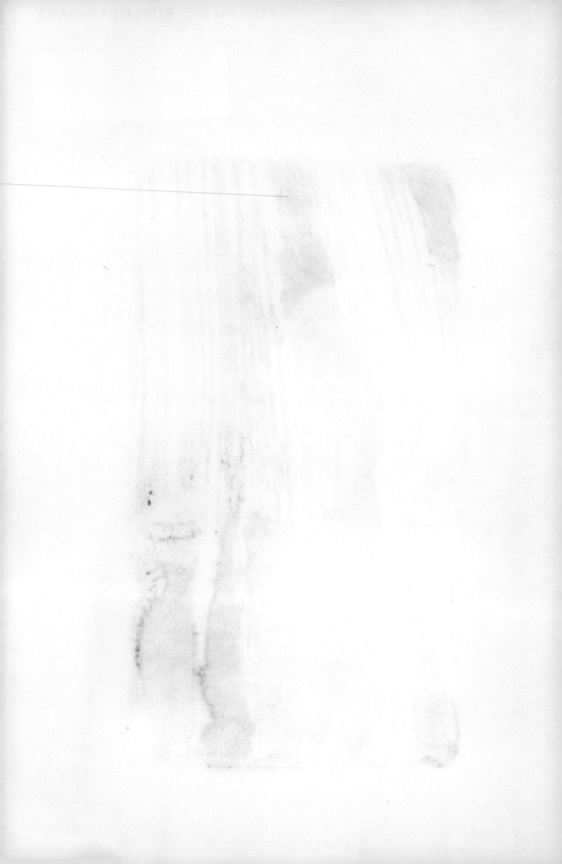

Corazon Aquino

By the same author

Down and Out in the USA: A History of Public Welfare

The New Feminism

SAN AUGUSTINE PUBLIC LIBRARY

019353

Corazon Aquino

The Story of a Revolution

LUCY KOMISAR

George Braziller

NEW YORK

Published in the United States in 1987
by George Braziller, Inc.

Copyright © 1987 by Lucy Komisar.

All rights reserved.

For information address the publisher:

George Braziller, Inc.
60 Madison Avenue
New York, New York 10010

Library of Congress Cataloging-in-Publication Data

Komisar, Lucy, 1942–
   Corazon Aquino : the story of a revolution.

   Bibliography: p.
   Includes index.
   1. Aquino, Corazon Cojuangco.   2. Philippines—
Presidents—Biography.   I. Title.
DS686.616.A65K65   1987   959.9′046′0924 [B]   87–6585
ISBN 0–8076–1171–9

Printed in the United States
First Printing, March 1987

To my parents

Frances and David Komisar

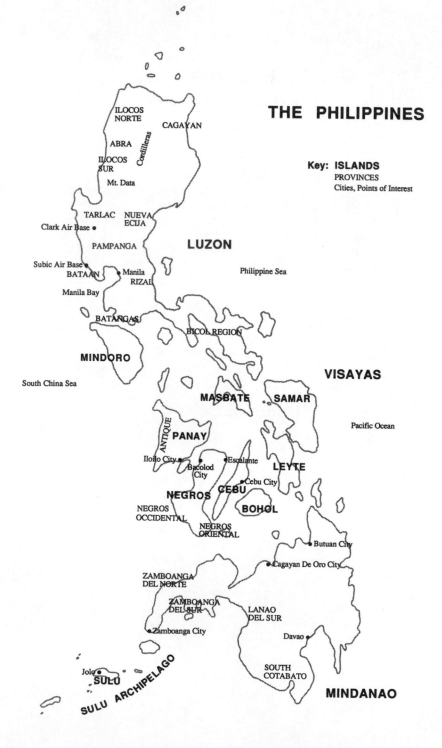

THE PHILIPPINES

Key: ISLANDS
PROVINCES
Cities, Points of Interest

ILOCOS
NORTE
CAGAYAN
ABRA
Cordilleras
ILOCOS
SUR
Mt. Data
TARLAC NUEVA
ECIJA
Clark Air Base
PAMPANGA
LUZON
Philippine Sea
Subic Air Base
BATAAN Manila
RIZAL
Manila Bay
BATANGAS
BICOL REGION
MINDORO
VISAYAS
South China Sea
MASBATE SAMAR
Pacific Ocean
ANTIQUE PANAY
Iloilo City
Escalante
Bacolod LEYTE
City
Cebu City
NEGROS CEBU
NEGROS BOHOL
OCCIDENTAL
NEGROS
ORIENTAL
Butuan City
Cagayan De Oro City
ZAMBOANGA
DEL NORTE
ZAMBOANGA LANAO
DEL SUR DEL SUR
Zamboanga City Davao
SOUTH
Jolo COTABATO
SULU
MINDANAO
SULU ARCHIPELAGO

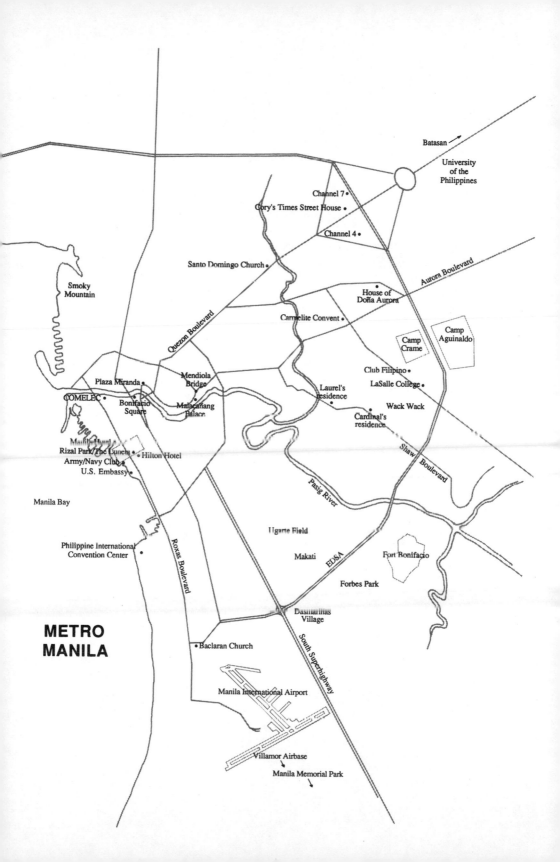

Batasan

University
of the
Philippines

Channel 7 •

Cory's Times Street House •

Channel 4 •

Santo Domingo Church •

Aurora Boulevard

Smoky
Mountain

House of
Doña Aurora

Carmelite Convent •

Camp
Aguinaldo

Quezon Boulevard

Camp
Crame

Club Filipino •

Mendiola
Bridge

LaSalle College •

Plaza Miranda •

Laurel's
residence •

COMELEC •

Bonifacio
Square

Malacañang
Palace •

Wack Wack •

Cardinal's
residence •

Shaw Boulevard

Manila Hotel

Rizal Park/The Luneta •
Army/Navy Club •
Hilton Hotel •

U.S. Embassy •

Manila Bay

Pasig River

Philippine International
Convention Center •

Ugarte Field

Roxas Boulevard

Makati

EDSA

Fort Bonifacio

Forbes Park

Dasmariñas
Village

METRO
MANILA

• Baclaran Church

South Superhighway

Manila International Airport

Villamor Airbase

Manila Memorial Park

METRO
MANILA

Contents

Preface

THIS IS AN UNAUTHORIZED BIOGRAPHY. Cory Aquino refused
to grant any interviews and instructed her brothers and sisters not
to cooperate because, explained the official who handles press appointments for the Cojuangco family, "She is writing her own book."

Her brother Jose "Peping" Cojuangco finally agreed to a meeting
because he is a political figure in his own right.

Some high government officials, and aides and personal friends
of the president were very helpful; others including Vice President
Salvador Laurel would not give interviews. The Aquino family was
extremely cooperative. I also talked with such leading players in the
drama as former Minister of Defense Juan Ponce Enrile and the
archbishop of Manila, Cardinal Sin. There were, of course, dozens
of others who helped provide the substance for this book, including
people who knew her as a "political wife"; those who were jailed
with Ninoy and stood by Cory during the years of martial law;
oppositionists who joined her in the challenge to Marcos; the people
who made the revolution and helped her establish her presidency;
military men who sought to destabilize her and others who defended

her; leaders of the Left and the Right; representatives of business, labor, peasants, and the church; and my colleagues, Philippine and foreign journalists.

The Philippines is an informal society, and people are routinely called by their nicknames in the press and public forums. To capture the feeling, this book follows that pattern. I also call the president "Cory," which is how she is known by virtually everyone in her country.

The quotations and events cited here were gathered from a wide range of sources, including interviews, newspapers, books, and the author's own experience. Descriptions of how Cory felt or what she thought are never invented, but are taken from her comments or from interviews. Source notes in the back refer to quotes or events on the cited pages; footnote numbers were not included in the text in order to avoid interrupting the narrative.

Cory Aquino is an extraordinary world leader, in the true sense of that word. Catapulted into her job by the assassination of her husband, she lacked both the experience and the mind-set of traditional politicians. Her religious commitment to nonviolence and reconciliation made her an anomaly in a world dominated by men who believe that policy must be effected by force. Philippine society is rent by violence—by the political violence of warlords, guerrillas, and troops locked in civil war, and by the social violence of poverty in a society where most people don't get enough to eat and the rich live behind high walls. If Cory Aquino, despite her inexperience and inevitable mistakes, can deal with those problems in her unique way, she will have contributed not only to her country's well-being, but to a new worldview of how leaders should act.

Lucy Komisar
New York City
February 1987

Corazon Aquino

Return

AUGUST 21, 1983. Benigno "Ninoy" Aquino had boarded China Airlines flight 811 from Taipei after a seven-day trip that took him from Boston to Los Angeles to Singapore, across the border to Malaysia, back to Singapore, to Hong Kong, and finally to Taiwan. He had gone the roundabout route partly to see officials from Southeast Asian countries to explain the purpose of his return and also in the hope of shaking Philippine President Ferdinand Marcos's security men.

The Marcos government had refused to renew the two-year passport it had given him when he went into exile in 1980. Never without a sense of irony, he had a phony Middle Eastern passport made in the name of Marcial Bonifacio "Marcial," for the martial law that had led to his seven-and-a-half year imprisonment until 1980, and "Bonifacio" after the military camp where he had been held as the premier figure in the opposition and the greatest challenge to Marcos's rule. He switched between that passport and a Philippine one, secured from a friend in the government, in which he had put his own name. But the security agents were monitoring his movements at every step.

His wife Cory had stayed behind in Newton, Massachusetts, a suburb of Boston, and he called her every day on that homeward journey. Over the phone, they prayed and read the Bible.

In Taipei, he received a phone call from Manila warning him not to come home. He reported the call to his brother-in-law, ABC newsman Ken Kashiwahara, who had met him in Taipei, but he did not say from whom it had come.

He spent most of August 20th talking to the journalists who had arrived to accompany him on the final leg of the trip. The next day, he telephoned Cory at 7 a.m. They talked, and she told him that Armed Forces Chief General Fabian Ver had warned the airlines that Ninoy would not be allowed to disembark and that any airline that brought him in would have to fly him out. Ninoy argued that more likely, because he was a Filipino, he would be arrested and returned to Fort Bonifacio. He told her that if she could get passports, she should take their three older daughters on a trip to Europe before coming home. Cory read the Bible to him. He also spoke to his children, and he cried. When the call was finished, he wrote each child a letter.

Then, he went to the airport to board the 11 a.m. flight to Manila. On the Boeing 767, he gave interviews and moved around the aircraft, shaking hands, talking with anticipation about the welcome he expected, cracking jokes, and telling photographers they had better be quick with their cameras because in a few minutes, it might all be over. He looked over the speech he would give at the airport. He had come, he would say, not for confrontation but to seek a genuine national reconciliation.

He knew a death sentence awaited him, but he would quote Gandhi: "The willing sacrifice of the innocent is the most powerful answer to insolent tyranny that has yet been conceived by God and man." He would warn that a nationwide rebellion threatened to explode into bloody revolution, that many young Filipinos had come to realize that freedom was never granted, it had to be taken. He would urge the people to understand that national reconciliation and unity could be achieved only with justice.

"Subversion stems from economic, social and political causes and will not be solved by purely military solutions," he would say. "It can be curbed not with ever increasing repression, but with a more equitable distribution of wealth, more democracy and more freedom."

4

Ninoy wanted a big homecoming. Opposition leaders had sought the cooperation of leftist groups, who could muster the greatest numbers for demonstrations, but they would not participate. They thought Ninoy must have made a deal with Marcos and that he was tied to the Americans and the CIA. So the moderate opposition, of which Ninoy was a part, transported people from as far as a three-hour drive away to meet him.

Thirty thousand people waited for Ninoy in the parking lot of the modern Manila International Airport. Many of them wore yellow ribbons or shirts, symbolizing homecoming, from the song about the freed prisoner, "Tie a yellow ribbon round the old oak tree." He had asked to meet with five people before he addressed the crowd: his mother, Aurora Aquino; his youngest sister Tessie; and opposition leaders Salvador "Doy" Laurel, Francisco "Soc" Rodrigo, and Lorenzo Tañada. They and the other leaders of the opposition—former congressmen and senators—waited in the VIP room. They could not get through to the field; the doors in the airport had been locked.

Laurel handed Aquino's mother a petition for writ of habeas corpus and asked her to sign it. They were expecting Ninoy to be arrested, and Laurel's law office had the writ prepared to deliver to the Supreme Court.

Just before the plane began its descent, Ninoy went to the restroom and put a bulletproof vest under the jacket of his cream-colored safari suit. He told Kashiwahara, "Don't forget to go to my house as soon as we land and have someone take my belongings to me in prison."

The plane touched down after 1 p.m. and taxied to Gate 8. Three khaki-uniformed soldiers boarded minutes afterwards. One soldier was from the Philippine Constabulary and two from the Aviation Security Command. The AVSECOM men took Ninoy by the arm.

"Where are we going?" he asked.

"Just down, sir."

"I'm coming with him. I'm his brother-in-law," said Kashiwahara.

Stay in your seat," said one of the AVSECOM troops. As Ninoy and the soldiers went out, the journalists on the plane rushed toward the exit door, but they were blocked by men dressed in white barong Tagalog shirts, the traditional Filipino embroidered overblouse.

Ninoy and his escorts walked onto the metal platform at the end of the passenger tube. Instead of going to the waiting room, the soldiers took him down the service stairs at the side of the tube.

The men in white blocked the door so the reporters could not follow. As they walked, two uniformed officers were on either side of him. Two soldiers in civilian clothes followed, and two more stood further up the stairs. Below, the ramp guards and maintenance crew had been ordered away from the service stairs.

Suddenly, one of the soldiers behind Ninoy called out in Tagalog, the national language, "Here he comes."

Another: "I'll do it! I'll do it!"

Then, "Fire!"

Eleven seconds after they left the plane, one of the soldiers turned rapidly, pointed his gun at the back of Ninoy's head and pulled the trigger. Ninoy plunged forward onto the tarmac. Seconds later, four more shots rang out.

Ninoy lay on the ground, blood oozing from his head and neck. Near him was another body, a man in a blue airport maintenance suit. He would later be identified as Rolando Galman, thirty-three, a known robber and killer-for-hire. The government would charge that he was a Communist hitman and that he had assassinated Ninoy.

The escorts and the men in white disappeared. Other soldiers jumped out of a blue AVSECOM van parked nearby and began firing furiously at Galman. Two soldiers threw Ninoy's body into the van, and the vehicle raced out of the field.

Authorities did not inform Ninoy's waiting mother and relatives about what had happened or where he had been taken. Kashiwahara told them Ninoy had been shot, but he did not know if he was dead or alive. They went to nearby Baclaran Church to pray, and then returned home. When they turned on the radio, they learned Ninoy was dead; his body had been brought to the military hospital at Camp Bonifacio. They went to the camp and argued with guards at the gate, who pointed guns at their heads until they finally allowed them to enter the camp and the hospital.

The only high government official who came to the hospital was Defense Minister Juan Ponce Enrile. His face showed astonishment at the sight of the bloody corpse before him. Marcos had asked Enrile to decide where the body should be autopsied and who should be present.

In Newton, Cory could not sleep. She was waiting for Ninoy's call. At 1 a.m.—1 p.m. in the Philippines—she prayed the rosary.

At 2:30 a.m., Cory's oldest daughter Ballsy answered the telephone. It was the Kyodo News Agency in New York.

"I want to talk to Mrs. Aquino," the reporter said.

"I'm sorry, she's asleep," said Ballsy. "Could I take a message."

"I want to verify the news I heard. Mr. Aquino was shot and is dead. What I got from Japan, AP and UPI have conflicting reports. I wanted to check. Thank you very much."

Cory, who had finally fallen asleep, woke up and asked what the call was about.

"Mom, they say somebody has been shot at the airport in Manila and they think it's Dad, and they want to know if we've heard."

Cory got on the phone. The reporter repeated, "We have heard from Tokyo that your husband has been shot."

"Are you sure?" she asked.

"Yes." Had she heard anything?

"No." Cory replied.

UPI and AP called shortly afterward. But the family did not accept the fact of Ninoy's death—they hoped the wound was not fatal—until a friend, Japanese Congressman Shintaro Ishihara, called from Tokyo. He said blood was seen spurting out of Ninoy's head.

Cory told the children the bitter news. They began to cry. She told them it was better their father was dead, otherwise he would be a vegetable; he had always said he would never want that to happen to him. Then she said, "We'd better pray, because there's nothing we can do."

Shortly afterward, her son Nonoy, twenty-three, saw the account of the assassination on the Cable News Network broadcast he had been monitoring all evening.

The Japanese Consul General Takeo Iguchi, a close friend, arrived to offer condolences and aid. By 3:30 a.m. other friends began telephoning and coming to the house. Cory and the children went to church at 6 a.m., then went back to the house to receive more sympathy calls and talk to the newsmen who had appeared. Later that day, she would do four television interviews and talk to numerous newspaper and magazine reporters.

She called her family in Manila and asked, "Do the people know?" She feared that a censorship black-out had hidden Ninoy's death and felt that after all they had gone through since 1972, they had few friends. She was astonished and relieved when her sister told her that throngs of people were coming to view the body. She asked that when she arrived she and the children be given some time alone with Ninoy.

Cory arrived in Manila on Northwest Orient Airlines at 8:05 p.m.

Wednesday after a grueling twenty-four hour trip from Boston. A slim woman of fifty with short, curly black hair, her round, bespectacled face had features that reflected her mixed Chinese–Spanish–Malay ancestry. She was with her five children and former Philippine Senator Ernesto Maceda, one of the opposition leaders who had been close to Ninoy in exile. She displayed little emotion. She went first to see her mother Doña Metring Cojuangco in Forbes Park, a wealthy, walled section of Manila, and then went home to the modest one-story wood frame bungalow on Times Street in the middle class neighborhood where she had lived for twenty years.

Thousands of mourners waited outside the house, and the lines of people who had come to view the body stretched for two miles. The first high-ranking diplomat to pay his respects was U.S. Ambassador Michael Armacost who had been so tight with Marcos that oppositionists called him "Armaclose." Workers who had to go to jobs by day came late at night or early in the morning. Cory was overwhelmed by the size of the crowd, by the display of love for Ninoy. It eased her sadness.

Inside, the house had been cleared of visitors. Ninoy lay in the coffin, still bloodied, his face marked by bruises and a gaping hole made by the bullet that tore through his chin. He was wearing the same bloody clothes he had on when he fell. His family believed the soldiers must have battered him in the van to make sure he was dead. They had not had his body cleaned and dressed, because his mother Doña Aurora had insisted, "I want the Filipino people to see what they have done to my son."

Cory leaned down and whispered to Ninoy that she would continue his work until the nation had freedom and democracy. She had no idea what that would involve. When she kissed him, she felt he was smiling at her. Her daughters told her that they also felt he was smiling.

That evening, Cory had an impromptu press conference on the lawn with the newspeople who were camped outside. She broke into tears twice as she talked to reporters. She told them that Ninoy used to say that courage, like cowardice, was contagious. She said, "If only one or two or three of you can show courage at this time, others will follow, and the truth about Ninoy will come out."

Thirty thousand people paid their respects to Ninoy at the Aquino home. Manila Archbishop Jaime Cardinal Sin came to the house to pray over the body and offer his condolences. Finally, the family decided to transfer the body to the Santo Domingo Church, the family parish, to make the public viewing easier. There would be a march from the house to the church, a few miles away.

Cory led the procession on foot. As it moved through the main business street of the area, passed office buildings, restaurants, and homes, people joined the march. Others lined the route. That day, there were 50,000 people who saw Ninoy's body carried to the church. They chanted his name and sang "Bayan Ko," (My Country), the nationalist song which had become the anti-Marcos anthem.

The body lay in state at the church except for the period that Cory took it to Tarlac, Ninoy's home in the sugarlands sixty miles north of the capital, for two days and nights of continuous masses and prayers. Some 150,000 people came to the small provincial town to view the body. Tens of thousands lined the roads as a motorcade of forty-five cars took the body back to Manila through the towns of three provinces of Central Luzon. Cory was astonished at the numbers and that the people had waited for hours under the hot sun just to glimpse Ninoy's hearse.

She turned down invitations by opposition leaders to rouse the people by bringing Ninoy's body to other key cities in the country. She said Ninoy had done his part, let him rest. The family was also tired, and the logistics of flying the body around seemed too difficult.

The funeral was ten days after Ninoy's death. People had arrived at Santo Domingo Church at 5 a.m. for the 9 a.m. service. Cory stood, composed and serene, under the high dome of the church's apse and looked out at the several thousand people who jammed the rows of dark wood benches. She told the mourners of her last phone conversation with Ninoy. She recalled the shock when she learned of his death and the comfort she drew from the sight of so many people demonstrating that she and her children were not alone and that Ninoy did not die in vain. If she and the children appeared brave, it was because Ninoy would have expected it and because of their faith in God. "Ninoy, who loved you, the Filipino people, is now loved in turn." The mass was carried live by some radio stations.

Then she and the Aquinos and Cojuangcos led a procession that reporters put at two million people in a country of fifty-five million. It began at 10:30 a.m. as the casket, surrounded by wreaths and yellow sunflowers, was placed atop a ten-wheeler truck used because the hearse had been damaged during the motorcades when mourners climbed on top of it. People had started lining the route before dawn.

Cory rode in a Toyota van as supporters followed the twenty miles on foot. The march lasted for ten hours.

Yellow and black streamers were tied to buildings, trees, and concrete overpasses. Crowds also carried ribbons, yellow flowers, and placards with Ninoy's picture. They applauded and chanted Ninoy's name, staying through the heavy rains that drenched the city for a few hours. That night, at the family's request, many of them would turn off their lights, light candles, and bang pots and blow horns in a city-wide noise barrage.

At the grave, people surged forward for a last look at the body, and Cory asked them to keep back. She was exhausted and dizzy from lack of food, but she thought, "I've never fainted in my life, and I don't want to faint now." Ninoy, in the same bloody clothes he wore when he was shot, was finally laid to rest in a concrete vault on a platform at the top of a grassy knoll in Manila Memorial Park at 9 p.m. A bugler played "Taps."

Cory shed tears as she saw Ninoy's body lowered into the grave. Then, the Philippine flag that had draped the mahogany coffin was presented to Cory by Doy Laurel, who was one of the pallbearers.

Afterwards, she was very composed, very strong, thought her brother-in-law Paul Aquino. He had seen her cry only two times, the night she arrived and at the actual burial.

Cory had done all her crying in Newton. She felt tears might upset her children and make other people uncomfortable. And, she believed, when you cry, things do not get done.

Growing Up

MARIA CORAZON COJUANGCO was born on January 25, 1933, the sixth of eight children of Demetria Sumulong and Jose Cojuangco. Both her parents came from families that were rich and politically powerful. Her mother's father was a senator. Her father, "Don Pepe," was a congressman, and his father had been a senator.

The Cojuangcos traced their lineage to Chinese traders from Fujian province who had done business in the Philippines and stayed to intermarry.

The family fortune had been started by Cory's great grandfather, Jose, a Chinese who still wore the traditional pigtail. He moved his family to Paniqui; about ninety miles north of Manila, during the last decade of Spanish rule in the 1890's when the railroad was being expanded northward from Manila. Cojuangco got an allocation of freight cars and filled them with dry goods going to the provinces and rice and other food products headed to the capital. Cojuangco's only son, Melecio, had four sons. One, Jose, would become the father of Cory. Another, Eduardo, would be the father of "Danding," one of Marcos's most notorious cronies.

In Paniqui, they say that Melecio's sister Ysidra, a beautiful, delicate woman with the white skin of a Chinese mestiza, was the girlfriend of General Antonio Luna, the chief of staff of the revolutionary armed forces. They reportedly met because Jose used to give important personages free rides on his railroad cars. In 1899, General Luna was called to a meeting by General Emilio Aguinaldo, his rival in a power struggle, and was assassinated. Because the revolutionary generals had charge of the funds which were used to buy arms and provision their soldiers, it is said that after Luna's death, Ysidra, still in her early 30s, was left with a fortune. The family became moneylenders and accumulated lands when mortgages could not be paid off.

Almost all the lands in the area were eventually owned by the Cojuangcos, who planted rice on most of it. They also had a 15,000-acre sugar plantation that stretched to three towns. The business was handled by Melecio's wife Tecla and Ysidra. Melecio went into politics and was elected to the Philippine Assembly.

The Sumulongs, on Cory's mother's side, were a landed and politically powerful family from the province of Rizal, adjacent to Manila. Their illustrious patriarch was Juan Sumulong, known as Don Juan. He was in his first year of law school when the revolt against the Spanish broke out in 1896 and he joined, becoming secretary of a provincial revolutionary headquarters. After the American victory over the Spanish and the Filipinos, the Philippines became a colony of the United States, which chose to rule through the aristocracy in which both sides of Cory's family were prominent.

Don Juan became private secretary to the Filipino civil governor of the province. Later he was a journalist, then a lawyer, and then a politician. He was vice-president of the National Progressive Party, but lost his attempt for a seat in the 1907 election. He served as a Filipino minority member on the U.S.-appointed Philippine Commission which ran the government.

One of Don Juan's clients was Jose "Pepe" Cojuangco. Pepe courted Don Juan's daughter, Demetria, and they wed after she received her bachelor of science degree in pharmacy. There was a lavish wedding party in Paniqui; guests from Manila arrived on a train loaded with food and drink.

Cory's parents moved to Manila soon after she was born so the older children could go to private school there, and Pepe could attend the meetings of the Assembly to which he had been elected a year after her birth. But she returned to Paniqui with her family on occasional weekends or vacations to stay in the large, square, two-story white stone and wood Spanish-style house across the yard from the tin-roofed rice mill.

The children held parties in the yard, and on election day, her grandmother and Ysidra would slaughter pigs and carabaos—a kind of buffalo—to prepare food to set out there for the voters supporting the Cojuangos' party. It was probably Cory's first taste of politics. Ysidra lived in the house until she died at ninety-three. But Cory's family would not have permitted Ysidra to tell the girl the story of her romance as they sat and ate at the long, white marble dining table of the old house. They were extremely conservative in social mores. Even when the children went to the movies, it was only with a parent or relative or in a large group.

To Cory, her father was a saint—he rarely got angry—and her mother was a disciplinarian and not very forgiving. Don Pepe was very patient and considerate of other people and, unlike most politicians, was soft-spoken and introverted. Cory would take after him. Her father managed the family's Paniqui Sugar Mill and later became president of the Philippine Bank of Commerce; both had been founded by Ysidra and the four brothers. Cory's mother was an enthusiastic campaigner for her husband and son. She would go house-to-house all through Tarlac, shaking hands and making small speeches to the Cojuangcos' followers. Cory, who was the quietest of her sisters, did not campaign.

Cory and her family spent most of their time in Manila, leaving the plantations to caretakers. It was a close knit family. Cory's best friends were her sisters, with whom she attended St. Scholastica's College, a private girls' elementary school run by Filipino and German Benedictine nuns for the children of the wealthy. Her favorite subjects were mathemetics and English, and she graduated first in her class.

Cory remembers meeting Ninoy for the first time when they were both nine years old at a birthday party for his father. Their fathers were friends because they were both congressmen—Ninoy's father representing the first district of the province of Tarlac and Cory's the second; the Aquinos also lived in Manila. Cory's father would become the godfather of Ninoy's younger sister, Lupita.

Their pleasant childhoods were interrupted by the shock of the Japanese invasion. Cory started high school at the Assumption Convent in Manila, but in 1946, a year after the war was over and with Manila in ruins, the family sought more congenial surroundings in the United States.

Cory, 13, was sent to high school at Raven Hill Academy in Philadelphia, a sister school of Assumption Convent. Her parents returned to Manila after a year, but their children remained in school in America. After a year and a half in Philadelphia, Cory transferred to the Notre Dame Convent School operated by the Society of St. Ursula in Manhattan.

Cory was a quiet, shy, unassuming girl; she was serious, bookish, a good student. Her high school yearbook picture caption is a quote from Pope Pius XII: "It is up to you to bring to the life you are entering, to the state you must help to form, an energy of true religious faith." Underneath, the yearbook editor added: "From what we already know of Cory, this might be called a prediction of the future. Beneath her gentle manner lies a friendly disposition and a quiet charm. . . . " She saw Ninoy again at parties when she came home for school vacations, but she was not interested. She wanted to marry an older man.

She then attended the College of Mount St. Vincent run by the Sisters of Charity at a quiet sheltered campus in Riverdale, a wealthy section of the Bronx in New York City. She majored in French and mathematics, thought of becoming a teacher or translator, and was active in the Sodality of Our Lady, a religious society for the study of liturgy. Years later, a classmate recalled, "She was always talking about Our Lady and her faith in religion. She visited the chapel about after every class; she always had her mantilla on." She was known for her charity and courtesy. A blind student lived in her dorm, and she walked the girl to classes.

Cory learned more than academic subjects from her teachers. "The nuns trained us in the traditional values," said a classmate. "That you must never do anything where your husband would lose face. If there was an argument, you gave in, because it's much more difficult for a man to back down than a woman. You never spoke against your husband publicly; you never did anything that would embarrass him."

It was not unusual to find Cory pictured on the society page back home. "Manila vacation," said the headline in the August 15, 1949, *Manila Bulletin* under a photo of her and her sister Teresita, prettily posed with a young niece in their garden. The young Cojuangcos,

14

both students at Mount St. Vincent College, had "arrived recently from the States to spend the summer holidays with their parents." When she was 18, she had a debut at the Fiesta Pavillion of the Manila Hotel, the elegant old Spanish-style premier hostelry of the city.

Cory met Ninoy again when she was home for vacation during her junior year in college. He was a reporter for the *Manila Times* and had won a reputation covering the Korean War. Cory was impressed. He was the most intelligent, most interesting, most articulate young man she had met. She admired his energy and industry. When the vacation ended and she went back to school, they began corresponding. She liked his letters, because they were not "mushy." She would say later that, "As a lover, he's not an emotional person."

"Ninoy was very secretive about the girls he courted," recalled his brother Agapito "Butz" Aquino. "He was not courting only Cory. He was an escort to Imelda at one function. Since he was a popular guy, he was a normal escort for these provincial beauty queens."

Imelda Romualdez, who certainly was a beauty, was a poor relation who spent some time during her teenage years at the home of her cousin, Daniel Romualdez, the speaker of the House of Representatives. His wife Pacing was Ninoy's aunt. Ninoy met Imelda in 1953 when she was a contestant in a beauty pageant. She did not make a hit at parties in Tarlac, because she was too tall a dancing partner for the Filipino men. Pacing Romualdez would call on Ninoy at times to squire Imelda and introduce her to his city friends. They saw each other frequently that year. Imelda would marry Ferdinand Marcos and tell everyone during martial law years that Ninoy had a crush on her.

Cory returned to Manila in 1953 and enrolled in the law school of Far Eastern University; she did not intend to become a lawyer, but was interested in law as a discipline. The university founder and president was her sister Josephine's father-in-law, and his family, the Cojuangcos and two other families owned the university, which had started as a school of commerce and accounting and, like many private institutions, was run for profit. She had started seeing Ninoy regularly and though he asked her to marry him, she said she preferred to wait. But she would stay in school for only one semester.

Cory did not have any other boyfriends. After she was convinced she would marry Ninoy, she did not look at anyone else. Her girlfriends used to tell her, "Cory you led such a dull existence!"

On one date, Ninoy's white Buick convertible was hit from behind by a jeep; the door flew open and Cory was bruised so badly, she had to spend the night at a hospital. When she finally got home, her parents told her never to ride in his car again. Later Ninoy told her, "You fell from that car on purpose, to force me to marry you."

"Ninoy was really running after her, but I knew he was also running after other girls," recalled Doña Aurora, "Then all of a sudden, he told me he'd be asking for Cory's hand."

Cory and Ninoy had had chaperones on their dates; now that they were engaged, it was expected that they could go out alone. But her conservative parents "wouldn't let you alone with your boyfriend even if you were going to get married tomorrow," Doña Aurora said. To avoid the problem, the engagement was short. Cory and Ninoy were married ten days later on October 11, 1954, at Our Lady of Sorrow Church in Pasay City, a suburb of Manila.

It was the wedding of the year between two of the country's most influential families, the land-owning Cojuangcos—already united with the wealthy Sumulongs—and the politically powerful Aquinos. There were 600 guests; President Ramon Magsaysay was one of the sponsors. The wedding breakfast was held at the Manila Hotel. Then Cory and Ninoy left for a honeymoon in the United States. They were both 21 years old.

Roots of Unrest

FILIPINOS LIKE TO JOKE that they lived for more than three hundred years in a convent, then spent the next forty in Hollywood. It is a humorous way of saying that except for the past four decades, modern Philippine history is the story of colonialism.

The Philippines is an archipelago of more than 7,000 islands, with a distance of nearly a thousand miles from north to south. The major divisions are Luzon in the north, the largest island; the Visayas islands in the center, including Panay, Negros, and Cebu; and Mindanao, the second-largest island, and the Sulu archipelago in the south. Although there are some mountainous regions, the climate is mostly tropical.

Filipinos are of Malay origin, with later mixtures of Chinese and Spanish called "mestizos." Explorer Ferdinand Magellan, searching for a new spice route in 1521 in an expedition sponsored by Spain, had landed in the Philippines and been killed not long after in a battle with a local chief. But other Spaniards arrived and conquered the islands. Manila was made the colony's capital in 1571.

The natives had worked their lands communally, but King Philip of Spain parceled out some of the lands to his followers and, asserting the West's concept of private property, conferred ownership in other cases on the "datu," the local nobles. Over time, the Catholic Church also acquired extensive holdings. When local government posts were established, they were often auctioned off. However, the Spaniards also allowed the old ruling class to continue to hold political power and made their positions permanent. The local aristocracy came to collaborate and sometimes intermarry with foreigners, and their descendents became the dominant class. A patron-client relationship of dependency and subordination that had existed before was deepened in the Spanish period. The landowners, officials, and the educated elite, or "ilustrados," often treated the peasants like slaves, imposing on them forced labor, taxes, monopolies, and licenses to travel. Though the Spanish ended slavery in 1692, debt peonage took its place, the result of high-interest loans incurred by villagers who could not pay their taxes. Church friars, who carried out local government functions, were frequently corrupt, charging the natives for compulsary masses and religious ceremonies. The Spanish colony was maintained largely by the Filipino elite; at the end of Spanish rule, there were only 2,000 Spaniards in the country.

After the opening of the Suez Canal in 1869 made travel easier and led to increased trading profits that could finance their trips, many of the upper class intelligentsia went to Europe where they absorbed the liberal and nationalist ideas of the late 19th century. As the Spanish had feared, they promoted reform movements at home, though not yet seeking independence. Educated Malay and mestizo priests also found themselves in conflict with the Spanish religious orders.

There was unrest among the masses, but it hadn't taken an ideological or nationalist form; and they were not attracted by the reformist intellectual movements. Then, in 1892, Andres Bonifacio, of a poor family, met with others of the lower class to organize a revolutionary society to overthrow Spanish rule and help the poor. Their goal was not reform, but independence. They won thousands to their banner and engaged Spanish soldiers for the first time in 1896. The fighting spread, and central Luzon became the center of revolutionary activies.

After the United States went to war with Spain in 1898 it sent Commodore George Dewey to attack the Spanish fleet in the Philippines. According to Philippine historians, the Americans persuaded the Filipino revolutionary general, Emilio Aguinaldo, to back them in their war against Spain by promising independence for his country. The American government has always officially denied this. The Filipinos achieved important victories, and in June that year, they declared Philippine independence, with Aguinaldo as president. The Americans, however, had no intention of keeping their word, and in the Treaty of Paris that ended the war, Spain ceded the Philippines to the United States for $20 million. President William McKinley issued the "Benevolent Assimilation Proclamation," asserting America's intention to remain in the new colony. Supporters of American colonization had varied motivations. Men like Theodore Roosevelt wanted to establish bases for American business and the military. Protestant missionaries saw a target for prosyletization, though the country had already been converted by the Catholics. And liberal reformers wanted to bring civilization to the non-whites. There was also anti-imperialist opposition to taking the Philippines, led by such people as Mark Twain, but it did not prevail.

In 1899, the tensions between the Americans and Filipinos erupted into war.

The Spanish conquest of the Philippines had caused the Muslim inhabitants to retreat to Mindanao and Sulu; they were not subdued until the late 19th century. The U.S. neutralized the Muslims during the war with Spain by persuading them to sign a treaty which the sultan believed recognized American dominance but maintained the Muslims' independence. For Washington, it was an acceptance of colonial status.

The Filipino revolutionary forces were divided. Once many of the wealthy realized the Americans were going to fight, they decided to collaborate. General Aguinaldo was forced to the hills by superior arms and tactics, many of his officers and men surrendered, and he was finally captured in 1901 by the forces of U.S. Commander General Arthur MacArthur. Guerrilla resistance went on for another year, with much brutality on both sides. Tens of thousands of Filipinos died, casualties were very light among the well-equipped Americans.

The Americans set up a governing commission with minority participation by members of the Filipino elite and slowly began to move more of them into administrative positions. Filipinos had the right to vote for local officials, but the limits on suffrage guaranteed that the elite would control those posts as well. Like the Spanish, the Americans depended on the elite to rule the masses and thereby strengthened its power. Some in the elite went so far as to organize a Federal Party urging permanent annexation to the United States. Nationalist attitudes, however, also continued in spite of strict censorship, fines, and jail terms for people guilty of advocating independence.

After the restrictions were loosened, the new pro-independence Nacionalistas contested the first elections to the Philippine Assembly in 1907 and won 59 seats to the 16 of the Progressives, who advocated only eventual independence. The sentiments of the people were clear. The Americans promised independence "as soon as a stable government [could] be established." But in their view, it would be a long time coming.

The Americans' public rationale for colonization—to improve the lot of the Filipinos—was carried out with mixed results.

The Americans publicly emphasized their promotion of education, though this was a benefit restricted largely to the middle class. The wealthy had their own institutions, and the poor could not afford the public schools. There was a crash education program in Tarlac and surrounding areas because it had been a center of opposition and was important as the rice and sugar bowl of the economy. Much less was done in the south.

The U.S. took major steps in public health in the first two decades, especially in the campaign against cholera, which was a massive killer.

Public works projects to build infrastructure such as irrigation, communications and harbors served the needs of the big farmers and businessmen.

The U.S. approach to the land problem was to take the minor step of arranging through the Vatican to purchase some of the "friar lands," which the church had acquired over the centuries, particularly in areas that displayed the greatest opposition to American rule, and they were resold to tenants. However, there was no interest in land reform or cheap credit for the masses of peasants.

The U.S. did nothing to disturb the unequal power relations in Philippine society.

After the revolutionaries were crushed, the Americans turned to the Muslims and defeated them as well. In 1915, the Muslims signed a treaty with the Americans that left the sultan authority only in religious matters.

But the Filipinos wanted independence, and Washington kept insisting the time was not right. The Democratic presidents wanted to move faster toward self-rule, while the Republicans put the brakes on. The Democrats, influenced by the trade unions and the sugar and linseed oil lobbies, wanted to prevent Filipino immigration and economic competition. The Republicans wanted cheap labor to work the plantations in Hawaii and farms in California. There was a push under Woodrow Wilson for "Philippinization," but that was halted under Warren G. Harding. Herbert Hoover vetoed an independence bill in 1930, claiming that the Americans were not finished with their "altruistic mission," nor were the Filipinos ready for self-government. It was passed over his veto, but then the Philippine Assembly rejected it because of internal political rivalries.

Finally, a new law was approved, a constitution modeled on the American charter was adopted in 1935, and the Philippine Commonwealth was launched. The Americans controlled only foreign relations and currency, though they kept their economic privileges, such as the right to own land, which was denied to other foreigners.

The rhetoric of the political parties championed independence, but for most politicians, parties were mechanisms to get into power to enjoy the economic spoils the Americans allowed them. One politician explained, "People went after election to improve their life styles through the public office they were holding." The dominant parties had similar philosophies and platforms—and none of them mattered. A politician joined a party because of family, friendships, regional ties, or attachment to personalities. Switching parties became common. Politicians built up personal followings through patronage and largesse. Some of them kept the local folks in line with private armies. Elections were typically won with "guns, goons, and gold," a phrase which entered the political lexicon. The members of the economic and political establishments made their deals with the local warlords, who proceeded to buy votes, intimidate or kill opponents, and stuff ballot boxes as was necessary to win.

Large elements of the peasantry and urban groups objected to the system, but there was no political mechanism for them to express themselves. Cory's grandfather, Juan Sumulong, said that the parties represented "almost exclusively the intelligentsia and what we would call the Philippine plutocracy, and that the needy classes have no representation in these parties." Their promises of social justice were simply rhetoric.

Most of the population were peasants who worked the sugar and rice fields as tenants under a feudal sharecropping system. In some cases, especially in the large Negros sugar estates, they were worse off as laborers without even the security of a tenancy agreement. Neither tenant nor laborer earned enough to live on, and they were always in debt to the planters, which made them virtual serfs. Those who had managed to hang on to or acquire some land were easily cheated out of it by powerful men who knew how to "fix" titles and win court cases. Traditionally, the division of the crops was 50-50, but if the landlord was powerful, he demanded and got much more. The peasant supplied the tools, animals, and labor, and the landlord's capital was deducted before profits were split. Sugar farmers were commonly cheated on weight and quality, the cost of fertilizer, payment for weeding the fields, and their right to excess sugar and to molasses. Tenants had to pay the owners fees for irrigation, for fish caught on the plantation's streams, even for the use of the hacienda's chapel.

The workers lived in hovels with grass roofs. They had no clean water, no access to doctors, and subsisted largely on rice, root plants and dried fish.

At elections, peasants were forced to vote for the landlord's candidate on pain of ejection. If the landlord lost a precinct, he and his security guards would find out who had voted against him and punish them.

Life for the peasants improved little from the transfer of Spanish to American control and in some ways worsened. The Americans' tariff-free policy favored the export of cash crops such as sugar and encouraged powerful men to acquire more land. Landlords had lived on their plantations. As they began to move to Manila and became absentee owners, as the population grew and land became scarcer in the 1920s, the feudal ties that had protected the peasants began to disappear. Landlords stopped guaranteeing subsistence to tenants, started to refuse them a large enough share of the crop or interest-free loans of rice to feed their families, and began to evict them from farms.

Peasant uprisings occurred in the 1920s and 30s, largely in central Luzon, where the patron-client relationship had eroded and where peasant unrest had historically been strongest. Peasants didn't demand their own land; they asked simply for improvements in the tenancy system—an increased share of the harvest, low interest loans, rice rations, and the right to organize.

For Luis Taruc, who was chief organizer for the General Union of Toilers, a militant union founded in the 1930s, the Cojuangco hacienda and sugar mill was like most others, which he said, "treated their tenants like their carabaos," the water buffalo that also worked their fields. The union sought relatively moderate changes—a representative who would watch the sugar weighing process, and better pay, better food, and better sleeping quarters for the sugar mill workers. Years later, Taruc would recall that he was "nearly killed" while organizing the Cojuangco hacienda workers. In general, those who protested plantation conditions were intimidated by security guards or the national constabulary or local police, had their huts burned, or were evicted and driven away. Owners also promoted company unions that pledged not to strike.

The Catholic Church at that time continued to be conservative, with priests and nuns obedient to the landlords who gave them contributions. The old churches had well-sculptured front-row seats with soft kneeling pews for the family of the hacendero, while the poor sat on hard benches or stood at the back. The union, in an early version of liberation theology, told the workers that Christ had come to earth to crusade for the rights of the poor.

The Americans did not attempt to solve the agrarian problem. On the contrary, they assured that it would continue by putting into power the same landlord class which had held sway before.

The Japanese invaded the Philippines the day after they bombed Pearl Harbor. During the war, the peasant movement spawned the People's Anti-Japanese Army, Hukbalahap in its Filipino acronym, or Huk. By the end of the war, it had 10,000 fighters. Taruc turned to organizing the Huks, and some of his recruits were from the Cojuangco hacienda. With the owners seeking safety in the cities, the peasants, who stayed on the land, planted rice, corn, camote—a kind of sweet potato—and sugar for their own use and served as part-time partisans helping the regular guerrilla fighters. Often, they farmed by day and were guerrilla fighters against the Japanese at night. They lived better than under the landlords. The southern part of the Cojuangco plantation was under Huk control; further south in Concepcion, the site of the Aquino farm, even the town's mayor was a Huk.

When the Americans returned, they pressed the congress to amend the constitution to allow them parity rights with Filipinos in developing agricultural, timber, and mineral lands, (exempting them from the rule that would ban corporations with more than 40-percent foreign participation), in operating public utilities, and in marketing U.S. manufactures. Washington said the Philippines would not get aid to repair the war damage unless it passed the measure, which would be in effect for twenty-eight years.

Most of the landlords and political elites in central Luzon had not resisted the Japanese and many, along with local officials and police, had collaborated with the occupiers. The Americans returned many of the local elites, including the collaborators, to their posts as local officials. The U.S. also gave posts to people who had fought with USAFFE (United States Armed Forces in the Far East) guerrilla units, many of whom had only collected intelligence and waited for the U.S. troops to return, or were simply bandits.

The Huks had looked forward to praise and medals for their resistance achievements. Some Huks, seeking formal recognition, provided lists of their members at the request of American authorities, and the men were promptly targeted for roundups, their names circulated among landlords and employers. U.S. military authorities allowed the people in the USAFFE units to keep their guns and rewarded them, but sought to disarm the Huks, who opposed economic parity for the Americans as well as the permanence of the U.S. bases, both of which would have to be approved by the new congress. Filipino officials appointed by the Americans arrested Huks on charges of refusing to turn in their weapons, communist subversion, and even pro-Japanese collaboration. In late 1945 and 46, police and civilian guards harassed, intimidated, arrested, and killed Huk veterans with the knowledge of the American military police. In one case, a few ex-USAFFE guerrillas came upon more than 100 Huks returning home, surrounded them, disarmed them, and massacred them. U.S. authorities later appointed the commanding colonel as town mayor. Many of the Huks who were killed were also members of the National Peasants Union. Taruc believed that the landlords were also responsible for the attacks.

Agrarian conditions had become worse after the war. The percentage of tenant farmers had risen, and landlords sought a greater part of the profits. Landlords and moneylenders charged as much as 150 and 200 percent for credit. Peasants who protested the rates or sharecropping agreements faced eviction. The government of President Sergio Osmeña forced the landlords to negotiate, and both sides finally agreed to a 60-40 division, but it was not enforced.

Landlords hired guards to intimidate tenants seeking their rights and targeted members of the Peasants Union.

Peasants in conflict with landlords used tactics such as secretly harvesting their fields, holding strikes, petitioning officials, marching, and demonstrating. If a landlord threatened peasants, they would summon aid by blowing on the tambuli, a crescent-shaped carabao horn. Stuttering short blasts of its penetrating sound meant an emergency. Three long blasts meant a big rally and alerted peasants to runners that sprinted through the fields from barrio to barrio with circulars to announce the meeting point.

Landlords with the aid of police, ex-USAFFE guerrillas, and civilian guards intimidated villagers who sought a larger share of their harvest or who joined or organized unions. They accused them of being radicals, agitators, communists, and socialists. The Concepcion municipal council passed an ordinance forbidding peasants from holding meetings without prior official approval. The civilian guards had started as the private army of the landlords. During the American colonial period, they became auxiliary troops for the police, their wages paid by the police and landlords. They were often local gangsters and thugs.

In 1945, peasant leaders joined with worker and leftist intellectual groups to organize the Democratic Alliance on a platform of relief for the homeless, removing collaborators from positions of power, and giving workers and peasants a share of the wealth. It sought a fair division of the harvest, recognition of trade unions, loans for tenants and small businessmen, and an end to landgrabbing and eviction of tenants. It also opposed the grant of parity rights to Americans.

The party's chief issues in the April 1946 campaign in central Luzon were the repression of peasants by the landlords and the government and the corruption of the politicians. During the campaign, the civilian guards intimidated the Democratic Alliance candidates and their supporters. Some party leaders were murdered. Nevertheless, six candidates, including Luis Taruc, were elected. After they won, congress refused to seat them on grounds of election fraud and terrorism allegedly carried out by the Huks. With the D.A. members gone, the parity amendment got its required three-fourths approval by one vote.

On July 4, 1946, the Philippines became independent, and politics took on added importance. It was a world still dominated by the business and landed oligarchy which had been returned to congress. Aside from a general pro-business, pro-American, pro-status quo stance, the parties had no ideological substance—or differences. The two important parties were the Nacionalistas and its offshoot, the Liberals. As before, the middle and lower classes had no influence on choosing candidates or making policy.

The presidential election was won by Manuel Roxas. A collaborator, he had been rescued from the Japanese by U.S. Pacific Commander General Douglas MacArthur, who put other members of the occupation government in prison. MacArthur, the son of General Arthur MacArthur, had become wealthy through his investments in the Philippines; many believed that he favored Roxas because of their business connections. MacArthur and U.S. High Commissioner Paul V. McNutt were behind Roxas's campaign to replace President Osmeña, which was aided by restoring to power, at MacArthur's insistance, the Philippine congress, two-thirds of whose members had also been collaborators. Roxas promptly awarded amnesty to Filipinos who had collaborated with the Japanese.

Repression increased after the elections as government security forces and civilian guards targeted Huk veterans and peasant union members. Several thousand peasants were killed and many more jailed, tortured, or disappeared. Finally, the Huks and peasants organized to fight back. They founded the Peoples Liberation Army, whose members were also called Huks. Luis Taruc became commander-in-chief, the post he had held in the Huk resistance. The army's demands were enforcement of the bill of rights, dismissal of charges against the Huks as well as against police and civilian guards, release of political prisoners, replacement of abusive officials, restoration of Democratic Alliance congressmen, and implementation of a land reform program beginning with a 70-30 distribution and leading to eventual abolition of tenancy. Most just wanted a bigger share and fair treatment.

The fighting between government troops and the rebels escalated. Supplied by the Americans with arms and equipment, government forces shelled and machine–gunned neighborhoods and destroyed villages with mortars, heavy artillery, and bombs and napalm dropped from airplanes. Police and civilian guards arrested and tortured peasants, raped women, destroyed crops, stole food and property, and burned houses. Some local officials required residents to buy passes to allow them to leave town; those traveling without them were subject to jailing, beating, or death. The Huks fought back with rifles, kidnapped and killed local officials, and also destroyed the property of landlords, who again took refuge in the cities.

By 1948 the Huk rebellion had some 5,000 to 10,000 troops. They went to the villages to propagandize, holding meetings and even performing theater pieces and singing songs. That year, President Roxas proclaimed that the Peasants Union and the Hukabalahap were subversive, illegal groups and all members were subject to arrest. The contrast with his amnesty for wartime collaborators was not lost on them.

After Roxas's sudden death in 1948, President Elpidio Quirino granted amnesty to the leaders and members of the Huks. Taruc returned to his seat in congress. However, the police and other authorities violated the truce and continued arresting people and stealing their property. The Huks did not want to give up their weapons which they needed to defend themselves. When Taruc discovered a plan to kidnap him and a relative was beaten by thugs looking for him, he returned to the hills. The peasant movement also went underground; many peasants were prompted by the repression to join the guerrillas.

The Huks got another boost in membership after the 1949 presiden tial election, when President Quirino's men intimidated and killed people supporting Nacionalista candidate Jose P. Laurel, who the Huks had backed in hopes he would be less oppressive. Many of Laurel's angry supporters joined the rebellion. From 1949 to '51, the Huk forces numbered 11,000 to 15,000.

Major Edward Lansdale, the chief of U.S. military intelligence in the Philippines, pressed the anti-Huk campaign, charging the Huks were "Communist inspired" and that their leaders were plotting revolution. (Eight years later, Lansdale, then a colonel, would be sent to Saigon to be chief of the U.S. military mission and then CIA station chief.)

Communists who were active in the peasant movement and among the Huks were indeed some of the important leaders. However, they didn't determine the movement's demands: most peasants were uninterested in their "land for the landless" slogan and fought only for a larger share of the harvests.

Major Lansdale, a former advertising man, advised Ramon Magsaysay, defense minister from 1950 to '53, to use a combination of force and reform against the Huks. Magsaysay acted to clean up the army and the police; they stopped massacring peasants and instead went after guerrillas in the hills.

The 1952 "Hardie Report" commissioned by the U.S. depicted the poverty and injustice of the countryside and recommended sweeping agrarian reform, including an end to tenancy, as the answer to the Communist threat it saw presented by the Huks. The rebellion reached its peak that year, then began to decline. The Huks were tired. They surrendered, were captured or killed, or fled to the mountains, their contact with their supporters in the villages broken, concerned only with trying to survive.

The Communists, who had dominated the Huks in some areas, extended their influence. Taruc broke with them; he says he quit, they claim he was expelled. Magsaysay became president in 1954, winning 70 percent of the central Luzon vote. The CIA directed his campaign, especially the "psychological warfare" division, and contributed massive funds. As president, again with American advice and financial aid, he adopted a policy he said would improve peasants' conditions with a better land-tenure system, easier credit, and technical aid. He set up agricultural extension services, health clinics, and landlord-tenant courts. He built bridges, roads, wells, and irrigation canals. He promised land to Huks who surrendered, though fewer than 250 families got plots. He pledged to reduce rents. He continued his efforts to make the military less abusive. Magsaysay didn't make deep changes in the system, many of his measures were public relations moves, but he provided hope, and his program convinced many peasants to give up their support of the Huks. Peasants began to be free to organize, assemble, and speak out. Tenants got 60 percent of the profits on rice though only half on sugar. They continued to press for fairer divisions of the harvest and cheaper loans.

When the Huk threat was overcome, the Americans pushed a more moderate program than the Hardie Report had called for. Peasants had votes, and politicians made lots of promises to them, but the reforms they adopted were minor and cosmetic, filled with loopholes favoring landlords and excluding lands planted with export crops. None of them dealt with the roots of the problem in the division of land and the system of share-cropping. The complaints of the generations that had spawned the Huks would fester and motivate new generations determined to abolish the land-tenure system.

It was a problem that would be central to the political lives of Ninoy and Cory.

Ninoy

THE AQUINOS TRACED their family history back to before the turn-of-the-century war for independence. The Cojuangcos were not politically strong then, but the Aquinos, also mestizos with Chinese and Spanish blood, were powers of Tarlac province. General Sevillano Aquino, Ninoy's grandfather, was a Filipino hero who fought against the Spanish and was imprisoned in 1897 and condemned to death. He was given amnesty and lived to fight the Americans a year later. It is widely believed in the Philippines that his men carried out the order to kill General Luna. Ninoy's father, Benigno Aguino, Jr., was a sugar planter. Ninoy spent his first three years in Concepcion, where his father leased a plantation he had lost through foreclosure. He moved to Manila after his father was elected to the National Assembly. Benigno Jr. would go on to be minister of agriculture.

The family plantation was one of the targets of Luis Taruc's peasant movement, and Taruc was briefly imprisoned by Ninoy's father when he was organizing the Concepcion farmers.

During the Second World War, the Japanese occupiers made Ninoy's father speaker of the House: Doy's father, Jose P. Laurel, was named president. The Aquinos moved into the speaker's residence near Malacañang, the presidential palace, and Ninoy played in the palace with Doy's younger brother. Their fathers were flown to Japan before the Japanese surrender; a month later, they were imprisoned in Tokyo by U.S. forces chief General Douglas MacArthur. Ninoy and the Laurel brothers, left in Manila, were shunned as the sons of collaborators, and they became closer. Ninoy remembered Doy as his only friend.

Nearly a decade after, when the Americans were pressing a military solution to wipe out the Huks who remained in the hills, Ninoy, who had become press relations officer and trouble-shooter for President Magsaysay, persuaded the president to let him try to negotiate. He wanted a peaceful end to the Huk rebellion. Finally, in 1954, promised amnesty for himself and his followers, Taruc arranged to turn himself in to Ninoy. Taruc explained that he was surrendering to the people, who were demanding peace at any cost. Magsaysay had also promised to institute land reform.

But the armed forces wanted to wipe out the guerrillas and end Taruc's leadership; they did not want him free. Without telling Ninoy, Magsaysay sprung a trap and ordered the military to arrest Taruc when he came down from the hills. Taruc spent fourteen years in military prison. Ninoy visited him in prison and said he was ashamed of what had happened. He offered to send his son to school.

Back from his honeymoon, Ninoy bought some farmland in Concepcion at an auction by the Development Bank of the Philippines whose governor was Cory's father. Conditions were rough while Ninoy cleared the land; so Cory stayed in Manila, and he came home on weekends. Then, some Concepcion landowners, in conflict with the ruling family, urged him to run for mayor. Cory, who had just had their first child, helped in the campaign and learned that the wife of a politician had no privacy. People would troop into their house at all hours. Although she was shy and uncomfortable, Ninoy forced her to campaign in public—even to ride in a carabao cart to promote a less patrician image. Ninoy, at 22, became the youngest mayor in the history of Concepcion. The couple moved from Manila to the sleepy sugar town and set up housekeeping in a big old five-bedroom wood house that got electricity only from 6 p.m. to 6 a.m.

Cory promised Ninoy that she would not have a career of her own, but would spend her time taking care of their children. Ninoy did not want her to play any role in his political life, not even as a loyal adviser. If she ever sought to give advice, he would not admit that she influenced him, especially before a group. She soon learned that she was not supposed to come out the victor in front of other people. It was what the nuns had taught her, and she accepted it. However, she also had to carry out the duties of the mayor's wife, taking sick people to a Manila hospital in the family car, attending wakes—sometimes afterward·she could not sleep—or helping to mediate local family disputes. She relieved her boredom by listening to radio soap operas, becoming a virtual addict. When she went to the town's one movie house, she brought a raincoat to cover the wooden seat and protect herself from the fleas. She picked a pediatrician in Manila to have the excuse of going there once a month.

Ninoy's political connections intervened at this time to pave the way for an important transaction by the Cojuangcos. A large tract of sugar land and a mill near Concepcion in San Miguel, where peasant unrest had continued, was owned by a Spanish company which had acquired it during Spanish rule. President Magsaysay told Ninoy that the Spaniards wanted to get out and suggested he acquire the properties so they would not fall into the hands of a political rival. Ninoy interested his father-in-law, and Cojuangco bought the land with about $3 million in a concessionary loan and loan guarantee from the government. Far from unusual, it was the fashion of the time for powerful families to borrow from the government to finance their private enterprises. Perhaps to put the face of public interest on the matter Cojuangco promised in a letter requesting funds to eventually sell the hacienda lands to small farmers. The agency approved the loan in 1958 subject to the condition that the hacienda be subdivided and "sold at cost to the tenants, should there be any, and whenever conditions should exist warranting such action under the provisions of the Land Tenure Act."

Hacienda Luisita was the largest and would become the most modern plantation on Luzon island. Pepe's brother, Eduardo, had wanted to be included in the purchase and broke with him over the matter, starting the conflict between the two wings of the family.

Ninoy became the plantation's manager and moved there in 1958, while Cory and their two children stayed in Manila. Ninoy told the workers that he was reorganizing the plantation and that they would be partners—that he was in favor of trade unionism and they should organize a union to negotiate an agreement. Ninoy told a close friend and political associate, "If I become president, first thing I will do is give the hacienda of my in-laws away." The tenants got a 60–40 share of the sugar harvest, but they still lived in poverty. Ninoy, however, would set up a little welfare state with free utilities, a high school, scholarships, sewing machines and lessons, and tenant villages with land for vegetable gardening. As on other plantations, a private army of security guards kept order.

During this period, Ninoy did some work for the U.S. Central Intelligence Agency. The Americans thought Indonesian President Sukarno was too leftist and had been supporting a group of rebel officers who sought to overthrow him. U.S. bases in the Philippines and Formosa were used to supply the rebels with arms. Ninoy acceded to a request placed through Philippine President Carlos Garcia to use Hacienda Luisita as a rebel training camp. Then he was asked to infiltrate Indonesia to make contact with the officers and try to get them together with an independent guerrilla group. The mission failed in spite of the backing of CIA bombers and mercenaries whom Ninoy called mostly drunks and racketeers. The coup attempt fizzled, the rebel colonels were arrested, but later released, and the U.S. switched its line and began sending supplies to Sukarno.

Ninoy was elected vice governor of Tarlac in 1959, the youngest man to hold the job. He was making his way up through the rough and tumble of Philippine politics. Ninoy was a political animal; he knew all the techniques and employed them with equanimity. He would say, "If your opponent uses terrorism, I think we should counter by giving our leaders ammunition." He was bright, energetic, fast-talking, magnetic, able to keep political audiences spellbound for hours. He was not intellectual or bookish, but street smart, wise in the ways of ward politics. He was known as "the wonderboy." He was also known as a ladies' man, common among politicians, who liked to flaunt their machismo. Cory knew he had affairs and did not like it. Columnist Max Soliven, who shared a cell with Ninoy for the first months after martial law, told him then, "Marcos hated you so much because he looked at you and saw himself."

Cory did not meddle in Ninoy's politics. His brother Butz, who lived with them in Concepcion for six months, felt she simply tolerated what Ninoy had to do as a politician, which often included feeding hordes of political lieutenants. Ninoy would give no notice and then arrive with two dozen people expecting to be served. There were maids, of course, but Cory was responsible for making sure everything went smoothly. She carried out her duty, but Cory was not the typical politician's wife. She was not overly friendly with political leaders; she did not "kowtow" or butter them up. She was uninterested in social events and stayed home unless she had to accompany Ninoy to a function connected with his political career. She preferred reading, watching movies, and eating out.

Cory did not talk much about politics, but, then, Ninoy usually did most of the talking in whatever group he was. "She was the perfect wife for Ninoy: she was in the background," said his sister Tessie. "Ninoy was always in the forefront, and there was absolutely no competition between them. Since Ninoy was lord of the crowd, you'd tend to forget Cory. But you knew there was somebody minding the kitchen and preparing the food." Years later, Cory would say that Ninoy's male chauvinism had kept her quiet.

After he became governor—again, the youngest ever—in a political reshuffle whereby the elected governor was kicked upstairs, Ninoy and Cory bought the bungalow on Times Street. It was an unprepossessing, undistinguished, ranch-style house separated from the street by a small yard and protected by a metal fence stuck in concrete and covered with vines. A thick, flat, concrete slab attached to the roof reached toward the street and served as a carport. There were only eight rooms, including a big living room which was usually full. People dropped by from 6 in the morning to late at night.

Ninoy commuted to his office in Tarlac by helicopter. As governor, his tasks ranged from running the "black propaganda" campaign against Diosdado Macapagal, successful presidential candidate of the rival Liberal Party, to dealing with the Huks, who were still in the hills creating problems for the government. In 1963, Ninoy changed parties. As a Nacionalista, he had spent a year and a half cut out of patronage and public works projects. Macapagal offered him the Liberal nomination for governor and a hefty budget for Tarlac province. Ninoy took it, explaining it was because Macapagal agreed to provide roads, bridges and other concessions for his Tarlac. He also ended up with a bigger quota for Hacienda Luisita, as well as marketing facilities to export abroad.

When Ninoy ran for governor in 1963, Cory helped campaign. While most of her work was door-to-door, once in a while, if Ninoy could not keep a date to be a godfather or sponsor of a wedding, Cory took his place. In Filipino society, such roles carried great social significance, akin to extending blood relationships. Years later, when

Cory was president, a provincial leftist leader would claim proudly that Ninoy was godfather to his son.

Ninoy became a political opponent of Marcos in 1964 when Marcos defected from the Liberals to the Nacionalista party and was named its presidential candidate. Ninoy had worked out a modus vivendi with the Huks. The group in Tarlac was led by Bernabe Buscayno— "Commander Dante"—the son of one of Taruc's guerrilla commanders. Most of his troops were sugar workers, some of whom lived on Hacienda Luisita. Dante would occasionally take sanctuary there; the roads to the hacienda were guarded by security men, but Dante had no trouble getting in. Sometimes the hacienda managers would provide Dante and his men with medical care. "You cannot say no. There is a clinic there with doctors," said Jose "Apeng" Yap, a close friend of the Cojuangcos who was then a Tarlac congressman. "It was part of our dialogue."

In 1967, after six years as governor of Tarlac, Ninoy sought a seat in the Senate, which was elected on a nationwide basis. After his decision to run, he sold his Concepcion farm to the tenants who worked it and told his relatives that they should do the same, because "the revolution is upon us." He wanted his mother to give her farm away, but she protested that she needed it to support herself. Ninoy said later, "The Huks are a necessary evil: they bring about social change." Ninoy also asked Commander Dante to campaign for him. They would meet in the barrios and the sugar fields to discuss the political situation.

Cory worked hard for her husband's election, visiting almost every factory in Manila. Every day, from 8 in the morning to 4 in the afternoon, she solicited voters at textile, cigarette and assembly plants or at community fiestas: "I am the wife of Ninoy Aquino. I'm sorry he can't be here, so I have come on his behalf." She also traveled to the provinces. She shook people's hands and gave them leaflets, but she didn't give speeches. Ninoy was the only Liberal Party winner, coming in second of the eight senators elected. He was the country's youngest senator.

The late 1960s, in the Philippines as elsewhere around the world, saw an agitation for change, the beginnings of mass movements, a cry for reform, and the threat of revolution. Discontent was evident on Hacienda Luisita, too. Tenants of the hacienda organized in 1966 to compel the Cojuangcos to honor their agreement to divide among themselves the land they had bought. The next year, the head of the land authority wrote Pepe Cojuangco to ask what had been done to implement the agreement. He replied that "it was doubtful whether the Central Bank had the power to impose that condition which was so alien to its function of stabilizing the country's monetary system." The tenants filed a court case through the Ministry of Agrarian Reform.

Students were holding rallies on the steps of the Congress to demand students' rights and to protest Philippine and American involvement in the Vietnam War. They opposed Marcos's decision to send Filipino troops to the war; the troops went, but they were army engineers, not combat forces. Ninoy supported the protests. He thought that neither the Philippines nor the Americans should meddle in the affairs of the Vietnamese. Nevertheless, radical nationalists considered Ninoy an "Amboy," an American Boy, ready to serve U.S. interests. They said he hedged when it came time to take positions on Philippine nationalism and the U.S. bases. He found the Americans useful, and managed to secure a lot of aid money for his province.

There was increasing criticism about Marcos's handling of the economy. Miracles were happening in Taiwan and Korea, but the Philippines, which had been economic leader of the region's developing countries when Marcos came into office, was left behind, still an agricultural economy while the others industrialized. Ninoy articulated the complaints against the Marcos government—its economic failures compounded by massive corruption. He served on a Senate committee charged with investigating official misconduct. He also criticized the growing military budget. Through a Senate committee investigating the Huk situation, he held meetings with some of the guerrilla fighters and concluded that they were not leftist ideologues: they were simply asking for land reform. Marcos accused him of coddling the Huks.

In December 1968, a breakaway faction of the Philippine Communist Party (PKP) founded the Communist Party of the Philippines (CCP), chaired by Jose Maria "Joma" Sison, a University of the Philippines professor, who had been expelled from the PKP because of his advocacy of the Maoist strategy of prolonged guerrilla war. In March 1969, "Commander Dante," who had met with Sison in Tarlac and then joined the CPP, founded the New People's Army as its guerrilla force. Ninoy allowed Dante to use Hacienda Luisita as his training ground and base of organization. Ninoy supplied the rebels with food and medicine and even printed Dante's book of guerrilla rules and regulations.

Ninoy had practical reasons of self-preservation for helping Dante. The NPA was powerful in central Luzon. It had murdered six mayors of one town in quick succession and so cowed the military that they set themselves a 6 o'clock curfew. The hacienda's thousands of acres of sugar cane could easily be set ablaze by the guerrillas. "Political hypocrisy aside," he told a friend, "can you name one central Luzon politician who has not dealt with the NPA whether for sympathy or merely as an act of survival?"

Militant activity grew in the capital as well. Marcos and Imelda, arriving at the Congress in January 1970 for his state of the nation address, were forced to flee demonstrators who greeted them with placards and a cardboard coffin. Police dispersed the crowds with truncheons. A few days later, violent protesters massed at the palace, threw Molotov cocktails into the grounds, stoned buildings and set a truck and a car ablaze. Firemen turned water hoses on them, and troops arrived and repelled the attack. Marcos went on television to denounce the rebellion.

A constitutional convention was convened in 1970 with the aim of replacing the 1946 constitution, drawn up when the country was a colony, with one written by the representatives of an independent state. There was strong sentiment to alter the special, semi-colonial relations with the U.S., including the articles that gave parity rights to Americans in ownership of land and natural resources. Marcos used bribery and cajolery to try to persuade the convention to abolish the two-term limit for presidents, but he had no success.

As the crisis intensified, Marcos appointed his justice minister, Juan Ponce Enrile, to head the ministry of national defense. Bombs went off in department stores, power stations, movie houses and other public places. They appeared to be the work of the Left. On August 21, 1971, unidentified men lobbed two fragmentation grenades at the stage of a Liberal rally in the Plaza Miranda that had been called to introduce the party's candidates for the Senate. Nine people were killed and ninety-five injured; the candidates were wounded, some receiving permanent injuries. It became known as the Plaza Miranda Massacre. Ninoy escaped harm because he had stopped off at a party for his goddaughter, the daughter of Doy Laurel, and arrived late. Later, people would believe testimony that Marcos had ordered the bombing.

Marcos accused the Communists and then Ninoy, because he had not been present. At midnight, three hours after the attack, Marcos suspended the writ of habeas corpus. When he announced the action two days later, he said a Maoist rebellion was underway. Twenty "subversive" leaders were imprisoned in Camp Crame; one was Len Oreta, Ninoy's close collaborator and the husband of his sister, Tessie. The wives or daughters of the wounded candidates campaigned in their places and won all but two seats.

Marcos restored habeas corpus the following January, but there were new bombings. It was a time of violent labor actions, of lawlessness—including police corruption and crime—and of a worsening economy. In 1972, Marcos was in the final year of his second four-year term, his last under constitutional rules. Some people thought he would use Imelda as a surrogate to continue in power. People spoke about Ninoy, Marcos's most articulate critic, as his likely challenger and successor. Ninoy had financed many local candidates the year before to build support for a 1973 campaign.

When the military round-up came on the evening of September 23, 1972, Ninoy was with some members of Congress who had been meeting in room 707 of the Hilton Hotel to discuss a tariff bill. At 11 p.m., the television news said Enrile had been ambushed. They laughed. In truth, Enrile had had his car shot up himself. At midnight, Colonel Romeo Gatan called on the house phone to say he had a letter from Defense Minister Enrile, that martial law had been proclaimed and Ninoy was under arrest. "We're coming up," he said. "Tell your boys [bodyguards] to go so we can avoid a confrontation." Several hundred troops had been deployed around the hotel. Ninoy was the first person to be seized. Then security forces arrested oppositionists all over the country. Marcos announced in an address over radio and television that he had declared martial law. He said it would stop the rebellion, wipe out the rule of the oligarchy and the elite and build a new society. During more than eight years of martial law, over 60,000 people would be jailed and thousands tortured, killed or made to disappear. TV stations and newspapers were taken over or closed; strikes and demonstrations were banned.

Local business groups, including the American Chamber of Commerce, passed resolutions and sent telegrams praising Marcos for instituting martial law because it would mean stability. It also meant more freedom for Marcos's friends and foreign firms to exploit the country's resources. The American-owned companies that grew and packed pineapple marketed under the Dole and DelMonte labels were being sued for illegally acquiring their lands. Peasants had been forced out by deceit and intimidation. After martial law, the suits gathered dust. Filipinos believed the declaration had been issued with the consent of President Richard Nixon. "No president of the Philippines would take such a drastic step without American support," said Apeng Yap. The growing nationalism was seen to threaten U.S. interests, including American bases; now in the middle of the Vietnam War, Washington could not afford to lose influence in such a strategic place.

Ninoy called Cory from Gatan's car and said he was on the way to Camp Crame. Her asked her to pack his clothes and go to her parents' house. Cory went to the camp a few hours later but was not allowed in. At 6 a.m. Ninoy's sister Lupita went to the camp gate and saw Philippine Constabulary (PC) commander Fidel Ramos, who let her enter. She talked to Ninoy briefly, then went back to Times Street to get Cory.

In the morning, military officers singled out prisoners, including Ninoy, from the 800 brought to the camp gym the first night and ordered them to step forward. The men thought they were going to the firing squad. The guards put them in a sealed truck and drove them to a barracks. They were put in a bungalow with boarded-up windows that the military had used as offices.

"We have been given a short reprieve," said oppositionist Soc Rodrigo, who was locked up with Ninoy. "Let us pray the holy rosary." They prayed, then started singing. Rodrigo led them in "Bayan Ko." Then Ninoy asked them to sing his favorite song, "The Impossible Dream." The next day, authorities sent a priest to hear their confessions. The prisoners believed they were going to die and took turns leading prayers.

Everyone in the group but Ninoy and Senator Jose "Pepe" Diokno was released after three months. Ninoy was to remain for most of his sentence in the cubicle in the bungalow in the middle of Fort Bonifacio, a military camp at the edge of Manila.

Cory went to mass daily during the initial months of martial law. Asking God for Ninoy's freedom, she began a period of sacrifice. She forbade the children to go to parties. She stopped going to the hairdresser and buying clothes. She finally ceased this regimen when a priest advised her it was best to try to live normally.

But life was not normal, as she was constantly reminded. She turned off the television whenever the faces of Marcos or Enrile appeared on the screen and was frightened and nervous every time she had to see military officials. She took a tranquilizer before her first visit to Enrile when she sought privileges for Ninoy. Her husband made her promise that she would not cry in front of the children or in public or beg the Marcoses to release him. He did not want either of them to display weakness.

In March, an article by Ninoy that Cory smuggled out of prison was printed in the *Bangkok Post*. Marcos was furious. Ninoy and Diokno were put on a helicopter with a presidential seal, blindfolded, handcuffed and flown to another military camp, Fort Magsaysay in Laur, Nueva Ecija, north of Manila. In Laur, Ninoy was confined to a thirteen-by-sixteen foot cell with a narrow opening in the boarded-up window for ventilation and a neon light that glowed day and night. He slept on a steel bed without a mattress. His clothes and glasses were taken—loss of the glasses caused him terrible headaches—and he was given only underclothes to wear. Afraid his food was poisoned, he lived on crackers and water. Ninoy's belongings were returned to Cory. "He won't be needing them," she was told. She wondered if he were dead or alive.

Cory and Diokno's wife went to see Jovito Salonga, a former Liberal Party senator who was one of their lawyers. "The more aggressive one was Mrs. Diokno," Salonga thought. "Cory was very shy; she hardly said anything." Cory overcame her shyness and, with Doña Aurora, ran from one military authority to another, only to be kept waiting interminably in anterooms. Her lawyers asked the Supreme Court for a writ of habeas corpus. Finally, Cory and her children were permitted to see Ninoy. He was behind barbed wire. His face was pale; he had to hold up his pants with one hand because he had lost twenty-five pounds. When they saw each other, Ninoy and the children started to cry. Cory was dry eyed. She had taken a ten-milligram Librium; the tears came when it wore off the next day. After more than a month at Laur, Ninoy and Diokno were returned to Camp Bonifacio.

Ninoy was a changed man. He had undergone a religious conversion in Laur. A few months later, he wrote Soc Rodrigo that he had asked what terrible crimes he had committed to deserve his fate; he had questioned the justice of God. Then, as he was praying, he began to realize how puny was his suffering compared to Christ's. He heard a voice tell him, "Why do you cry? I have gifted you with consolations, honors and glory which have been denied to the millions of your countrymen." The voice said, "Now that I visit you with a slight desolation, you cry and whimper like a spoiled brat!" Ninoy went on his knees to beg forgiveness.

He knew he was undergoing a test, and he resigned himself to God's will. "In Laur," he told Rodrigo, "I gave up my life and offered it to Him . . . picked up my cross and followed Him." He said that during his long hours of meditation, he had found inner peace. "He stood me face-to-face with myself and forced me to look at my emptiness and nothingness, and then helped me discover Him who has really never left my side; but because pride shielded my eyes and the lust for early and temporal power, honors and joys drugged my mind, I failed to notice Him. There is something providential in the persecution of tyrants," he said. "If only for my conversion, I should owe the tyrant my eternal gratitude!"

Cory was tested as well. A military officer at the camp showed her a dossier of Ninoy's alleged affairs. The tactic made her furious. She knew it was part of a plot to weaken Ninoy by estranging her from him, and it was all the more reason for her to stick by him.

It was a time of bitterness and self-pity for Cory and Ninoy. Those first few years, there was substantial support for martial law among businessmen and some political leaders who saw Marcos as a counter to crime and violence. Some believed his arguments that he would wipe out the oligarchs and the warlords. Cory and Ninoy were angry at the people who appeared to give Marcos the benefit of the doubt and were willing to sacrifice the lives and liberties of his opponents. It was a lonely time. So many were afraid to be seen with her; so few were willing to help them. People snubbed her and seemed to go out of their way to be unkind. She did not tell Ninoy about those slights or of the time she spent weeping or the nights she was unable to sleep. She did not want to burden him with her own anxieties. Even Doña Aurora never saw her cry.

The Church was officially neutral on martial law. Only about twenty of the 110 bishops condemned it. However, at the local level, priests and nuns aware of the suffering of their poor parishioners and the growing human rights violations by the army and paramilitary groups began to sympathize with the radical critics of Marcos's rule. Some would disappear or be killed; others joined the New People's Army.

In 1973, Marcos promulgated a new constitution which changed the system to a parliamentary government and wiped out the limitation on presidential terms. One provision established that the incumbent would have all the power of the president under the 1935 constitution, all the power of the prime minister under the 1973 document, and the power to legislate by decree. There was a parliamentary government, but no parliament. Marcos's constitution allowed Americans to keep their lands by selling them to nonstock foundations which they controlled and permitted foreign manufacturers to sell their products themselves rather than through Filipino distributors.

Ninoy had been held in prison without charges. Finally, in 1973, he was accused of murder, illegal possession of firearms, and subversion. The trial was scheduled for 1975, but he refused to appear before the military tribunal, and after the court ordered him to do so, he went on a hunger strike. Cory called on members of the opposition, university students, and others to attend daily prayer services. She had consulted regularly with opposition leaders on what strategies Ninoy ought to follow in prison, how he could continue in the struggle against martial law, and she met with them every night during the hunger strike.

After thirty-nine days, Ninoy collapsed and was taken to a military hospital. He was emaciated, and his breath had the odor of bile. A priest gave him the annointing of the sick. The next day, Cory told him, "That's enough. The Lord fasted for forty days and forty nights, and you should not fast more than the Lord."

"No," he said, "I can still make it one more week."

"Ninoy, we already announced last night that it's finished," Cory said.

His years in prison were a harsh experience for the sheltered, convent-bred woman. Cory would call the time her "first great suffering," and say it taught her that, "If we are to be real Christians, we have to accept suffering as a part of our life." She said the experience was "the making of the new Cory Aquino." For the first time, she identified with the poor who were ignored, harassed or repressed. Tessie noticed that the years of imprisonment seemed to have moved them both to a higher level of spirituality. They settled down to a prison life that called forth in Cory determination to overcome the humiliations of the system and to carry out the demands of her new role.

Her life revolved around prison visiting days, which were Wednesday and Saturday. The immediate family came on Wednesday from 3 to 5, but Saturday was reserved for Cory. She was required to remove all her outer clothing for a search by a female attendant before and after each visit. She hated that; she felt she had been violated.

In accord with the practice of Philippine prisons, she was eventually allowed to spend the weekends in Ninoy's cell. Making love with him there made her nervous because the room had a videocamera and she had been warned of a one-way mirror and listening devices. On her first conjugal visit, she arrived lugging a big suitcase.

"Why the suitcase, Cory?" he teased. "You're only staying here one night, not one week."

She said nothing, but opened the case and took out a dark blue towel and some rubber bands. She asked Ninoy to cover the intrusive video camera and secure it with the rubber bands. Then she took out a dark blue sheet, and they covered the mirror, fastening the sheet with masking tape.

But she was nervous nonetheless. He told her, "Look, we're married, so what do you have to be worried about?" She replied, "Even if we're married, I still want this to be private."

The children would come on Sunday and sit on the cement floor on mattresses they brought with them. Dim light came through the windows which were largely blocked with plywood.

Ninoy conducted the Wednesday visits as meetings. His relatives sat silent before his rapid-fire talk. Even from jail, he seemed to know more than people outside. For Cory and the others, the visits were like reading an international magazine. He started with world events, followed by national affairs, then he would go to local politics and finally, to entertain them, gossip. They wondered how he got his facts and figures, because the authorities did not initially allow him to have newspapers.

Once in a while, he would ask his visitors to make noise to prevent his conversation being picked up by the hidden microphones he was certain existed. Then he would whisper something to Cory or his sister Lupita. Ninoy, in prison, was trying to keep the opposition alive, trying to make people aware of Marcos's violations of law and human rights. But except for the leftist groups that went underground and distributed mimeographed broadsides, there was little organized protest.

Cory had been in the background during Ninoy's political career.

Now she became his political stand-in, the one person he could confide in and trust to carry out his confidential tasks, to take messages between him and his political allies, often smuggling them past guards in a thermos jug or in her young daughter Kris's clothes. She carried sensitive information that required explanations and responses. Ninoy was extremely inquisitive, and she had to be prepared with detailed answers. He helped train her for the role. He would pose a question and then tell her how to answer it. She said her thirty hours with him every weekend were a political "brainwashing."

Cory became Ninoy's spokesman and conducted press conferences on his behalf. He would dictate the details. One day when he was instructing her to call a press briefing, Cory's face betrayed her displeasure. He whispered to his mother, "She does not like this. She does not like this job, but she has to do it." When Cory asked him what would happen if he were killed, who would take his place, he told her new leaders would emerge.

Cory got help from nuns to distribute Ninoy's statements and to appear in support at the hearings that were held during those years. But she would not forget the clergy who appeared to be too pompous and afraid to speak up for them and other victims of the Marcos regime.

Meanwhile, Marcos sought to wipe out the fortune of Ninoy's political bankrollers, the Cojuangcos. First, he blocked the release of a loan secured to put up a sugar refinery. Then, he raised the capitalization required by banks and refused to allow the Cojuangcos' bank to merge, an option given to other institutions. Danding bought the bank. Marcos denied the family's bus company a fare increase allowed other transport firms, and Imelda's brother, Benjamin "Kokoy" Romualdez, acquired that. Pepe Cojuangco had died and Hacienda Luisita now belonged to Cory and her brothers and sisters. The Central Bank governor wrote them requesting information about what they had done to comply with the agreement to divide the property among the tenants.

In 1977, a military court sentenced Ninoy to death by firing squad for murder, subversion and illegal possession of firearms. Cory cried in public for the first time. The lawyers filed an appeal for a stay with the Supreme Court, and international press reaction was so strong, that Marcos backed down.

Seeking to improve his image, Marcos reestablished the National

Assembly and called elections for 1978. He announced that the martial law ban on meetings and speeches would be lifted for sixty days. He had wanted to liquidate the existing parties, but former Speaker Jose B. Laurel, Jr., elder son of the former president, wanted to preserve his Nacionalista Party, and proposed that Marcos form the New Society Movement, KBL in its Tagalog acronym, to group all his supporters. Doy Laurel ran under that umbrella.

Ninoy and the opposition leaders decided to run a campaign in Manila. He was afraid he was being forgotten; Marcos forces had started a rumor that he had gone crazy, and he thought the campaign would expose the evils of the regime even if the candidates had no chance of winning. They organized Lakas ng Bayan (Strength of the People) with the acronym, Laban, or "fight." Ninoy headed the capital region ticket against a slate led by Imelda Marcos.

Cory was against participating in the campaign. She thought it was a futile exercise and tried to dissuade Ninoy. But he told her, "It only takes a few courageous souls to awaken the people." In the beginning, so few spectators attended campaign rallies that she thought the people did not care. Sometimes they came to a meeting, but hung back in the shadows in fear. Ninoy told her not to lose hope. She saw that he was right; by the end, the crowds were huge. Cory gave occasional campaign speeches, but she did not enjoy appearing in public and set seven-year-old Kris on stage to rally support for her father. The candidates often met at Cory's house where her role was to serve them coffee.

Marcos ordered Enrile to declassify intelligence files linking Ninoy to the CIA, and Enrile accused him of being an agent and also of having changed parties to get Hacienda Luisita. Allowed to go on television from his cell Ninoy admitted the CIA charge, saying he had worked at the request of the Philippine government, a reference to his involvement with the Indonesia colonels' failed coup. But he reminded Enrile that the hacienda had been bought the year before he changed parties, and said, "The minister must have forgotten; it was his law firm that transacted this."

As the opposition's crowds got larger, Marcos became worried and banned the traditional election-eve rallies. The opposition reacted with a call for a noise barrage. The city was in an uproar; it was a harbinger of "people power." People went into the streets to bang pots and pans and boldly made the Laban "L" sign with the thumb and forefinger to the police. Some of them heeded Cory's call to produce a noise barrage outside Fort Bonifacio so Ninoy could hear and feel less alone, but the next day they learned he had not heard a thing. Cory was emotionally worn out when the vote was over. Marcos's party swept the election—Doy Laurel got his seat—but many thought Ninoy would have won in an honest count. "This is the end," she told Ninoy. "It is useless fighting Marcos in an election."

Nevertheless, Marcos began to feel that Ninoy, even in jail, was a profound annoyance and potential threat. In December, 1979, while Ninoy was on Christmas furlough, Marcos offered to free him if he left the country. Ninoy sought the advice of political friends, who advised him to go to America. He decided to go and was back in Fort Bonifacio awaiting Marcos's order for his exile when he felt heart pains while jogging in the prison yard. It took a week for a doctor to arrive; after an examination in a local heart center, during which he had another attack, doctors said he needed surgery. He asked to go to the Baylor University Medical Center in Dallas where a Philippine doctor and family friend had performed a similar operation on his brother-in-law. Carrying out the fiction that this was a medical leave and not exile, Ninoy promised to return when he recovered and not to engage in politics while abroad. In May 1980, after seven years and seven months in solitary confinement, he was allowed to leave the country to undergo a triple bypass operation.

Just before he left, the Agrarian Reform Ministry started a suit against the Cojuangcos for compliance with the Hacienda Luisita agreement signed more than two decades earlier.

After the open heart operation, Ninoy informed Marcos he was prepared to come back, but was told he could stay away as long as he liked. He accepted a two-year fellowship at Harvard University's Center for International Affairs followed by another at the Center for Southeast Asian Studies at Massachusetts Institute of Technology.

The years in Boston were to be the happiest Cory had known, the kind of married life she had dreamed of. She called it Camelot, a second honeymoon. She and Ninoy were together most of the time. They lived in a large Tudor-style red brick house on Commonwealth Avenue in Newton and had a circle of friends from the universities and the Church. The house was across the street from Boston College, a Jesuit institution where their third daughter, Viel, was studying. They also bought a seventeen-acre country estate in Brookfield, which five years later would be put up for sale for $500,000.

The Filipino community welcomed them cordially, but Ninoy did not always appreciate their helpful suggestions. At a dinner party, a Filipino woman said Cory ought to learn to drive. Later, Ninoy told the woman, "Leave my wife alone. I like her the way she is."

Still, he seemed to have doubts that she would acquit herself well in the rarified atmosphere of Boston. She liked to read light best-sellers, and Ninoy told her not to talk about them. "Nobody reads best-sellers in Harvard," he said. He also told her not to discuss the World Series when she was with Harvard folks, because they did not bother with such things. Once, at a party, she asked a professor if it was true that no one at Harvard watched the the World Series. "Of course, we do, but secretly," he replied.

As the exiled leader of the opposition, Ninoy received a steady stream of Filipinos and other visitors. He was hungry for news of what was happening in the Philippines and seemed to know almost as much as he had back home. One visitor was astonished: "He even knew when a general had been transferred to another command."

One of those who visited was Doy Laurel, who would also telephone Ninoy from Manila or Hong Kong with news. Somebody once told Ninoy, "Be careful, you might be fighting Doy later on."

"No, we won't fight," answered Ninoy. "Either I become the president and he is the vice president or he becomes president and I the vice president. That is what we agreed."

"But if he insists on being the president?"

"I'm younger. I'll give in," answered Ninoy.

Ninoy met with Imelda Marcos in New York in December 1980. She accused him of financing squads to assassinate her and her husband. She also showed him a videotape of a reception in which former President Richard Nixon called her "the angel of Asia."

Marcos seemed tired and appeared less in public. There was speculation that he was ill and might soon die. Cory told a visitor, "We have to be very careful with that; we've been hearing the same story again and again. It sounds like it's being fed to us." Her advice was not put forth as social or political analysis, but as common sense.

Usually, Cory stayed out of political talk. Jovita Salonga noted, "In the political discussions around the table, I don't recall that Cory ever made a comment." She would pour coffee, then be gone to attend to the children. But behind the scenes Cory was playing a greater role. During his imprisonment, Ninoy had gotten used to her making statements to the media. In Boston, he would ask her to read drafts of his speeches and instead of just correcting grammar, she would suggest substantive changes.

She and Ninoy developed a new spiritual relationship and a commitment to work for peace and freedom through nonviolence and reconciliation. He wrote that he now had developed a Christian Socialist vision, noting that capitalism cared about political liberty but not much about social and economic equality, while communism valued the reverse. He felt Christian Socialism combined the best of the two systems. Ninoy visited Nicaragua, Cuba, Libya, and Iran to see what had happened to countries that had made a revolution and concluded that nobody would gain from revolution in the Philippines: the social dislocation and devastation would bring thirty years of backwardness. He was convinced the only way to fight Marcos was through parliamentary struggle.

For all her delight at being with her husband, there were some negative aspects of Cory's life in Newton. She was sometimes peeved at having to serve Ninoy's constant stream of guests. When a visitor gave her his underwear to wash, she threatened Ninoy, "Either he goes, or I go." She also suffered from a recurrence of asthma which was aggravated by the cold. Once, a big rain flooded the basement, and Cory, who had never had to do manual labor, emptied the water. The exertion caused an asthma attack, and she told Ninoy, half joking, "I can't stand this life here. If this keeps up, I will have to go home, and you stay in exile."

But Ninoy was thinking of home, too. He felt that he was getting isolated from the Philippine struggle. It was an ordeal for him to be thousands of miles away from the political drama being played out at home. In 1981, Marcos lifted martial law, but he continued to rule by decree, controlling both the parliament and the courts. Marcos announced presidential elections for June, then warned Ninoy not to return home for the contest.

Laurel had become disillusioned with Marcos, and he, his brother and other politicians had organized Unido (United Nationalist Democratic Organization), a coalition of Liberals and Nacionalistas opposed to the regime. Laurel wanted to run against Marcos, and he and Lorenzo Tañada came to see Ninoy in Boston. They agreed that if Laurel ran, Ninoy would return home to manage the campaign. Cory was against the idea. "Doy, I'll never talk to you again if you insist on running for president," she told him. But after another

47

meeting with Ninoy in Tokyo, Laurel changed his mind. It was a show election, and Marcos won a six-year term by an 80–percent majority. Afterward, U.S. Vice-president George Bush congratulated Marcos on behalf of the Reagan administration: "We appreciate, Mr. President, your respect for democratic principles and procedures."

Ninoy saw Imelda Marcos again at the end of 1982. He told her he wanted to return home and gave her his passport, which she promised to renew. He never saw it again. In May 1983, Imelda, who was accustomed to buying everyone, offered him a share of power: "Why don't you come with me to the Philippines and together you and I will be invincible." He said, "Thank you, but no thank you, I've always been an opposition man." Then she offered him a blank check to set him up in business in the U.S. He refused: "I'm a very simple man: I don't have a lot of needs." The third alternative was a threat: "If I can't convince you to come with me or stay here, if you insist on coming home, we will not be able to control even our friends." She said that he would be arrested on his return and that an assassination plot against him had been discovered in Manila. "I'll take my chances," Ninoy told her.

Although Ninoy had always talked about returning to the Philippines on his own volition, he believed he might be forced to leave the U.S. now. He had been warned by the State Department not to engage in political activity, and after the inauguration of Ronald Reagan, things got tougher for him. Secretary of State Alexander Haig had visited Manila in 1981 and promised to go after anti-Marcos "terrorists" in the United States. FBI agents subsequently began harassing anti-Marcos leaders. Ninoy had difficulties re-entering the country after he went to Jeddah; he told friends the Americans were giving him a hard time because Marcos had asked them to prevent him from traveling. FBI agents were once embarrassed by arriving at Ninoy's house while he was being interviewed by Ted Koppel on ABC-TV's "Nightline." Ninoy tried to see President Reagan several times, but was turned down.

Finally, in 1983, he contacted friends telling them he had gotten word his visa would not be renewed and asking if they could help him find another refuge. He said he was considering Spain or West Germany, where he had gotten offers of help. But in those countries, without the large Filipino populations of the U.S., he would have been out of the mainstream, out of touch. He was sure that Marcos was very ill, Marcos's cronies were shipping their money out of the country, and a meeting with a New People's Army representative convinced him that the guerrillas were preparing to move. At this critical moment, he felt he was needed to reorganize the political opposition which was dissipating itself in factional fighting. Finally, he decided to return in time for the parliamentary elections scheduled for 1984. His message would be national reconciliation to prevent a bloody confrontation.

He wrote a letter to oppositionist Angelito "Lito" Banayo saying he had begun to absorb the Gandhian thinking on active nonviolence. He said the moderate opposition was amateurish at the game of violence. If it were to involve itself in such a struggle, it would be eaten up by the revolutionaries, who were experts. He expected he would be jailed if he returned, but thought Marcos's illness meant it would not be for long. His mother warned him that Armed Forces Chief Fabian Ver had reportedly said, "Once Ninoy is in the plane, he's already a dead duck." "They're just trying to scare you," he told her. "Why would they kill me, make a martyr out of me."

Cory did not want him to go. She knew they would have to return, but did not want it to be so soon. She told him that Marcos would not listen to him, that he was completely calloused. "Do you think you are ready for another long term of incarceration?" she asked him.

"This time it won't be so long," he replied. "I have my heart problem, and we can always use that as an excuse." Once he had made up his mind, she knew she could not change it. She and the children would remain in the U.S. Ninoy knew the risks and did not want to endanger his family. Still, Cory hoped the future might not be as dim as she feared. In June, she wrote a haiku that read,

> *The worst of my life*
>
> *is over, I hope.*
>
> *And may the best,*
>
> *please come soon.*

But when she read it to Ninoy, he said, "I don't think you have experienced the worst yet. There is so much we have to do."

Cory was frightened. She talked with a psychiatrist about how to deal emotionally with Ninoy's decision to return and face prison or even death. How could she get through more years like the ones that had followed martial law? She asked if tranquilizers would help. The doctor told her it would be easier, because she knew what to expect. He did not prescribe drugs.

Ninoy's return had originally been planned for August 7, but Enrile sent him a telex asking him to postpone the trip for a month so the military could investigate and foil rumored assassination plots. Ninoy compromised and decided to come back two weeks later.

The day before he left Boston, he held a press conference. At dinner, Cory served him Peking duck, his favorite dish. Neither of them could sleep that night. It was summer, but Cory felt cold, clammy, and nervous, and she put on thick socks.

"You know, this is exactly how I felt after you were arrested, the day of martial law," she told Ninoy.

"Oh, let's not talk about it. I told you long ago this is what we have to do," he replied.

"I just wanted to let you know how I felt," Cory said.

In the morning they went to mass, talked to some friends who had come to bid Ninoy farewell, and then Cory and the children drove him to the airport. They could feel each other's sadness. On the way, he said good-bye to his favorite places. "Good-bye MIT, good-bye Boston." He asked Kris to buy a poster of Boston to hang in his cell at Fort Bonifacio.

"See you in two weeks' time," Cory and the children said as they told him good-bye. "Just call me up at every stop," she said. They were to follow after she packed and closed up the house. Neither of them thought the assassination plots were real.

Ninoy took off from Logan Airport Saturday, August 13, at noon. Eleven days later, his widow arrived in Manila to bury her husband.

The Opposition

NINOY'S KILLING had a profound impact on the country. It was disastrous for an economy already marked by capital flight, factory closings and rising unemployment. The assassination caused a massive hemorrhage of capital: hundreds of millions of dollars were slipped out of the country through the black market by businessmen uncertain about the political future. There was little money left to finance businesses, and many companies were near collapse or went bankrupt. Joblessness increased. Banks closed. The peso was devalued by 00 percent. Prices went up. The popular discontent was palpable.

The situation worsened with the collapse of the world prices of sugar and coconut oil, two of the country's main exports. Economic growth fell to zero percent and then declined even further. Some 70 percent of the population was living below the poverty line. In towns, the poor were squatters in hovels of old wood, tin and cardboard. In the countryside, they dwelt in grass-covered huts. They lacked electricity, water, sanitation. They survived by scavenging, catching fish, digging dirt to sell for construction, peddling in the streets, scratching a few grains of rice out of bad earth, and working as servants in the homes of the rich and middle class, who generally had two or three maids. In Manila, several hundred families lived at the foot of a garbage mountain, called Smoky Mountain, named after the methane gas emitted from the decomposing matter. They spent their days following the dump trucks at the top of the hill and then rummaging through the fetid heaps for bits of plastic, tin cans, and bottles they could sell for pennies. Children and adults dodged vehicles to walk in the streets selling cigarettes, candies, and newspapers to the occupants of cars and jeepneys, the colorfully painted open vans set on jeep bodies that provided transportation to most of the population.

Much of the poverty could be traced to Marcos's policies. In Mindanao, he had promoted the advent of the multinational companies such as the Malaysian-owned Guthrie Corporation, which with $12 million from a World Bank affiliate and the promise of good jobs for local workers, bought or forced more than 500 peasant families off land it wanted to plant with palm oil trees. One former farmer employed there said, "Even though I had only a small farm, our income was enough for subsistence. Now I can't afford to buy vegetables. We want to go back to farming, but we don't have any land."

Since Marcos came to power, some 300 local and multinational corporations, most of them American, had grown to dominate the Mindanao economy. Bishop Antonio Mabutas, former head of the National Bishops Conference, said modern agribusiness had never spelled progress for Mindanao, just profits for the corporate owners.

Filipino business managers outside Marcos's circle also felt oppressed. They were tired of paying bribes and kickbacks or higher prices extorted by trade monopolies. "Nobody can import meat, because there is a group run by Danding Cojuangco," explained Jose Romero, executive director of the Makati Business Club, which included many of the country's premier business leaders. "It has to be cleared by the bureau of imports, and the red tape there perpetuates the monopolies." It meant higher prices for consumers. "Just restore the market system," he said.

With the crisis caused by the assassination piled on top of a corrupt and exploitive economic structure, it seemed hard for conditions to get any worse. Marcos needed to do something to regain credibility. He set up a commission to investigate the airport killings, but it was dominated by his supporters and he disbanded it after it was clear its composition would make any conclusion it came to useless for public relations purposes. In October, another body was established, to be known as the Agrava Board, after its chair, court justice Corazon Agrava. The other members were a businessman and industrialist, a corporate lawyer, a law professor, and the head of a pro-government labor federation.

Cory said she and her family would not cooperate with the board; they did not think justice was possible under Marcos. She also did not think the board could provide security to any possible witnesses to the shooting. Later, she would explain, "Even in the beginning, I wasn't really interested in finding out who did it. I think most of the people know anyway who killed Ninoy. I don't know if there are really people who believe it was Galman [the alleged hitman murdered with Ninoy], but the way I've been hearing it, everyone seems to be convinced it was one of the military escorts. I'm more interested in finding out who ordered it." One theory, reported in the press, was that Imelda and Armed Forces Chief Ver hatched the plot out of fear that Marcos would die and Ninoy, with U.S. support, would lead the opposition to take control of the country. Imelda wanted to be her husband's successor. The board's investigations and hearings would go on through the year, with broadcasts over Radio Veritas, the Catholic radio station, winning rapt audiences.

The U.S., worried about the Communist insurgency, put pressure on Marcos to reform the military; Washington wanted him to replace Ver with Philippine Constabulary chief Lieutenant General Fidel Ramos. Marcos ordered Ver on leave for the duration of the investigation and trial, and named Ramos acting chief of staff. But Ver kept his office in the palace, his command of the Presidential Security Guard and the National Intelligence Security Agency, and his power.

Ninoy's family had been astonished by the massive outpouring of emotion and support for him. They would not accept the idea that Ninoy's sacrifice had been in vain and decided to finish what he had started. Cory said she would support the opposition's efforts but would not play a direct role herself. Other people would emerge to take Ninoy's place. She was often the hostess for meetings of the political opposition, providing a neutral ground and refereeing with the authority she was granted out of the oppositionists' deference to Ninoy's widow.

After Ninoy's interment, there were prayer rallies virtually every night for a month, protesting the killing, calling for the release of political prisoners, and demanding the return of democracy. Family and friends called some of them; sectoral groups organized others. Local political leaders in various municipalities also held meetings. The most active opposition groups were the "sectoral organizations" and new "cause-oriented" groups, not the traditional politicians. These social action and interest groups of students, teachers, lawyers, workers, peasants, and slum dwellers mobilized thousands of people for street marches and demonstrations. Their leaders and the opposition politicians began to work together in a broad political front where ideology was not discussed. They all sought to keep alive the sentiments of outrage and opposition, and the politicians were not averse to promoting themselves in their own communities.

The turnouts were massive. In mid-September, some Makati business leaders and lawyers organized a rally at Ugarte Field at the back of the stock exchange, choosing the financial center to jolt the international community. Makati was the business section of the city. Its high, modern structures contrasted sharply with the rundown buildings in the other parts of town, and it included many of Manila's walled communities where the wealthy lived. The organizers imported 500 people from other areas, because they were afraid they couldn't get enough business district participants. They need not have worried; 100,000 people showed up and shouted for Marcos to resign. People tore up paper and telephone books to throw as confetti from the windows of office buildings. Cory was not there; she was still grieving.

The Makati rallies were repeated every week. For the first time, the middle class, the Makati businessmen, even the traditionally conservative clergy became involved. The mass outpourings to view Ninoy's body and to salute his funeral cortège showed that people had the will and the courage to move into the streets and convinced the opposition they had to continue the mass actions to pressure Marcos.

On the eleventh anniversary of the declaration of martial law, Cory addressed her first mass meeting. She was very nervous, uncertain of what to say. She led a crowd of several hundred thousand at Bonifacio Square in front of the neo-classical Greek main post office building in a pledge of commitment to freedom, sovereignty, and democracy, and to fight united and nonviolently for Ninoy's ideals. But a largely student group marched on Malacañang and eleven people were killed and two hundred wounded in an exchange of gunfire and homemade bombs. The rally had joined the Left and the Center, which would happen again only on occasion. The centrist "yellows" were the middle class, the business community, the moderates and social democrats whose focus was getting rid of Marcos; the "reds" were the trade union workers, students, and nationalists who saw American domination as the country's key problem. Cory tried to bridge the gap between the moderates and radicals, meeting with the Left and appearing at some of its rallies.

On what would have been Ninoy's fifty-first birthday, November 27, tens of thousands of people rallied downtown at the Rizal Memorial Park—the site of a large grandstand and a favorite place for political meetings, known popularly as "the Luneta"—to hear mass and listen to speakers call for Marcos's resignation. Many wore the yellow T-shirts and headbands that were to become the symbol of the movement; yellow streamers fluttered over their heads; yellow balloons bobbed above the crowd. The crowd chanted Ninoy's name and then sang happy birthday to him. A street theater company portrayed Marcos as a Dracula-like "King of Darkness." Cory thanked them all for the "most extraordinary birthday gift in the world." She said, "You cannot tell how much loneliness has been relieved by this outpouring of love by so many people." She added, "I hope Marcos listens to us and resigns." That afternoon, the radicals—this time demonstrating separately—gathered more than 30,000 adherents at Bonifacio Square.

The rallies would continue sporadically over the next two years. The phenomenon came to be known as "the parliament of the streets." Cory was not one of the key "street parliamentarians," but she was in demand as a speaker and appeared at many of the events. In the months after Ninoy's death, she gave dozens of speeches and hundreds of press interviews. She told the public that Ninoy's death would have no meaning unless it spurred them to action against the dictatorship. Her speeches were largely accounts of her suffering and quotations from Ninoy. At the Makati Rotary Club in December, 1983, she read Ninoy's speech about democracy and the need to speak out against one-man rule which he had written in 1977 as his final statement before the military commission that was trying him. She called on the listeners to have courage and not be afraid. In January, Butz led a long march "from Tarlac to [the Manila Airport] tarmac." When the military said the protesters could not march to the airport, live radio appeals and phone calls to activist groups roused masses of people; the military let them proceed.

Cory's first important political decision was whether to boycott or participate in the 1984 vote for National Assembly—the election that Ninoy had returned home to contest. A group of business and professional people collected signatures of important community and political leaders, including Cory, on "A Call for Meaningful Elections" and sent it to Marcos. It listed six conditions for their participation, including repeal of the presidential power to make laws, repeal of repressive decrees, general amnesty and release of political prisoners, authority for the parliament to approve important appointments, declarations of martial law, and suspensions of the writ of habeas corpus, and procedural electoral reforms. The demands were not met.

The Aquino family was divided. Butz and his sister Lupita Kashiwahara, along with the organizations of the social democratic and radical Left, supported a boycott. They thought participation would legitimate the Marcos regime and that honest elections were impossible.

Cory postponed announcing her decision until after the national convention of PDP-Laban (the Philippine Democratic Party had merged with Ninoy's Laban) because, she said, "through the years of martial law, I have developed an aversion to unilateral decisions that are, one way or another, imposed on people whose lives are affected by them." By delaying her announcement, she could take other views into consideration. But she had already made up her mind. She told a political ally she would elect participation because, "This is the form of struggle Filipinos can accept." It was the way Ninoy would have done it.

Finally, in a ten minute talk on Radio Veritas, February 29, Cory asked listeners to understand the position she was taking. At no time in her life had she felt more alone than in the past few weeks when she tried to come to a decision. She had spent hours in meditation and prayer and had repeatedly consulted the advocates of both sides. "I for one wish with all my heart to avoid the suffering and pain that violence will inevitably bring," she said. "More than anything else, the fear of violence is what weighs heaviest in my heart." She had seen that the majority of people were for participation, because the path to reconciliation and national unity through elections was the only way by which the violence she abhorred might be averted. Participation was not an "act of surrender," she said. She called on the opposition to keep its options open and to prepare to participate actively in the election. Then she added, "Mine is only one voice. I speak not as a political leader."

The next day, she appeared with other opposition leaders at a rally at Ugarte Field and urged voters to go to the polls. She told them that if Ninoy had boycotted the 1978 elections, "we would not have known that so many of our countrymen were supporting the opposition, as evidenced by the noise barrage of April 6, 1978." She said, "It is unfortunate, but I cannot please everyone. I decided what I thought Ninoy would do in the same situation."

Cory was invited to campaign throughout the country and went to major towns and cities. She got used to writing speeches and appearing before crowds who greeted her with banners of yellow. Most of her talks were about her life with Ninoy. She would close by saying that if he were willing to suffer and sacrifice his life, they also had a duty. She acknowledged ruefully that while she was improving as a public speaker, she had not learned to use humor: "When I crack a joke, people sit still, as if it were another one of my sad stories." Reporters began to ask her if she were thinking of running for office. "No, I don't think I'm cut out for it," she replied. She told one interviewer, "When Ninoy was alive, I was just a wife and mother. Now I am a widow and mother. There are many, many Filipinos more intelligent than I and who are recognized political leaders. I speak for just one person—Cory Aquino."

The election was held May 11. Opposition candidates won fifty-nine out of 183 seats. They estimated they would have won twice as many had the election been honest.

No central opposition organization developed, but the movement continued. On August 21, 1984, statues of Ninoy were dedicated at the site of his murder at Manila International Airport and at the Santo Domingo Church, where Cardinal Sin celebrated mass with 200 priests and ten bishops. The Cardinal called for national unity and reconciliation between the opposition and the government. Sin, a genial, portly man with the face of a Chinese mestizo, who had become archbishop in 1974 at the age of 46, had taken a conservative church aligned to the wealthy and powerful and seen it move toward a concern for the poor and oppressed. "Where do we go from here?," he asked. "Where are all the mass actions since the death of Aquino a year ago leading to?" The Cardinal, who understood well the morass of Philippine politics and self-serving ways of opposition leaders, answered, "The option of a new political alternative must lead to a unity beyond the reach of personal ambitions."

Cory told the 5,000 people who had packed the church and spilled outside, "It has been a year of justice delayed, but it has also been a year of courage and sacrifice by the Filipino people. It was the year of the people's victory over themselves, over their timidity before their rulers, over their fear before their oppressor's might."

After the service, crowds lining the streets cheered and honked car horns as Cory led a four-hour march from the church to a rally at the Luneta. Yellow streamers flew from the buildings and trees. Supporters continued to arrive from march gathering sites around the city until close to a million people were massed at the park. The men who had been detained with Ninoy marched under a special banner, "Cell Mates of Ninoy Aquino."

In September, police—in ironic but brutal symbolism—attacked marchers commemorating the declaration of martial law with truncheons, tear gas, and water cannons. Marcos was angry that the rallies and demonstrations were creating panic in the business community, especially among the multinationals. He hoped that force would scare off the rank and file. Two people were shot dead and dozens injured. An "indignation rally" was called, led by Butz and other leaders of the "parliament of the streets." Security forces turned water hoses on them and attacked with truncheons, rocks, and smoke bombs. Cardinal Sin denounced Marcos and called on him to stop the "saturnalia of sadism and violence" by the security forces. He asked the middle classes to stand with the students and workers. However, Sin did not call for the dictator to step down. He said his policy was one of "critical collaboration."

In October, the Agrava Board released the results of its eleven-month investigation. All but the chair concluded that a military conspiracy was behind Ninoy's assassination, and they named Chief of Staff General Fabian Ver, three other generals, twenty-two military officers, and one civilian. Agrava herself said she did not think Ver had been involved and cited only a general who was the former AVESCOM chief and six of his men. Cory said that the chief conspirator had been left out of both versions. "Wasn't Ninoy's assassination a political decision of the gravest import so that no military man, no matter how high in authority, would think of making that decision on his own? Can Mr. Marcos, in Ninoy's words, 'wash his hands of my blood'?" She said that from the time of his arrest, everything that happened to Ninoy had to be cleared with Marcos—from his detention and trial to the conditions of his release. "Are we now going to believe that the assassination of Ninoy was planned and executed without Mr. Marcos's foreknowledge or expressed approval?" She argued that Enrile and the military establishment that detained Ninoy had done so on Marcos's order, that the president had directed transfer of his case to a military tribunal, and that the tribunal had been under Marcos's control. She said, "Justice is not possible while Marcos is still in power."

Back in the U.S., President Reagan, campaigning for a second term, declared, "I know there are things there in the Philippines that do not look good to us from the standpoint right now of democratic rights, but what is the alternative? It is a large communist movement to take over the Philippines." He said, "I think that we're better off, for example, with the Philippines, trying to retain our friendship and help them right the wrongs we see rather than throwing them to the wolves and facing a communist power in the Pacific." The opposition was shocked and dismayed.

The "parliament of the streets" carried on. In 1984, Cory decided that Ninoy's birthday celebration should not be so political. She would have preferred only a mass at Santo Domingo Church. "People will be too tired always attending rallies on his death and his birthday. This time let's give the people something," she said, and organized a celebration with singers and musicians. She was afraid the attendance at the mass rallies would dwindle and Marcos could make an issue of the reduced numbers. She asked participants to bring canned goods and old clothes to give to the poor and to political prisoners. But people wanted to demonstrate, and they did. Seven marches set off from around the city to meet at the Luneta where tens of thousands celebrated Ninoy's fifty-second birthday with a mass, cheers, firecrackers, sirens, and a noise barrage.

In spite of Cory's hesitation in playing an activist role in the opposition, people transferred to her the role Ninoy had carried. And finally she accepted it. Cory's eldest daughter Ballsy tried to explain the change that came over the new widow. "A lot of people don't understand my mother and what happened to her. When we were growing up, she was always in the kitchen. She was always with us. Her role was really with the children. She knew where her place was. But when my father died, everything changed."

"Cory Aquino became a real Cory Aquino only when Ninoy died," said Ninoy's sister, Tessie. "Everybody had to notice her, because Ninoy was gone."

The Candidate

SUDDENLY, Cory was faced with another political task. Rumors were spreading that Marcos's poor health, or increasing international pressures, might force him to call an early presidential election, before the scheduled end of his term in June 1987. Though he denied it, Marcos, was believed, correctly, to be suffering from systemic lupus erythematosus, a cyclical degenerative disease that attacked his kidneys and left him increasingly weak. Speculation grew as he sharply reduced his public appearances.

Washington was becoming embarassed by the repressive actions of its ally and worried about his failure to contain the communist insurgency that threatened the stability of the American air and naval bases in the Philippines. It was leaning on Marcos to reform the "crony"-dominated economy, the abusive military, and the corrupt political system. Committees in both houses of the U.S. Congress were holding investigations into Philippine use of aid funds and proposing cuts in military assistance. The International Monetary Fund (IMF) was making it clear that it would not grant new loans without moves toward economic and political stability.

The Candidate

A plethora of opposition leaders waited to take Marcos's place. The problem was to forge opposition unity around a single candidate. The people who had organized the call for reform before the legislative elections set up another group. They feared that the fragmented opposition would not be able to unite if the sudden departure or death of Marcos opened the way to a presidential vote. Following months of informal talks, in November, 1984, they set up a "convenor group" of people who would not be viewed as candidates, but who could bring together potential candidates to agree on a selection process. The convenors were businessmen Jaime "Jimmy" Ongpin, former senator and civil liberties leader Lorenzo Tañada, and Cory. Many of the meetings were held at her house. She rarely spoke, but when there was a conflict among the various political personalities, she would step in and restore stability, if not harmony, by calling on the need for unity.

At the first meeting, Tañada turned to Cory and said, "Why do we have to go through this whole thing? Why don't you be the candidate?" She promptly dismissed the idea. "I don't think I should be the one," she said. "I will play the role of unifying the opposition any way I can."

Eleven potential candidates were invited to sign a declaration of unity: all but Laurel, head of Unido, now the most important opposition party, and Eva Estrada Kalaw, head of a conservative faction of the Liberal Party—and a cousin of Ninoy—signed. Laurel and Kalaw thought the accord could block their own chances. Laurel said he had problems with a paragraph calling for the removal of U.S. bases. Kalaw said the process was undemocratic. Laurel had been preparing for the presidency for years; since Ninoy's assassination, he had traveled around the country several times and built up a political machine. In a country that thinks in terms of political dynasties, he felt it was due him to follow the path of his father. Shortly after the agreement was signed, the convenor group agreed that if an election was announced, it would organize a convention of parties and cause-oriented groups to choose a candidate.

In December, Cory noticed a newspaper account that opposition leader Neptali Gonzales, who was dean of the law school at the Far Eastern University, had suggested she run for president. He thought only she could end the squabbles on who should lead the divided opposition. She later recalled it as the first public mention of the idea. "Please stop your crazy ideas," she told Gonzales.

"Are we going into politics?" Doña Aurora asked her.

"No, I know what this is," Cory replied. "We can attend rallies, but after we attend we can go home peacefully. If I'm president, I don't think I can ever sleep with the problems in my head."

At Christmas time, she visited several leading political prisoners, including a rebel priest, a former government executive, and a former college president to discuss the political situation and begin a dialogue.

Laurel meanwhile sought to recover the initiative for Unido by setting up the National Unification Conference to choose a candidate. He sought to mute the criticism that it was organized to. annoint him by stepping out of the chairmanship and giving equal representation to all parties, but he still controlled it.

"We badly need a minor miracle," Cory said as she appealed for unity."

The trial of Ver and his co-defendants began February 22. It would last for seven months. The case was heard by a three-member court which Marcos appointed. The prosecution failed to introduce evidence against the defendants, and the court ruled out whatever incriminating testimony slipped through. The judges ignored the eyewitness account of a passenger who told how she saw one of the military escorts shoot Ninoy on the plane's steps.

The NUC conference was scheduled for March. Cory was invited and wanted to go, but the convenor group and signers of the unity declaration pressured her not to go. They said it would be a proclamation of Doy Laurel. Jovito Salonga, head of the left faction of the Liberals, told her, "We have a ring with a precious stone. You are that precious stone. By attending the meeting, it would be like giving away the precious stone. But we leave it to you to decide." Her unhappiness at their refusal to let her seek unity between the two groups brought tears to Cory's eyes, and she wiped them with her handkerchief. The day before the convention, she ran into a woman law professor who gave her some pointers on how to be more assertive in dealing with men.

The NUC decided to attempt to set up a selection process for delegates to a national convention to choose a candidate. But after the meeting, Cecilia Muñoz Palma, a member of parliament and former Supreme Court Justice who had been made NUC chair, aroused Laurel's ire and suspicions, when she told the regular Monday morning journalists' roundtable at the Manila Hotel, "If there's one who could unify the opposition, it is Cory, if she would agree to be a candidate." There were angry reactions from the Laurel camp.

Cory was angry, too, at the convenor group's insistence she not go to the NUC meeting. "I feel like I'm being manipulated," she told Soc Rodrigo. "I don't like it." They were treating her as Ninoy's wife who used to serve coffee, she thought, even though the circumstances had altered altogether. A few days later, Cory told Tañada and Ongpin that she wished she could be regarded as a person in her own right rather than as just Ninoy's widow. Ongpin advised her to be more assertive.

The convenor group met the next night. She spoke for an hour without notes. "When I joined this group," she said, "I thought I would be a unifier, and now I find myself just part of one faction. If this is going to be the case, I'd rather pull out of the group. If you want me to stay in this group, I want to play a more key role." She said she was being ordered about. When it came to what she wanted, they all clamped down on her. They were inflexible.

"Look," she said, "You people are probably all smarter than I am. You may even be right 95 percent of the time. But I think that maybe 5 percent of the time I may have some of the right answers. And I am not going to allow myself to be coerced into not doing something I believe I should do. You always say I am very important to you. If I'm so important, why can't I do what I want to do? I cannot be useful unless I can have my independence." She added, "We seem to forget that it is Marcos who is our enemy, not one another." The emotion of the moment caused tears to fill her eyes again. She felt that that evening was a turning point for her.

The group pleaded with her to stay on and gave her a mandate to negotiate with Palma on unity and devise a formula for selecting a candidate, provided Palma was given a similar mandate. Palma got NUC approval the next day.

In late March, Marcos dropped out of sight. "The flu," his spokesman said. "A virus." The opposition smelled a snap election, an election held before its time.

A month later, Cory reported to the convenor group that she and Palma had agreed to have Unido, the Liberal Party, PDP-Laban and a meeting of cause-oriented groups each choose a candidate. A convention with delegates from each of the groups would make the final choice.

But others were beginning to call on Cory to run. She told them,

"Have pity on me. I think I have already done my share, and if it comes to a question of paying one's dues, I think I have more than paid mine." At a meeting in April, the convenor group and the NUC agreed to support a single ticket.

The U.S. was watching developments closely and pressing Marcos. In May, CIA Director William Casey arrived in Manila. The local press reported that Washington wanted early elections. A new mandate would promote confidence in Marcos's government and strengthen it against the insurgency. A month later, former U.S. Ambassador Michael Armacost, now Undersecretary of State for Political Affairs, arrived and reportedly also told Marcos that early elections should be held, but Marcos stated the elections would be as scheduled, two years later.

In May, Laurel offered Cory Unido's vice presidential nomination. She declined, saying it conflicted with her effort to unify the opposition. In June, a Unido convention named Laurel its nominee; it was clear he had the support of most traditional opposition leaders. The other parties held off picking a candidate because of internal conflicts, but they promised to choose quickly once an election was announced.

Meanwhile, the cleavage between the Left and the moderates was becoming more pronounced. In January, when the convenor group had decided to hold a convention to choose a candidate, the parties involved agreed to broaden the participation by including the mass-based and sectoral groups, but they asked, "Who do we talk to? There are so many." Lorenzo Tañada, Pepe Diokno, and Butz Aquino were directed to form an umbrella group, and they put together the founding conference of Bayan, an acronym for National Democratic Alliance; the word meant "nation." The leftist leaders, who had been organizing workers, peasants, students, and clergy in anti-Marcos resistance for years, had a network of cause-oriented and sectoral groups, but had agreed to share the leadership of Bayan with the smaller sections of the opposition. A third each would come from the Left (also called the national democrats or nationalists), the social democrats, and the liberal democrats. But, the Left did not keep the bargain and elected leftists to more than half the executive; the moderates responded by pulling out and forming Bandila, which meant "banner," and was the Tagalog acronym for "Nation One in Spirit and Purpose." It was headed by Butz Aquino. The congress declared it would endorse either Cory or Salonga for president.

Some of Cory's friends cautioned her against being used by the Left, and she turned down an invitation from the leftist Nationalist Alliance for Justice, Freedom and Democracy to speak at a rally on the second anniversary of Ninoy's assassination. She said she had already agreed to speak at another event, the Bandila rally. The year before, both groups had demonstrated together.

Cory went to mass at the Santo Domingo Church on the morning of August 21; then she and her supporters marched the nine miles to the rally in Makati. Laurel had just finished speaking when the first "Cory for President" banners were unfurled. The leftist demonstration went on across town. Attendance figures for each ranged from 20,000 to 50,000, depending on who was doing the counting.

Later, Cory told a press conference that the moderate opposition was offering an alternative to the Communists seeking Marcos's ouster. "We know that we cannot possibly have the Communists taking over. It will be shifting from one authoritarianism to another," she said. "If the moderates are not successful, I have very little hope for a peaceful transition."

Public dissatisfaction with Marcos had grown, even among moderate businessmen who had initially cheered martial law as a defense against leftist disorder. Increasingly, people in the opposition came to believe that only Cory roused public faith that could unite the opposition. There was widespread suspicion of Laurel in the opposition. Though he had been close to Ninoy during his exile, he had run on the KBL ticket in the 1978 elections and had not broken with Marcos until 1982, when he resigned from parliament saying it was useless and a rubber stamp. He was a conservative, traditional politician with a reputation for opportunism.

Pressures continued for Cory to accept a draft. She was the favored candidate of many opposition business leaders and industrialists. But in September, she told radio listeners that asserting her own candidacy would conflict with her efforts to unify the opposition. "Perhaps it would be better not to mention my name anymore," she declared. "Get organized, not for Cory Aquino, but for the good of the nation, which is the unseating of Mr. Marcos who is responsible for all of our hardships."

"What do I know about being president?" she asked her long-time friend, Flory Aguas.

She was indeed not acting like a candidate. Questioned about her economic program, she told the Management Association of the

Philippines that she was only a housewife and not well-versed in economics, but she believed the government should be honest, credible to the people, and not spend more than it earns. A business friend told her later, "Cory, please don't underestimate yourself."

She thought that the decision would never have to be made, that people were think of her for the snap election, but that it was more likely that local elections would take place instead in May '86. She prayed, "Please Lord, please make us have local elections."

But her relatives were already gearing up for a campaign. Her brother Jose "Peping" Cojuangco, her brother-in-law Paul Aquino, and her cousin Emigdio "Ding" Tanjuatco started the core of an organization, "without her knowledge," Tanjuatco said. They began getting in touch with political friends, screening names to determine coordinators for each province, drawing up a financial plan, and setting up a primitive intelligence and security mechanism. A few times she walked into Cojuangco's office when the group was meeting. They tried to be evasive, but they guessed she knew what they were doing.

Meanwhile, the convenor group was worried that Laurel was undermining the unity effort. It organized Laban ng Bayan "Struggle of the People," a coalition of the other opposition groups, to force Unido to negotiate and launch another candidate. Cory endorsed the group, but was not actively involved in its formation.

At a meeting of the board of directors of the Ninoy Aquino Foundation, newspaper publisher Joaquin "Chino" Roces said to her, "If you are not going to be the candidate, you have no right asking somebody else to be the candidate if the people want you."

She was silent.

He continued, "Suppose the people want you to run? What would be your answer?"

She replied, "How do I know that the people want me to run?"

He would soon prove it. One day in October, half a dozen people sat sipping coffee and talking about the political situation at the Taza de Oro, a simple restaurant looking out on Manila Bay. None of them were political leaders or involved in the groups then meeting to find an opposition candidate. They included Roces, who had been detained with Ninoy at Camp Bonifacio and saw his newspaper closed during martial law, and a former bank president, a hotel consultant, and other businessmen. They wanted Cory to run for president and wondered how many others in the country felt the same way. It was the beginning of a "Draft Cory Aquino for President" drive that aimed to gather a million signatures on a petition to convince her to run.

In mid-October, "Cory Aquino for President" opened its headquarters in the Plywood Industries Building owned by Roces's brother. Volunteers were sent to find signatures among people leaving churches, shoppers at public markets, office workers, and commuters waiting at rapid transit stations. When Laurel asked her about the campaign, she told him it was done without her encouragement. And when people asked her if they should put their names on the petition, she told them "My family and friends are not signing."

A week after the campaign was announced, Cory was at the Century Park Sheraton Hotel lunch of Sigma Delta Phi, the alumnae association of a Michigan-based sorority, to give a speech entitled, "My role as a wife, mother and single parent." Over lunch, the women asked if she would run for president.

"I do not seek any political office," she replied. "However, your question is one which I cannot answer definitely for now."

"What if there is a draft?" they asked.

"There is no such thing as a draft in this country, only typhoons and strong winds!" she quipped. She added that two conditions had to exist before she decided, first that Marcos call a snap election, and second, that the signature campaign collect a million names endorsing her candidacy. She did not think she would be considered in a regular election nor that Marcos would call a snap vote. She also felt people would be afraid to sign—one million signatures would be impossible to raise. Other people were not so sure. PDP-Laban and Bandila announced Cory as their nominee.

One day she walked into the Cojuangco Building office where her relatives' quasi-secret campaign group was meeting and asked, "When a certificate of candidacy is filed, does the income tax return have to be filed with it?"

Tanjuatco was delighted. "I like it when you talk that way!" he replied.

In October, U.S. Senator Paul Laxalt, representing President Reagan, visited Marcos, who indicated that there might be an early election. Laxalt told him it was a good idea.

On the evening of November 2, Cory relaxed by watching tapes of "Falcon Crest" and "Dynasty," then took some allergy medicine and went to bed. She was not to get much sleep that night. Ballsy woke her at 1:30 a.m. to say Ken Kashiwahara was calling from San Francisco. Kashiwahara told her Marcos, interviewed by David Brinkley on NBC television, had informed U.S. audiences that he would order snap presidential elections.

The next morning, Palma phoned to say she would call a meeting of the political leaders. Cory remembers, "That whole day was so confusing, as I went from one meeting to another, I felt that I could no longer escape what was becoming increasingly inevitable."

Later in the week, someone showed her a survey that indicated most people did not understand the concepts of justice and freedom; what they cared about was jobs, food, and housing. She thought to herself, "My God, how do we reach out to our people?" On Sunday, November 10, she asked a priest to answer that question. She wondered if the people realized that Marcos had caused their suffering and that the opposition could give them a better life. The priest told her it was necessary to personify ideas such as justice and freedom to the people, and that a candidate needed to be very different from Marcos.

Cory began to realize that it would be hopeless to get the other prospective candidates together. She would have to run; otherwise, she would blame herself for not having tried, and she would always ask herself if she could have made a difference. At dinner that night, she told her children and son-in-law how she felt. She said she would say the same to Laurel. Her children did not want her to run. "Why do you have to be a martyr like Dad?" asked her older daughters.

The next day, she went to an all-day retreat at the convent of the Sisters of Perpetual Adoration—the Pink Sisters. She prayed for Marcos and Laurel and for the people connected with Ninoy's assassination. As her candidacy had become more and more possible, the convenor group had stopped inviting her to its meetings. On the day Cory went to the convent, the convenor group met at the Club Filipino, a traditional center for the opposition that had been the home of the nineteenth century reformist intellectuals, and endorsed her as its nominee.

The next morning her mind was clear. She told Doña Aurora she had decided to run, that she would never forgive herself if she did not accept the challenge. "I do not think Marcos will let us win," she said. "We will try. This is a challenge I cannot run away from anymore."

She wanted to talk the matter over with Laurel, who was then on a two-week visit to the United States speaking to Washington officials and Filipino communities about the elections. Laurel arrived home November 13; Cory, Doña Aurora, Butz, and Lupita went to the airport to meet him. They talked that evening at Times Street, discussing the current political situation and how they could work together in the future. They agreed to consult each other. Cory told Laurel that she had thought things through and that the candidate they should offer the people was someone who had both moral leadership and was clearly a victim of the Marcos regime.

Then she said, "Doy, I hope we don't quarrel, because this would really upset my mother-in-law so much. She always reminds me that the Aquinos and Laurels have had this very long-standing friendly relationship, and I remember, Ninoy would tell me that right after World War II, when classmates and friends just abandoned the two of you, you gravitated toward each other."

What followed in the next weeks was a test of wills. Cory would say, "I'm really running." Laurel would say, "I asked you before if you were interested and you said no. Now I've already gone through all the organization." But he would add that he did not want a fight between the Aquinos and the Laurels. In his mind, he was preparing to give in.

Cory did not want Laurel for vice president. She did not think that Laurel met the standards required to run on a platform of moral leadership. She thought he would be unacceptable to her supporters and lose her votes, especially from the cause-oriented groups. Some of her advisors thought that she should take him for practical reasons—he had an organization.

At an NUC meeting November 15, there was a discussion of whether the NUC or Unido would be registered as the "dominant opposition party" in the election. Laurel accused Palma of seeking to overrule the body's decision and register the NUC. He lost his temper and shouted at her that she was dictatorial. He was suspicious of her loyalties; she was supposed to be neutral, but he had received reports that she was committed to Cory. The party listing was important for a man who staked his future on the power of a political machine. The dominant opposition party had the right to name poll watchers, an important organization building block. It afforded prestige to local leaders and protected their candidates; none of the opposition parties trusted the others to tally their votes honestly.

When Cory heard about the blow-up, she was very upset and

went to see Palma. The incident was another turning point for her. "That's the reason why I cannot accept him as president," she said. "That's why I really cannot." She decided that she would not let Laurel be the candidate. Unity talks collapsed.

Cory told friends how the decision whether to run for president weighed on her. "The tremendous responsibility scares me," she told Soc Rodrigo. "I feel it's a heavy cross on my shoulder, but I can't afford to drop it." One day Rodrigo and Palma took her to the Carmelite Sisters for prayers. "Pray for me," she asked them, "because I have this very big problem. I need divine guidance."

As she was trying to make up her mind, she had a recurring dream that she had visited a church and looked into a casket she thought held Ninoy's body. But it was empty. She believed that Ninoy had been reborn in her.

Cory finally took the decisive step. She called the family together and told them she would run for president. "We must present someone who has been a victim. I may not be the worst, but I am the best known." On November 18, the Laban ng Bayan coalition announced that it was supporting Cory's candidacy. Five days later, Cory and Doy met again; she told him she was determined to run.

The conflict heated up as Cory's backers accused Laurel of being overly ambitious and hungry for power, not very different from Marcos. His people countered that Cory was inexperienced and unqualified to be president. Many of Cory's advisers shared her view that he should not be on her ticket. Some thought he would drag her down; others coveted the spot for themselves. But Palma and Rodrigo urged Cory to take Laurel as her vice-presidential candidate. "What is your alternative?" Rodrigo asked. "There will be two opposition candidates." She argued that her advisers told her that even if there were two opposition candidates, she would win.

Cory went to bed at night praying, "Ninoy, please, have mercy on me. Help me."

Roces called Cory the night of November 25 to say "I just want you to know that at this very moment we have reached the million signatures." She said thank you; she was grateful, but that she would not make an announcement of her candidacy until Marcos announced snap elections.

She went to Tarlac for a mass and rally on Ninoy's birthday two days later. She told the crowd of more than a thousand, "I've been asking the people to be involved—but not in the Cory Aquino for President Movement—and now that they are involved, I cannot just tell them to stop." She repeated what Ninoy had said: "I will never be able to forgive myself if I live with the knowledge I could have done something and didn't do anything. This is what is in my heart and mind." She said she knew they had grown impatient waiting for her to declare her candidacy, but asked them to wait until Marcos signed the election bill. But, after the rally, she told the people across the table at lunch at Hacienda Luisita that Laurel had been trying to persuade her to support his candidacy, but he did not realize how determined she was to run. A few days later, she agreed to accept a formal presentation of the one million signatures.

When she met with Laurel again November 30, she told him, "Doy, I know it is very difficult for you to accept my candidacy because I am a woman; but it seems that the public perception is that I can generate more votes than you." She offered him the vice presidency, and he said he would think about it.

At church the next afternoon, she told Ninoy and God, "If you are trying me, I just want you to know I'm about to collapse. I've been taking all these trials. You better help me soon." The one million signatures were blessed, and she thanked her supporters, adding, "If I were a traditional politician, I would be very happy standing before you tonight. But I am not and so I am very nervous when I think of the difficult days that lie ahead." She looked out at the 4,000 people who carried yellow banners and placards that said, "We love Cory," and "Cory, you are our only hope." She said she would make her decision after the bill was signed. "I assure you, you will hear what you want to hear." The crowd erupted into applause and cheers of "Cory, Cory, Cory"; people pressed around her, wanting to touch her, or shake her hand. They lighted the night with candles on the walk to her Times Street home where the signatures, tied with yellow ribbons, were formally presented.

The next day, the court that was hearing the murder and conspiracy case against Ver and twenty-five others handed down its verdict: not guilty. It supported the defense claim that hitman Rolando Galman had shot Ninoy on Communist orders. A thousand people marched through Makati to denounce the verdict with signs that said, "We shall not forget and forgive the killers of Ninoy" and "Prime Suspect" under Marcos's photo. Another group marched on Malacañang and burned an effigy of Marcos at the foot of the bridge leading to the palace. Protesters banged pots and exploded firecrackers; cars dragged tin cans. The streets were bright with burning tires.

Cory was not surprised at the verdict. "My number one suspect is Mr. Marcos," she told a press conference. "Since he was not even mentioned among those accused, it's really not of much concern to me whether one or all would be acquitted." She added that the verdict validated her decision not to participate in the investigation. Ver had been suspended after his indictment, but Marcos took him back at once and announced a reorganization of the military. It would turn out to be merely cosmetic. That same day Marcos signed the bill setting the election date as February 7. Cory dispatched Lupita to tell Laurel she would declare her candidacy the next day.

Cory made the long-awaited announcement at a press conference in Makati, December 3, at the auditorium of the Mondragon building, a modern white concrete and glass office block owned by one of her supporters. She said the major issue of the campaign was credibility—that Marcos had none. Asked her qualifications, she said, "I will probably give more than a million Filipinos hope that I can bring about change." To the charge of inexperience, she said it was true, she had little training, but experience was not the answer: Marcos had too much experience.

Her comments on the U.S. bases were conflicting. She would respect the agreement on their existence till 1991, but she would work for their eventual removal and would not allow any other foreign bases on Philippine soil. However, she also said she wanted to be flexible. "Who knows what will happen between now and 1991? I'd much rather wait for developments and act accordingly. I don't want to be rigid in my stand."

Her economic program would aim to solve the problems of hunger and poverty. She would work to establish credibility and integrity to attract local and foreign investment. She said she hoped to convince the insurgents to return and reject force as the way to achieve change. "All they have to do is pledge allegiance to the republic and denounce all forms of violence."

Responding to a question, Cory said she had offered Laurel the vice presidential slot. "We are still talking."

Cory noticed that every time a question was posed, she could see the opposition leaders with her become tense. She felt that if they could rush up to the stage to help her with notes, they would do so. After she answered the questions, she saw them sigh with relief. She told herself she would soon scold them for having such little faith in her. When she stopped talking, her supporters in the audience let loose their emotions; they cheered, cried, and chanted her name.

Marcos caused her some embarassment by getting a local judge to order, the day she announced her candidacy, the expropriation of Hacienda Luisita and its division among tenants and farmers.

After the press conference, Laurel said he would meet with Cory to continue talking about a single opposition slate, that her announcement had not prejudiced their talks. But then he canceled the meeting, angry when he learned of her statement that he was considering the vice presidency. Opposition businessmen, political leaders, and others continued to try to get them together. There was also U.S. pressure on Laurel to take second place on the ticket. Washington had preferred Laurel for president, but acknowledged the power of the emotional support for Cory.

Laurel suggested to Soc Rodrigo that, since they had exhausted their human resources, they leave it to a higher power. "Let us go to Cardinal Sin and give him two slips of paper, "president" and "vice president." Then we will kneel down and pray and draw lots who should be the candidate," he told him.

When Rodrigo told Cory of the plan, she smiled, "My goodness, why should we draw lots on a matter like this?"

By Thursday, December 5, Cory and Laurel were talking again. Laurel had agreed to the vice presidency.

The next day, she called the Laban ng Bayan coalition to a dinner meeting at the Cojuangco building. "May I invite you to a press conference with Doy Laurel at the house of his brother on December 8. We will make an announcement you all have been waiting for."

That morning, Butz Aquino, answering questions following a speech before a conference of Islamic organizations, was asked whether there was agreement. He replied that most probably there would be an Aquino-Laurel ticket. Laurel reacted to the premature announcement with fury the next day. He had gone to his beachhouse in his home province to rest without telling his party chiefs or even his wife of the decision, but had planned to do so before the announcement. When he got the newspapers with Butz's comment, he rushed home to find his house filled with worried party leaders. Laurel responded to their consternation by denouncing the "purely speculative" and "malicious" report he had agreed to accept the vice presidential slot. His party leaders demanded that if he took second place, he had better get well-defined terms—jobs and candidates for local elections.

Cory and Laurel met Saturday night. He made a final effort to get her to run as his vice president, but when it was clear she would not budge on the presidency, he asked that he be appointed prime minister and be given the cabinet post of his choice, that a quarter of the other cabinet jobs go to Unido people, that he be consulted on all appointments, that she honor his commitments for nominations in the 1986 local elections, and that if the snap election was called off, Cory endorse him in the regular election.

At 2 a.m., Cory called Emanuel "Noel" Soriano, secretary of the convenor group. "May I ask you to call everybody we invited to the press conference and tell them not to go, because I'm not going. I'll explain it later this morning." At 7 a.m., Cory and Soc Rodrigo went to see Laurel at his house. "Why did you not tell me before you wanted to run?" he said to her, unburdening himself of his resentment. "Had you told me from the beginning you would be amenable to being the presidential candidate, I would not have involved myself. In fact, I was asking you if you had any desire, I would step aside. But you said no." He set his final terms for an accord. "Now I am asking you to run under Unido, because it is the only political party that has the chance of being the dominant opposition party."

Cory replied that she did not want to have any party, she wanted to be above parties.

"All I ask is that you place Unido on your certificate of candidacy," Laurel said. "On your banners you can place all the parties you want." She refused, and the meeting broke up.

Back home, Cory and the Laban leaders listened to Laurel's announcement on the radio. He said Cory had initially agreed to run on the Unido ticket which was the only way to guarantee—in a field with several vice presidential candidates claiming to support her—that her votes be counted for him, but that she had backed out.

She in turn told her advisors that Laurel had delivered a list of demands that "if I had accepted would make him president of the Philippines." They were indignant. "They're blackmailing us." However, they finally agreed to Laurel's demand for a cabinet post, promised best efforts on the prime minister's job which was up to parliament, pledged to give Unido thirty percent of cabinet jobs if individuals were acceptable, and to consult on minor appointments. They agreed that Cory would not run in regular elections, but refused the other demands.

Cory was desperate. She blamed some of the older politicians like Salonga and Tañada for being too hard-headed. "What's happening? Am I in control or not? It's my life." She told them, "I am going to meet the press. I want blanket authority to come to terms with Doy Laurel on my own." They backed down. Now, the only issue was whether she would run under the banner of Unido. She told the journalists waiting under her carport that she had declined to run as a Unido candidate, because she had been endorsed by Laban. But she said that the coalition had agreed to list the ticket under a Unido-Laban ng Bayan coalition.

Laurel rejected the new proposal, saying the election code banned candidates running under two parties. He said now Aquino would have to be his vice presidential mate. The general secretary of Unido, declared, "Doy's humility has been abused."

That evening, Cory went to visit Cardinal Sin in his sprawling white villa. She sat across the table from him in his office. "Your Eminence, I have prayed over this. And I have made up my mind. I will run."

"Cardinal, Ninoy is inspiring me," she said. "It seems that he is talking to me, telling me that I should run." She said she had gotten this message while she prayed at the Pink Sisters convent.

He told her, "I would like to know the conditions by which you are running. Do you have a political machinery?"

She said she had none.

"With whom are you going to run?" the Cardinal asked.

She said she could not run with Doy Laurel.

He replied, "Cory, you cannot do it alone. You are a housewife. You have no political party, no poll watchers, no national organization. You should run with a party because then you have a machinery. It is foolish to run if you are going to lose."

She replied, "Your Eminence, before I came here, I made up my mind. Whatever you tell me to do, I will do."

Monday, December 9, Laurel filed his petition for candidacy, blaming Cory's advisers for the collapse of talks. "If she had negotiated alone, we would have reached an agreement," he said. Indeed, Tañada, Salonga and PDP-Laban leader Aquilino Pimentel were trying to keep her from running on the Unido ticket. Salonga and Pimentel wanted to be her running mates. Laurel said he was still open to reconciliation and named representatives to meet with her people. Cory filed her papers two days later, but each side put out feelers to the other.

That same day, Marcos's KBL had a convention and with little enthusiasm chose Arturo "Turing" Tolentino as his vice presidential running mate. Marcos picked him to add credibility to his ticket. Tolentino had been a senator until martial law dissolved the parliament and then was the only KBL candidate to win in Manila during the National Assembly elections in 1984. Marcos appointed him foreign minister in June 1984 but fired him nine months later for publicly criticizing the president and his policies. He had a good reputation as a constitutional lawyer, and Marcos thought he might pull votes in Manila where twenty percent of the electorate lived. He was also too old to be a threat to Marcos or Imelda.

Cory visited Cardinal Sin the morning of December 11. She told him "I am now sure to run. It is God's will."

"All right," said the cardinal. "Kneel down. I will bless you. You are going to be president. You are the Joan of Arc."

Later that day, the cardinal saw Laurel. "You are wise in the ways of politicians," Sin told him. "But you are not attractive. Nobody will vote for you. Cory is very attractive. First of all, she is a victim of injustice. The sympathy of the people will go to her. Join with her, and you will win."

Cardinal Sin saw a tear roll down Laurel's cheek. He knew Laurel must be fighting his pride. The Cardinal said, "Tonight at 12 will be the deadline. Now go out and decide."

That day, Doña Aurora told Cory, "The Laurels are coming over and they want to meet you. Can you bring Peping or any of your brothers?"

At 7 p.m., Laurel and his brothers, former speaker of the House Jose B. Laurel, Jr., and former ambassador to Japan Jose Laurel III, arrived at the comfortable home where Doña lived with the family of her daughter Maur Lichauco. Cory's "seconds" were her brother Peping and Doña Aurora. They met for only thirty minutes in a family room lined with books.

The Laurels appeared to have made up their minds before they arrived, and Cory had decided to run on the Unido line. "We've agreed that Doy should run as vice president. Let's talk about conditions later," said one of his brothers. After five minutes, the talk turned to banter. Cory and Laurel agreed to meet at the Commission on Elections in three hours, and both sides called their supporters. Government employees cheered as the candidates arrived with families and friends at 10:30 p.m. It was an hour and a half before the midnight deadline.

The Campaign

THE CAMPAIGN started the next day. At a press conference, Cory joked about the late hour of the last night's events. "As you can see, it's a contest of who has the bigger eye bags."

They set out in a motorcade that started in the Laurel family compound in Manila and stopped at his birthplace in Batangas province to hear mass. Laurel's supporters had not had time to make new banners: the ones they unfurled, in his party color, green, said, "Laurel for president," and the word "vice" had been crudely inserted. Cory and Laurel would travel across the country together in separate cars and planes for most of the campaign.

Back in Manila that evening, Cory met at a friend's home with members of the Reform Armed Forces Movement (RAM), a group of young officers who had been speaking out against corruption and unprofessionalism in the army. They told her they wanted to support her, to see to her protection, because she represented an effective opposition that could bring about a representative, pluralistic democracy.

She replied that she wanted her own relatives to protect her. Her chief bodyguard would be her son-in-law, Eldon Cruz, her cousins, nephews and Hacienda Luisita guards. The Reformists offered to train her people. She agreed that they needed it; her shoulder was sore because people in the crowd had pulled her, and her security officers did not know how to handle even such simple situations. The officers would also use their contacts for intelligence work to uncover threats to her security.

A few days later, before the first big campaign rally in Manila, Cory went to Santo Domingo Church for mass with 2,000 supporters. Then she led them on a two–hour march to join some 50,000 people gathered at Bonifacio Square with yellow and green banners and balloons. There were fireworks, cheers and shouts of "Cory-Doy."

The themes of her campaign were to be honesty, sincerity, simplicity, and religious faith. She said she had suffered a lot under Marcos, "but I don't seek vengeance, only justice, not only for Ninoy, but also for the suffering Filipino people. Here I am, asking for your help to topple the Marcos regime." She called on them to "join me in my crusade for truth, justice and freedom." "Think less of ourselves, think more of our country," she told them.

She answered Marcos's charges of inexperience. "I'm very different from Marcos," she said. "I'm not a politician. I don't know how to tell a lie or take advantage of others. I'm not a dictator. I thank God I'm really very different from him, because if we really want to save the country, we need a leader very different from Marcos."

As if to demonstrate that as vividly as she could, she promised she would not live in Malacañang, the palace that had housed both Spanish and American colonial governors. "The Philippines is a suffering country, and thus it is not right that the leader of such a country should live in ostentatious splendor."

The strategy of the campaign was to cover as much territory as possible and tell Cory's personal story. She told Doña Aurora that her campaign message would be her sincerity and determination to clean up the government. "I might sound like a politician, promising this and that," she told her. "I don't want to promise what I cannot do. What I will tell them is that I have been a victim of this regime. The people will believe me. We have suffered a lot. My sincerity will be real and will make people free from fear."

At rallies, she began by telling of her husband's imprisonment. Often people were teary-eyed when they heard of the humiliation and fear of those years. As she told of the life and death of Ninoy—

and told them how Ninoy had died for them—it bore not a little similarity to the Christ story. Then she would talk about why she, who had been a victim of Marcos, was carrying on the fight and what she would do as president.

Cory surprised even some of her backers. "She was oozing with sincerity," thought Antonio "Tony" Cuenco, a provincial political leader. "Even though she was not a good speaker, not a bombastic speaker as we politicians picture speakers on stage; I was surprised for the first time in my life. Here comes a lousy speaker talking to them in a monotone, and yet everybody was all ears and many were crying, especially the girls and old women, whenever she would relate her sad experiences." They loved her for her sincerity, her honesty, her simplicity. They grieved with her for the loss of her husband.

She drew wildly enthusiastic crowds wherever she went. Teenage boys with yellow ribbons around their heads climbed on trees and atop cars or ledges to get a better view. Others hung out of windows. Yellow confetti rained from buildings along the routes. Even government employees in uniform risked their jobs to join the crowds. In the town of Tarlac, 10,000 people lined the streets; some farmers gave the Laban sign from the tops of their carabaos. Those who could remember said it was a bigger reception than even Ninoy had gotten.

Some compared the spontaneous emotional reaction of the public to a "mild mass hysteria." One observer called it "Corymania." People, mostly women, sought to touch her hands or feet or hair or the hem of her dress or to have her touch religious items they held up to her. It was like they had reacted to the Pope, an observer said. One woman kissed a photographer's campaign press pass that had Cory's picture on it. If security men were rough to people who surged around her, she told them not to push so hard.

It was a campaign not of the old style, with professional politicians and their beneficiaries, but with civic leaders, women's clubs, businessmen, and local community organizations pitching in their support. With money in short supply—the Cory campaign sold its T-shirts while Marcos gave his away—it depended a lot on volunteers, on middle-class women like those who signed up as "Cory's Crusaders" or on businessmen who printed leaflets and used their own vans to go into the provinces to campaign. Poor people wrote signs on pieces of cardboard and made flags of yellow bedsheets, towels, old curtains, shirts, rags, or faded banana leaves. Newspapers were turned into posters to tack on the walls.

Her closest advisers were members of her family—Peping was chief strategist, Paul ran the secretariat, Butz worked with cause-oriented groups and did a lot of campaigning, Lupita ran the press operation. Cory treated her staff as a worried mother would, concerned about whether they had eaten. She traveled by car and pickup trucks over dirt roads often muddied from the rains. Sometimes she flew in small private planes or helicopters. She was usually accompanied by her sister Terry Lopa and one of her daughters. She seemed to have limitless energy and stamina, helped, perhaps, by massive doses of vitamins in a combination of seven daily pills. She might speak at a dozen rallies in a day, from 8 a.m. until near midnight.

Most of the talks were off-the-cuff. She gave prepared speeches to elucidate policy at a handful of major events—most of them to business groups—but the provincial speeches repeated her personal travails and then touched on general problems such as the country's debt, people's poverty, and Marcos's stolen riches. A reporter asked Lupita Kashiwahara if she could not do something about Cory repeating "the same old sob story" all the time. Lupita replied, "That is the theme."

There was, in the beginning, a complaint that Cory and Laurel were not saying anything substantive about major issues. They were not proposing an alternative plan of government. Cory promised people justice and a fair share in the system. She pledged to dismantle the monopolies controlled by Marcos and his friends. She would release all political prisoners and call a six month cease-fire between government and rebel troops and initiate a dialogue with the Communist forces. She said that the guerrillas would be granted amnesty if they agreed to lay down their arms. She argued it was only the injustice and repression of the Marcos administration that had driven the guerrillas into the Communist fold. While she would not sway the hard core NPAs, she could convince the majority who were not really Communists to return. Giving them that chance did not mean being soft on communism. Her inexperience led her into a few gaffes. "I will retire the old generals; there are a lot of colonels interested in my election," she once said. "What do I think of the Soviet Union? I don't know. Till now, I have never thought about it."

Reporters asked her if she had political ideas other than her husband's. "Sometimes I wonder," she replied. "I don't know. . . . Sometimes I can't differentiate anymore where it is Ninoy and where it is Cory." She acknowledged, "I learned a lot from Ninoy. Ninoy taught me well. I cannot do everything that Ninoy did, but I promise I will try my best." She said, "I do not pretend to be politically brilliant." She said she would get fifty dedicated men and women to help her run the government.

Cory had several sessions with economists and business leaders such as Jimmy Ongpin and Noel Soriano to brief her on the causes of the country's economic problems, which were deemed to be monopolies and too much government interference. The solutions, they told her, were breaking up the monopolies, privatization, and spending only as much as was earned. But they warned her against getting too specific on anything.

In her speeches, Cory did not explain in much detail how she would solve the economic problems that had provoked the conflict, how she would confront the 20 percent unemployment, 40 percent underemployment, and inflation moving toward 25 percent other than to say she would establish the integrity and credibility that would encourage local and foreign investment. She said she would implement "true land reform," but did not say what that meant.

Her advisers agreed that the Marcos land-reform program was good; it just had not been carried out. In a brainstorming session for a speech that touched on land reform, she and her advisors discussed the problems of the sugar industry, where it did not make sense to parcel out land to individual farmers. Perhaps farmers should be made part owners of the corporation, someone suggested. Hacienda Luisita could be a model. Cory said it would be a good idea; it was a matter of persuading her brothers and sisters. Cory was treasurer of Jose Cojuangco & Sons, the holding and management company for the hacienda and other enterprises, including a sugar refinery, marketing corporation, distillery, and two realty firms.

When the government's expropriation order of the hacienda was raised as an issue, Cory declared that the move was politically motivated and that the hacienda's policies were benevolent. She said the 6,000 workers who belonged to a union had a collective bargaining agreement and had not gone on strike since the Cojuangcos took over in 1958. "We pay our sugar farmers the highest wages in the industry," she said. They got up to $2.90 a day, most only for the seven or eight months of the year when they were needed. "It is not economically feasible to produce sugar on a small scale," she added, but promised that if she were elected, she would use Hacienda Luisita as an example of how true land reform should be implemented. She would discuss with her brothers and sisters "how we can get a better share of profits for the workers in Luisita." Perhaps they could "share in the profits or become co-owners," she said.

Cory moved decidedly away from her original position on the American bases. She had signed the Laban coalition program calling for removal of the bases, but she told journalists, "I am leaving myself flexible." During the campaign, her brother Peping went to Washington and returned to tell Cory that people there wanted her to call for an extension of the bases. "What else do they want? I said I will respect the bases till 1991 and that's it," she replied. She would reach a firmer policy regarding the bases in 1989, two years before the expiration date of the agreement. She also complained publicly that Marcos had gotten only $180 million a year for the bases, while other countries with smaller installations got heftier sums—Spain $415 million, Greece $501 million, and Turkey $938 million a year.

The groups of the Left also made demands. Bayan called on Cory to pledge a "genuine" land reform, nationalization of banks and support for a policy of national industrialization instead of the liberal import policies demanded by the IMF and World Bank as a condition for loans. It also called for release of political prisoners, abolition of repressive decrees, and dismantling of the crony monopolies, all of which she agreed to, and abrogation of the bases treaty, which she did not.

When Cory declined to adopt its positions, Bayan, which was well-organized in Mindanao and the Visayas, called for an election boycott. Boycott advocates said that the election was a sham, that Marcos would not allow himself to be voted out of office, and besides, they were fighting not only Marcos but the elitist control of the economy. Faced with the demand for economic reform, Cory, they said, would side with her class. But their own members were divided and many worked for her election, including Bayan's chairman, Lorenzo Tañada.

The election was posing ever greater problems to Marcos. He had hoped to show to the Filipinos and Americans that he was the only one who could lead the country. He sought a victory as a new mandate for his counterinsurgency and economic policies. He had a powerful grassroots machinery built on government officials that included a network of district captains in every neighborhood, or "barangay," in the country. He controlled most of the media. But opposition newspapers had begun publishing. He could not very well close them and maintain the image of a free election. And the once divided opposition had united. It was talking about high prices, unemployment, government graft and corruption, and human rights violations—all charges on which Marcos knew he was vulnerable. Cory had turned out to be an attractive opponent. People showered sympathy on her for the death of her husband, they lauded her sincerity and courage, and they saw her as their only hope for change. Now, speculation was beginning that Marcos might find an excuse to cancel the elections.

Marcos charged that Cory was inexperienced and naive, that her rule would cause instability. He said some of her advisors were close to the Communist Party, and accused her of ties to the NPA. "Are we going to have another Vietnam, another Kampuchea, another Iran, Nicaragua, El Salvador?" he asked. He predicted a victory by the Communists if she were elected. Ignoring the evident contradiction, he also charged Cory with seeking the intervention of foreign countries: he meant the United States. Confounded by the challenge of a neophyte who was female to boot, Marcos declared it was "kind of embarrassing to be running against a woman" and made some off-color remarks about her sex.

Some of his statements had a surreal quality given the fact of his dictatorship. He said that the opposition would make a partnership with the Communists, leading to the loss of Filipino freedoms. "If that is their purpose, then ours is the nobility to rise again as a people. We are an independent country, ours is a noble race. We must not let that freedom be lost." He declared that his economic recovery program was in place and the insurgency problem soon would be solved, but that an opposition victory would undo his reforms. And he warned that if Cory won, the military might take over the government, and civil war would follow, leading to bloodshed and economic chaos "for quite a while."

There were rumors that Marcos might stage a coup if Cory won. The Reform Armed Forces Movement announced its members would not obey orders to alter the election results for Marcos and would support Cory if she won. It urged its fellow soldiers to work for "clean and honest elections." It built on military dissatisfaction with such practices as promotions made according to friendships and political ties and the siphoning off of money meant for arms and supplies that caused soldiers in the field to wear rubber thongs instead of boots and to lack other military equipment.

Marcos made few forays outside the palace, and when he did, he no longer had the drawing power that had produced crowds in his past campaigns. Even in his home province of Ilocos Norte, the roads were not lined with cheering supporters. His rallies were relatively subdued affairs; most of the crowds were made up of school teachers and children or civil servants ordered there for the occasion. Others were peasants or urban poor his district captains had paid to attend with T-shirts and a few dollars. The audiences, many transported to the sites in trucks or buses, spent most of the time watching singing groups and movie stars. Often, after people were paid or their attendance noted, they drifted away even before Marcos spoke. By Christmas, Cory had campaigned before a quarter of a million people, while crowd estimates for Marcos's few trips amounted to much less than 10 percent of that. At first, she had been apprehensive, but after seeing the crowds, which she called "fantastic, unbelievable," she was convinced she would win.

During the campaign, the beginning of the conflict between the Laurel and Aquino camps was evident, each side pressing for the right to designate poll inspectors. Some of Cory's people indicated that they did not think Unido was working very hard for their candidate, and there were rumors toward the end that Marcos would arrange for Laurel to be elected vice-president and serve with him. In Cebu, an important island in the Visayas, the political rivalry was so intense that Cory had to go to two rallies, one run by Maria Victoria Osmeña-Stuart, chairman of Unido, and the other by her cousin, John "Sonny" Osmeña, more closely identified with Cory. The cousins each wanted to be mayor. The Osmeña family oligarchy—which included former President Sergio Osmeña—had run the city and sometimes the island for decades, and the cousins assumed it was theirs by inheritance. Cory divided the election inspectors among the two Osmeñas and two members of the National Assembly who had been elected in 1984.

There were colorful moments such as her visit to the tribal regions of the north, an NPA stronghold. In one town, she was greeted by Kalinga tribesman in loin cloths who danced to the sounds of brass gongs. The people held signs protesting abuses by the military and the government's takeover of their lands. Many Kalinga had joined the guerrillas after the Marcos regime seized their ancestral lands and displaced 100,000 people to build a dam on the Chico River. The project had been suspended and Cory promised to end it.

There was some unhappiness when she visited Bataan and failed to say anything about a controversial nuclear power plant that had been off line because of local opposition. The crowd of 3,000 residents wanted her to promise to dismantle the reactor that had cost more than $2 billion to build. A government commission had found that the 620-megawatt Westinghouse pressurized water model had an obsolete design and 4,000 defects. She partly rectified the matter a few days later, saying, "The nuclear plant must go."

Marcos countered her charges of his economic misrule by saying the crisis had been due to international factors beyond his control—a decline in the price of exports such as sugar and coconut oil and the oil price hikes of the seventies. He warned that the opposition would end free enterprise and private property. He said one could not regard the NPA simply as ordinary Filipinos with grievances against the government. Cory had said at a late night press conference that "So long as the Communists renounce all forms of violence, we welcome them. We will certainly need everybody's help." Marcos seized on that to renew his charges that she was linked to the guerrillas.

Three days later, Cory responded, "I will not appoint a Communist to my cabinet." She added, "I can't possibly be a Communist, because I am a very devout Catholic and, as we all know, there is no God in communism." Later, she would express surprise at her discovery that so many poor people were afraid of communism. "All along, I always thought it was just the rich and down to the middle classes. But it was the poor themselves who asked, 'Is she really a Communist?'" She was relieved that the charge had come early enough. "If Marcos's think tank had saved this for the last two weeks, I would have been dead."

Joma Sison, the Communist Party chairman who had been in military detention for ten years, announced from his cell at Camp Bonifacio that he hoped the Left boycott would not be too active. He said he did not expect much from the opposition "in terms of outright anti-imperialism and anti-feudalism," but there would be some gains in the realm of "anti-fascism."

In the new year, the opposition's issues began to be better defined. Cory and Laurel had begun campaigning before they had even adopted a common platform. On New Year's Day, Cory witnessed an agreement signed by Laurel, representing Unido, and Salonga for the Laban ng Bayan coalition, which adopted a minimum program of government. They promised to respect the bases agreement up to 1991. That departed from the coalition stand calling for the bases' removal. They called for a ban on storing nuclear arms in the country.

The program also called for dismantling the 1973 martial law constitution, reorganizing the government, and writing a new constitution within eighteen months. It promised unconditional amnesty for political prisoners. It called for abolition of the business monopolies that hurt the public interests. It pledged to grant workers the right to organize, bargain collectively, and strike. It said it would distribute land to the tillers and landless peasants and give them credit, marketing and technical support.

Marcos became more active in striking back. He argued that Cory knew that Ninoy and others in the family had participated in organizing the Communist party with Sison. He added that he had no reason to kill Ninoy because he had already been sentenced to death for subversion, murder, and rebellion.

Cory's first major speech was to a collection of business organizations in a lunch at Manila's Intercontinental Hotel. She promised to stop government interference in business, although the government would be there "to protect the poor and the disadvantaged." She would dismantle the monopolies and stimulate investment in labor-intensive, rural-based, and small and medium-sized agricultural enterprises. In line with nationalist sentiments, she said utilities and natural resources would be reserved for Filipinos, but foreign investment would be welcome in areas where local capital was inadequate. She would delay the import-liberalization program and roll back some of the taxes recommended by the IMF and the World Bank. She reiterated her support for land reform and workers' rights. The business leaders cheered her, some with tears in their eyes.

She told a crowd in one provincial town—with a curious genuflection to local machismo—"I'm a woman, but I'm ready to lay down my life for the country. I will restore honesty and sincerity in government." And in Ilocos Sur, northern Philippines, which was Marcos country, she told them, in language that almost echoed the passion of the Christ they were celebrating, "Ninoy fought for you, he suffered for his beliefs, and I am here to continue his fight."

She got a massive welcome in mid-January in Cebu, where 200,000 out of a city of 600,000 gathered in the streets from the airport to downtown. It took the motorcade four hours to go a distance normally covered in thirty minutes. When her open jeep ran out of gas, she jumped onto the truck that was carrying the news photographers. Later, 10,000 people jammed the Basilica of the Holy Child and spilled out into the churchyard. "I continue to be amazed" at the public reaction, she told the press.

A brouhaha erupted after Muslim secessionist leader Nur Misuari said from Fez that he had met with Butz Aquino in Madrid and reached an agreement that, as president, Cory would recognize Muslim independence in Mindanao and several other southern islands. Butz said he had not signed any such agreement, only discussed peace possibilities, and that they had agreed on local autonomy but not secession. Butz had privately asked Misuari to minimize cheating in the Muslim regions. Misuari did more than that. He instructed his commanders to campaign for Cory. Cory said there was no deal, but that if she won, she would hold talks with the separatists, who had been fighting a guerrilla war for thirteen years, and she would respect Muslim aspirations for autonomy to the extent that it was compatible with the territorial integrity of the nation. Marcos accused her of treason for wanting to dismember the country.

Imelda Marcos threw out her own accusations: "Our opponent," she told an audience of 1,000 dockworkers at a Manila rally, "does not put on any make-up. She does not have her fingernails manicured."

Cory sought out the victims of the dictatorship. In Escalante, on the sugar island of Negros, she visited the house where emergency medical treatment had been given to the victims of a military massacre three months earlier. Soldiers and members of the Civilian Home Defense Forces had fired into a crowd that was protesting the thirteenth anniversary of martial law, killing twenty and wounding thirty-one. "Like you, I am a victim of Marcos," Cory said, and she promised justice.

In Antique province, she visited the bridge where during the 1984 parliamentary elections a dozen opposition supporters were ambushed and massacred on the order of the local warlord Arturo Pacificador. She lit a candle and said prayers in honor of the dead. One of the widows embraced her, crying, "Cory, you are my last and only hope for justice for our husbands." She promised they would have it. "We are both victims of the injustice of the Marcos regime," she told another widow.

As the campaign went on, rumors grew that Marcos would not

allow an honest vote, as he repeated that an Aquino win "would mean a bloody confrontation." She promised direct action. "If the votes are clearly in my favor and the president tries to frustrate the people's's will, I will call for people to demonstrate peacefully in the streets, and I will even lead those demonstrations." She added that she would retire Armed Forces Acting Chief of Staff, Lieutenant General Fidel Ramos, "who is already retirable." She suggested that if she lost because of gross cheating and terrorism, the moderates would give up on the election process and the radicals would take over the leadership. She added that she would never join the insurgency.

Cardinal Sin issued a pastoral letter warning of a "sinister plot" to frustrate the people's will, including bribes to teachers, district campaign managers, and others to buy their votes. Sin told the people that they could take the money but that "money offered to you in no way obliges you to vote for a particular candidate."

Cory outlined her program for peasants and workers in Davao City, Mindanao, where the squatters slum, Agdao, a collection of shacks, shanties, and cinder-bloc houses crisscrossed by dirt and mud roads was so tightly controlled by the NPA it was nicknamed "Nicaragdao." She said that Marcos had promised them land reform, but had sent land grabbers instead, protecting them with unsavory military men. He had promised better housing, but had subjected them to hamletting, where the military refused to let people into NPA suspected areas, or freely to leave and enter their own towns.

She criticized the displacement of farmers left "at the margins of agricultural monopolies" with large tracts of land awarded to Marcos's cronies or foreign investors. The goals of her land reform would be greater productivity and equitable sharing of the benefits and ownership of the land. She would seek land reform suited to the needs of the small farmers, landless workers, and communities of tribal Filipinos. "For long-time settlers and share tenants, land-to-the-tiller must become a reality, instead of an empty slogan." For the landless, there could be resettlement and cooperatives. She stressed that land first had to be used to sustain people's need for food; then attention could be turned to creating wealth-producing industry.

She pledged that she would apply the same policy to Hacienda Luisita, even though sugar land was not covered by the land-reform law. "I shall sit down with my family to explore how the twin goals of maximum productivity and dispersal of ownership and benefits

can be exemplified for the rest of the nation in Hacienda Luisita."
She did not, however, propose extending the land-reform law to
cover land other than that used for rice and corn. Large sectors in
Mindanao were used for pineapples, coconuts, rubber, palm oil,
trees, and lumber.

She promised also to improve the lot of the workers, declaring
that a large proportion of them were "broken victims of the avarice
of individuals and of an oppressive social structure and hostile labor
laws." She knew workers wanted fair pay, decent conditions, and
meaningful participation in the decision-making process of business
and industry. But when they sought to organize, they were subject
to "harassment, intimidation and violent dispersal by goons, by the
police or by the military." She promised to end repressive laws and
dismantle the "economic structures which keep workers in a state
of quasi-slavery." She meant that she would abolish the Marcos
monopolies.

The original draft of the speech had included a proposal to give
teachers the right to organize and strike. Her advisers thought it
was a good idea, but she said, "Maybe not. The teachers may like
that, but the parents won't. You might gain the votes of the teachers
and lose the votes of the parents."

She said the NPA insurgents in Mindanao had been driven to war
in pursuit of their vision of a just society, that "they are our brothers
and sisters" who had "given up on the capacity of the Marcos regime
to give relief to their just grievances." She promised to "immediately
declare a cease-fire with the rebels," release political prisoners, and
begin a dialogue with the insurgents that would lead to a redressing
of their legitimate grievances. The next day, she visited the tomb of
Father Tulio Favali, an Italian missionary, who had been murdered
by paramilitary troops in 1985.

The paramilitary Civilian Home Defense Force (CHDF), under control of the armed forces, would continue to claim victims during the
campaign. While she was in Mindanao, a PDP-Laban campaign chairman was gunned down by a man witnesses said was a CHDF
member and the bodyguard of the local mayor. This was the first
casualty of a number that would grow to dozens.

Cory's intelligence discovered death plots against her, too, and
sometimes she seemed to escape danger by luck. Once, on the way
to a town in Mindanao, Cory's plane was prevented from landing
by a torrential rain. The party flew on to the next stop and later

found that at the first airport there had been an unexpected welcoming party of men armed to the teeth.

In Zamboanga City, with close to 50,000 people in Pershing Plaza (named after the U.S. World War II general) an explosion sounded at the farthest perimeter of the crowd. On the platform, the men's faces showed tension. The crowd surged. Cory, serene, turned to the person beside her who pressed her hand as if to say it's nothing. Then the explosion got closer. It was a grenade. There were some injuries but no deaths. Cory and her party cut short the rally, got into their cars, and went off to the next event. Later, a reporter asked her if she had been frightened. "I was too tired to care," she replied. "Anyway, I've always been fatalistic about these things. If it's my time to go, it's my time to go."

On the island of Negros they were in the region controlled by Marcos warlord Armando Gustilo, who was accused of ordering the Escalante massacre. Halfway through the town, Cory's driver received a walkie-talkie message not to proceed further. He turned back, but half the motorcade, with Laurel's car, did not get word and went ahead. A security guard came to Cory's car and said, "There's a hot spot inside the town. You shouldn't proceed."

"If we stop right now, people will think we are afraid," said Cory. "Let's not show them we are cowards." They moved on, past people in the streets standing tensely, some of them making the Laban sign surreptitiously. CHDF troops stood grim-faced along the route. The "hot spot" consisted of two machine guns on top of city hall. Usually they were just for show; that day they were manned. The motorcade passed through.

Cory knew Filipinos cared a lot about courage. It was a trait on which Marcos had played. Cory could do the same. She called Marcos a coward with fake war medals, who had not come to Mindanao for ten years to see the horrible effects of his greed, brutality, and ignorance. She called on him to "stand up like a woman and answer charges of his cowardice with truth . . . if he dares." Marcos, apparently flummoxed by it all, reacted by declaring that Filipino women should confine their preachings to "inside the bedroom."

She riposted in a speech before the Manila Rotary Club asking, "How do you deal with an inveterate liar?. . . . What do we do with the overgrown child struggling to lie his way to a re-election?" To his charges of her inexperience, she conceded that she could not match him. "I admit that I have no experience in cheating, stealing, lying, or assassinating political opponents." She was applauded dozens of times and at the end received a standing ovation. When Marcos, rambling, addressed the businessmen later, they sat on their hands.

He increased his public appearances as the campaign drew to a close. He was carried on stage by his security men and gave speeches that bordered on the incoherent, his voice quavering. People wondered whether he would be able to go on or whether he might call Imelda to take his place.

Meanwhile, the bishops, increasingly concerned about electoral fraud, issued a pastoral letter warning about violations "on a level never experienced before." They called on people not to participate in this "conspiracy of evil."

Cory made a return trip to Bataan, and this time she said what the people wanted to hear. She was cheered when she pledged she would not allow the nuclear plant to operate because it was costly and unsafe. She backed the complaints of the workers in the export processing zone. She spoke toughly to Marcos, warning, "I dare you, Mr. Marcos, to crack down on the opposition. I dare you to demonstrate to the world that you are a born coward, and that you are too stupid to answer the charges and issues against you with anything but bullets."

The end of the campaign was a fitting and prescient conclusion. The day of Cory's final mass rally in Manila, people from points all over the city began marching and arriving in cars and jeepneys early in the morning. Finally, over a million people, waving flags, shouting joyously, grinning, flashing the Laban sign, jammed Rizal Park for a meeting that lasted almost ten hours to hear opposition politicians, entertainers, and finally Cory, who promised that they were near the end of the first stage of the journey that had begun on the tarmac of Manila Airport in 1983. "The yellow revolution," she said, "has shaken off the shackles of the Marcos dictatorship. . . . There is a new politics in our land: people power." "Cory, Cory, Cory!" the crowd screamed. White pigeons with yellow ribbons tied to their legs were released into the air.

She sent a message to Marcos: "As the old dictator lurks in his palace with his dwindling band of cronies and his false medals for comfort, I warn him, do not cheat the people on Friday." Already, she said, there were reports of the old tricks of intimidation and fraud. She told him he would not get away with it. "On Friday,"

Cory promised, "out of the ashes of twenty years of misrule, there will be a new beginning."

The next day, at the same site, Marcos gathered only a few hundred thousand people, many of whom admitted they were paid to attend. As he spoke, their interest wavered, and many wandered away.

The campaign had lasted fifty-seven days. It had taken Cory to sixty-eight of the country's seventy-three provinces to address over a thousand rallies. Marcos had spoken at only thirty-four rallies in twenty-two provinces, but he had had the advantage of government-controlled television that virtually ignored the Aquino campaign.

The Catholic bishops repeated Cardinal Sin's advice to the poor that it was okay to accept money for their votes—as long as they voted their conscience once they were alone with the ballot.

Election

THURSDAY, FEBRUARY 6, election eve. Homobono Adaza, an Aquino supporter and political leader from Mindanao, commented in pastoral metaphor, "The fields are golden and the grains are ready for harvest. But there are not enough hands to gather the harvest, and in some areas they are harvesting each other's heads."

Marcos had never been defeated in his political career since he won his father's congressional seat in Ilocos Norte in 1949. The Aquino camp figured it needed to get two-thirds of the total vote to overcome the massive cheating it expected from him. Anticipating the worst, Cory warned Marcos that her supporters would not accept fraud. She would ask for peaceful demonstrations, but if they had no effect, the people might not listen to her. Marcos replied that her threats of "civil war" indicated her desperation.

Cardinal Sin urged Filipinos to "turn the other cheek" rather than meet electoral violence with more violence. But he also said the Church was considering a campaign of civil disobedience in case there was fraud.

U.S. Senator Richard Lugar arrived in Manila at the head of an official American observer delegation and delivered Reagan's message that credible elections could produce a substantial increase in U.S. aid.

NAMFREL, the National Citizens Movement for Free Elections, backed by the Catholic Church, business organizations, labor and civic groups, had been set up in 1984 as the citizens' poll-watching arm and had limited fraud enough to allow the opposition to win a third of the parliamentary seats. NAMFREL would play a crucial role in the presidential vote. Marcos, pressured by the Americans to accredit it, would accuse it of being part of the opposition and financed by the CIA. It was based on the nation-wide organization of the Church. Cory would think then, as she had before and would again, if she did not have the Catholic Church, she might as well call it quits. The Church had the only organization that could compete with Marcos and his party.

NAMFREL had some 800,000 volunteers to cover nearly 90,000 polling places and certify the ballots of a prospective twenty-six million voters. The people would be voting in sixty cities and 1,500 towns. It would take several days for the official total to be announced, but NAMFREL would run a quick count based on the carbons of the government Commission on Elections (COMELEC) precinct tallies. Members of the Reformist military group were given NAMFREL IDs so they could have access to polling places and NAMFREL headquarters. And Cory's top staff secretly set up its own count which would be faster than NAMFREL's, with several thousand people feeding in numbers directly from the polling booths. The results would be given to Radio Veritas.

Friday, February 7, election day. Cory, with a retinue of security men and reporters, arrived at 7:30 a.m. at the Central Azucarera de Tarlac Elementary School on Hacienda Luisita. She was greeted by hundreds of cheering tenants, then waited on line three minutes in a classroom with cracked wooden walls until three people ahead of her had voted. After she cast her ballot, she went to a front lawn a few houses away and told the reporters, "Today is my day. I have never been more confident of anything in my life. I am going to win." Then she returned to Manila to the house of some friends in Makati. Her whereabouts were kept secret.

Marcos cast his vote at the Don Mariano Marcos Memorial Elementary School, named after his father, in his hometown, Batac, Ilocos Norte.

As some twenty million others would do that day, they put their thumb prints on their ballots and on detachable, numbered coupons. They were also given papers that listed the four candidates for president and the five for vice president. The ballots had two lines on which to write their choices. They went into make-shift booths, then a minute later handed the ballots to the election officials who separated the two parts. Each was slipped into a separate compartment of the ballot box. The polls were scheduled to close at 3 p.m. to allow a daylight count.

The thought that the presence of hundreds of foreign journalists and observers might mitigate against Marcos's use of guns, goons, and gold was apparently naive. Thirty opposition workers were murdered. Unido inspectors awoke to find their cars vandalized; some were kidnapped or terrorized by goons. KBL leaders gave out bribes of $1 to $5 or bags of rice to buy votes. Soldiers asked Unido and NAMFREL representatives to leave their posts.

The Regional Unified Command in Mindanao campaigned openly for Marcos. Marines landed in Naga City and with other armed elements surrounded the municipal building and stopped the vote canvass. Paramilitary troops terrorized some precincts. They had been issued weapons by Marcos people or the military. In Tarlac and other provinces, military commanders submitted lists of their soldiers to be counted as Marcos votes.

In Makati, jeepneys disgorged squads of "flying voters" who, with firearms prominently stuck in their belts, entered the polling places to vote, then drove on to the next poll. In numerous cases, thugs pushed their way into the voting sites, terrorized the election officials and watchers, and seized the ballot boxes. In one polling place, Cory was not even listed as a candidate, and in another town the tally showed results from twelve more precincts than existed. The opposition would conclude later that it had lost 10 percent of the vote through deliberate under registration and slowdowns in opposition strongholds, 10 percent through ballot-box stuffing, "flying voters," and falsified returns, and another 5 percent through bribery and intimidation.

The results came in slowly to the two quick-count headquarters. One, run by COMELEC, was set up in the huge, air-conditioned hall of the Philippine International Convention Center, one of Imelda's boondoggles. The other, run by NAMFREL, was set up in the gym of LaSalle College.

With only a fraction of the count public, Cory went on Radio Veritas to claim victory. "The Marcos spell is broken," she said. "The myth of his invincible machine has been shattered against his guns, against his goons, and against his gold. The Filipino people have prevailed," she said. "The trend is clear and irreversible. The people and I have won, and we know it." She said election returns from around the country proved it. Her "secret count" gave her a margin of 800,000 after 14.9 million votes had been counted.

The next day, security officers checked reporters carefully as they filed into the Mondragon auditorium. Cory, acting with assurance, told them she hoped to meet with Marcos soon to make arrangements for a smooth and quick transition of government. Asked what she wanted from the Americans, she said, "Maybe they can impress upon Marcos how very necessary it is for him to concede." She said if he refused to give up, she would lead daily, peaceful street demonstrations. Afterward, she drove to the Makati Municipal Hall to show her support for the hundreds of people, most of them youths, who had held a vigil there, since the night before, to guard the ballot boxes.

Speaking on Radio Veritas that night, she called on people to keep defending the ballots and not to believe the count broadcast by the government media. "These are the lies of desperate men," she declared, saying that every report confirmed her victory. She predicted that she would win by 55 percent.

On Sunday, she went to thanksgiving masses at the Santo Domingo and Baclaran churches. The Baclaran Church was packed, and some of the thousands of worshipers spilled out into the grounds and nearby streets to listen over loudspeakers. Cardinal Sin, dressed in vestments of yellow and green, the colors of Cory and Laurel, said the election was a proof of "people power" and "a collective expression of solidarity." He praised the NAMFREL volunteers and said, "God will not forgive Marcos" if he betrayed his countrymen. Her supporters cheered, "Cory, Cory" and flashed the "L" sign for Laban. Cory's speech was suddenly interrupted when security men hustled her from the altar. Someone had spotted a man with a gun tucked in his waistband standing at the front of the crowd. He and another man fled when people began shouting that he was armed.

In some places, canvassing had not even started. The opposition charged that the delays were part of a plan to change the results to be submitted to the Batasan (assembly). Marcos was delaying returns from his strongholds until he saw how many votes he needed to win. More volunteers were sent to guard the ballot boxes.

In the days after the vote, opposition leaders argued over what would be done if Marcos stole the election. Some supported a wait-and-see attitude; others pushed for more immediate and aggressive action. Cory asked opposition leaders to visit certain provinces to check on the delays, collect the official tally sheets to bolster her case, and give moral support to the people.

She also waited for the Church to act. Before the election, Cardinal Sin had said the bishops would meet by the following Thursday to determine their post-election stance.

The Reform Armed Forces Movement released a statement condemning the fraud: "There are serious indications that the people's will has been thwarted." The officers called on their colleagues to refuse to use force or violence against freedom-loving Filipinos who were asking to be heard.

On Sunday night, thirty-eight computer technicians who had been tallying the count at the government convention hall walked out to protest the government's manipulation of the figures. The numbers they had in their computers were being altered before being posted on the giant screens.

Senator Richard Lugar said at a press conference before his departure on Feburary 10th that he and the observer group had witnessed and heard disturbing reports of efforts to undermine the integrity of the election both during the voting and the counting process which was then underway. He said they believed that manipulation of the count was taking place.

Back in Washington, later that day, President Reagan, ignoring the counsel of State Department advisors, issued a statement that in spite of the charges of voting fraud, "there really is a two-party system in the Philippines," and he suggested that fraud could be occurring on both sides. He indicated that he expected Marcos to win and he would support him. He called on Marcos and Cory to "work together to form a viable government" and to "work to implement reforms." He said the U.S. would remain neutral, and that after the vote was counted, "we then hope to have the same relationship with the people of the Philippines that we've had for all these historic years." However, he said, "Both sides must work together to make those reforms which are needed to ensure a stable democracy."

Journalists covering the election wondered if Reagan was talking about the same country they were in. The opposition was outraged. "There you are, being cheated, your people are being killed, then a coalition with Marcos is proposed," said Cory's press spokesman Rene Saguisag, reflecting widespread disgust with the American president.

Reagan then announced he was sending special envoy Philip Habib "to help nurture the hopes and possibilities of democracy." Cory was not impressed, noting that Habib's last assignment to end the civil war in Lebanon had not been a notable success.

On Tuesday morning, a country inured to electoral violence was shocked when Evelio Javier, the popular ex-governor of Antique province, was gunned down by thugs, hired by Marcos warlord Arturo Pacificador, outside the provincial capital building where the votes were being counted. The next day, Marcos, taking his cue from Reagan, announced plans to form a council of state that would include the opposition.

At a packed press conference at the Cojuangco building campaign headquarters that day, press officer Teodoro "Teddy" Locsin read Cory's answer to Reagan. She was angered and wondered whether Reagan had seen the election violence on American television or heard reports from the observers he had sent. She suggested that before he made further comments about the election, he should check with his own embassy, foreign observers, and the media. "No Filipino president has ever received the overwhelming mandate at the polls that I have been given. I would wonder at the motives of a friend of democracy who chose to conspire with Mr. Marcos to cheat the Filipino people of their liberation." She called on the U.S., without mentioning it by name, "not to make the mistake, in the name of shortsighted self-interest, of coming to the support" of Marcos. U.S. Ambassador Stephen Bosworth rushed to her headquarters to say Reagan had been misunderstood. She said she would await a fuller explanation from Habib. Cory and her advisors believed that the U.S. had no political will to bring down Marcos. It would take large demonstrations throughout the country to convince Reagan to act. Ongpin saw the alternative as civil disobedience or as some moderates moving to the Left.

Cory also appealed to the military. She said she "knew that the guns of some in the military and the police were aimed to silence our voices and steal our victory," that many of them witnessed or participated in those attempts; but she appealed to their patriotism, saying it was never too late for "truth, courage, and honor."

In the days of uncertainty following the election, people became restless and wondered why Cory was not taking action. Leaders of one of the volunteer groups presented her with the idea of a workshop of leaders of key opposition forces, and she agreed. On Thursday, Cory met at the Mondragon building with 350 leaders, including businessmen, professionals, politicians, the urban poor, clergy, and the military, to discuss the protest campaign they would launch. The alliance taking shape included moderate and social democratic opposition groups, the Church, and reformist elements in the armed forces. It did not include the radical Left, represented by Bayan.

Many of the leaders of the moderate opposition pressed her to take a stronger stand and hold marches or rallies, in the hope that they might lead to storming the palace and forcing Marcos from power. One of the workshops even called for armed struggle. She was appalled at the idea. She told everyone that as far as she was concerned, if they wanted to remove the dictator through violence, they could find themselves a new leader.

She rejected the idea of demonstrations, afraid they could explode in violence. She also did not want to do anything that might be interpreted as linking up with the radicals; such an alliance would give Marcos an excuse for a crackdown, or the well-organized radicals could impose their leadership. It was easy to shut out Bayan because it had lost its claim to representation by boycotting the election. When she was asked if she would accept the participation of Bayan, whose million members and nationwide organization would provide experienced leaders and troops for the civil disobedience campaign, she replied, "I have not talked with Bayan people. Tañada told me they would like to talk to me. I told Tañada that it is better that they talk to him." And she did not want to propose stronger actions until she was convinced that the people were ready to carry them out.

She did not much like another proposal that they dump horse manure in front of the U.S. Embassy to show their disgust at Reagan's policy. "Oh my gosh," she said. "I don't believe we should do that, because it's so unsanitary and unhealthy." Given the circumstances of the crisis, her well-mannered sensibility made the audience explode in laughter.

A committee processed the workshop recommendations and came

up with a series of nonviolent actions. In the following two weeks, she would tour the country to ask her supporters to carry them out. On Marcos's inauguration day, there would be a memorial service for the election victims at Santo Domingo Church. The next day, there would be a general strike, a noise barrage, and teach-ins on nonviolence. The president of the Philippine Chamber of Commerce and Industry, a federation of eighty business associations, would later announce that members should allow workers to join the one-day strike.

On Thursday, February 13, the Catholic Bishops Conference deliberated into the early morning as members argued whether to take a strong position. Imelda Marcos visited the bishops to ask them not to issue a statement. She had been to see Cardinal Sin several times during the week; one day she gave him a cross, covered with diamonds and dedicated "lovingly yours." He took it to sell and give the money to Caritas, the Catholic charity. This time she arrived at 3 a.m. to ask him to intervene in the bishops meeting. He refused. "Madame, don't come here at night," he told her in his jocular style. "The people might suspect that you are sleeping with me. It is not good. Come early in the morning." He would repeat the story to reporters afterward: "It is not good she comes at night. First of all, this is the House of Sin. What do you think of that!"

Despite the nervousness of the Papal Nuncio at a strong statement, the bishops called the elections "unparalleled in the fraudulence of their conduct." The 120-member conference condemned the systematic disenfranchisement of voters, the widespread and massive vote-buying, the deliberate tampering of the election returns, the intimidation, harassment, terrorism, and murder. It warned that a "government that assumes or retains power through fraudulent means has no moral basis." And if such a government did not correct the evil it had inflicted, it was the "moral obligation" of the people to make it do so through nonviolent struggle, "active resistance of evil by peaceful means—in the manner of Christ." The statement was read at Sunday services around the country.

The new Soviet ambassador took this opportunity to astonish everyone by presenting his credentials and congratulating Marcos.

A week after the vote, Cory said she would not honor the proclamation of the parliament. She said it lacked the capacity to arrive at a credible result. The Commission on Elections gave 10,807,197 votes to Marcos and 9,291,761 to Cory. A week after the Batasan had begun the count, it proclaimed Marcos and Tolentino the winners. The opposition walked out when the majority refused to delay the proclamation. Most of the official returns had been challenged by either Unido or the KBL for failing to comply with legal requirements, being statistically improbable, tampered with, or based on spurious documents.

"Mr. Marcos controls his Batasan, so what?" declared Cory the same night. "We never doubted the votes of his puppet members of the Batasan. But when Mr. Marcos called an election, it was not with the intention of having to be rescued from defeat by his own assemblymen. He is finished. He has had to use one trick after another to try and rescue himself from defeat: fraud, intimidation, violence, cheating in a super slow COMELEC vote count, to the final panic of rushing the canvass through the Batasan. Yet nobody believes he is still president. Because the one vote he does not have is that of the people. Even before I am finally declared winner of this election, I think we can all agree who is the biggest loser: Mr. Marcos. No tinsel and celebration of the President's make-believe win can hide his loss of moral and political authority. He is beaten. When is he going to go?"

While the government election commission showed Marcos to be the winner, the independent NAMFREL tabulation, based on 70 percent of the precincts, was 7,835,070 for Cory and 7,053,068 for Marcos. Later, it would issue a report that Cory might have won by a margin of three million, if the vote had been fair. The report cited 750 documented cases of fraud in 86,000 precincts. It said more than six million votes were questionable, and there were more than three million voters whose names disappeared from the voter lists or who were visibly disenfranchised through ballot-box snatching, fraudulent counting, the transfer of voting places, slowdowns, or even the failure to hold the election in some areas.

Reagan issued another statement on Saturday. He repeated his comments of how the elections had furthered the two-party system, but he added, "It has already become evident, sadly, that the elections were marred by widespread fraud and violence perpetrated largely by the ruling party." He said, "It was so extreme that the election's credibility has been called into question within the Philippines and the United States." But he still did not want to break with Marcos. His advisors told him to be cautious, not to jeopardize the U.S. bases.

In the midst of the crisis, Cory salvaged a moment for her personal life and attended the wedding of her daughter, Pinky. No politicians were invited.

The first step of the mass action campaign was a "Triumph of the People" prayer rally on Sunday, February 16, at the Luneta, where she would reveal the program of nonviolent protest against Marcos. Her advisors told her the rally was a mistake; they thought people would not come out for it. Some suggested the rally be held in a smaller square, so a sparse turnout would seem less obvious.

"Look," she told them. "If the people are not behind me, I want to know. If they are behind me, I want to know. I have to know once and for all if people still believe that I won." If there was not a large turnout, there was no point in leading a population who would forget so quickly their anger at the conduct of the election. She was almost alone in her decision.

But the response was overwhelming: nearly two million people marched from all over the city to the meeting, first to hear three bishops and thirty-five priests, from the top of a flatbed truck, say mass and read the bishops' letter, and then to hear Cory, from the same platform, call for a nation-wide general strike on the first working day after Marcos's inauguration as well as an immediate boycott of newspapers, television stations, banks, and several big companies owned by his cronies. People groaned as she announced a boycott of San Miguel beer, the country's favorite.

"Well," she said, "We all have to sacrifice."

She asked them to delay payment of their water and electric bills until they got their final cut-off notices.

"I am not asking for violent revolution," Cory said. "This is not the time for that." It was a time, she said, for a nonviolent struggle for justice, of active resistance of evil by peaceful means. The big turnout was the boost she needed. All she had to do was keep reaching out to the people.

There was, however, some disappointment in the crowd as there had been among many opposition leaders. They thought her proposals were too cautious, her call for a boycott a weak response, hardly much in the way of defying the regime. They wanted her to call for mass strikes of transit and government workers, and street demonstrations. "The majority of us felt that she could have asked for more and people would have gone with her," said Noel Tolentino, an organizer of the post-election "civil disobedience" campaign, which actually did not involve civil disobedience.

But she defended her policy. "Many of my supporters are just beginners," she said. "So rather than alienate these newcomers, I thought it best to engage in these so-called tame proposals, because If I cannot even get enough people to stop drinking beer, how can I expect them to work harder."

The next morning, Habib and Bosworth met with Marcos. Habib told him he had to make democratic reforms and share power with the opposition or he would lose U.S. military and economic aid. Marcos countered that he would abrogate the bases treaty if Reagan halted U.S. aid to protest the fraudulent election.

In the afternoon, the Americans went to see Cory. They arrived at 2 p.m. in a black limousine. "What can I do for you, Mr. Ambassador?" she said coolly as Habib was ushered into her office at the Cojuangco building. She warned the U.S. against supporting Marcos, and said the crisis "will only be resolved by a swift and orderly transfer of power to the Aquino presidency that the Filipino people have chosen overwhelmingly at the polls." "Don't see me anymore if you have to insist that I should cooperate with the government of Mr. Marcos," she told them.

Later, in a statement, she said, "Although this is a Filipino matter, which will be resolved by the Filipino people, we expect the understanding and support of friends of democracy everywhere. There was nothing healthy or democratic about the violence, intimidation, cheating, and bribes, with which Mr. Marcos sought to snatch victory. Anyone who seeks to obscure this blunt point is not helping the Filipino people, but would be betraying their fight for democracy." She criticized Reagan's statement that the election, in which the winning party had been cheated of its landslide victory, had furthered the two-party system. Then she announced she would travel around the country to call for her mild form of civil disobedience and nonviolent protest. The bishops endorsed the campaign. The first stops would be Cebu City, and Davao in Mindanao.

Cory and her chief supporters also began contacting ambassadors of European countries and Japan to ask them not to recognize Marcos. One group met with Habib to ask him to persuade Reagan to cut off economic and military aid.

On Wednesday, Cory began her provincial swing, with a rally before 20,000 supporters in Angeles City, site of the U.S. Clark Air Base.

The next day, the twelve-nation European Parliament condemned the election as fraudulent and gave its support to Cory. But the

Americans were still hedging. On Friday, Cory met Habib again; he proposed a formula based on sharing power with Marcos. She told him she would not share power and to tell Reagan to cut all aid to the Marcos government. She refused Habib's request to provide details of her plans. "Wait and see," she told him. Cory did not trust Reagan.

That afternoon, she flew by private plane to Cebu about 400 miles to the south to promote the civil disobedience campaign.

On Saturday, Habib would meet with Marcos and hear his fears of a plot to carry out a coup and assassinate him. Habib would warn him to make democratic reforms and share power with the opposition or risk losing U.S. military and economic aid. Then, he would return to Washington later that day. It was February 22, destined to be a landmark in Philippine history.

Revolution

JUAN PONCE ENRILE, 62, was a trim man with thick black hair and rimless glasses set on a chiseled face etched with deep wrinkles. The illegitimate son of a prosperous attorney who had a brief liaison with a peasant washerwoman, he had gone to Manila from his rural home in northern Luzon to claim his parentage when he was twenty-one. His father, who had not known of his son's birth, gave him his name and an education, which included law school at the University of the Philippines where he was second in his class. His classmates were members of the country's elite, including Doy Laurel, and Joker Arroyo, who would be one of Ninoy's lawyers. Enrile won a scholarship to Harvard and got a master's degree in 1955. He returned to be a partner in his father's firm, with major corporate clients, and also taught law. He went to work for Marcos in 1966 and held various cabinet posts until he was appointed secretary of defense in 1970. He lost a bid for the Senate in 1971.

During his service to Marcos, Enrile was cut into the banking, coconut, and logging industries and became a multimillionaire. Next to Marcos, he was the most powerful man in the country. Then, in the 1980s, he began to be excluded. General Fabian Ver, a Marcos relative who had been his driver and bodyguard, was named chief of staff in 1981, and he and Imelda, with Marcos's support, helped Enrile's political opponents in his home province of Cagayan.

Enrile responded by beefing up the Ministry of National Defense (MND) security force headed by Colonel Gregorio "Gringo" Honasan with more training and arms. Some people at the time suspected he was building a force for a coup.

Ver's son Irwin in 1983 filed a report to Marcos on the activities of the Security Group, which included training for assassination and kidnapping. Marcos was told that these activities were directed against him, and he confronted Enrile with the report. Enrile and Ramos talked with Marcos in July 1983 about their relationship with the palace and president's people, especially Ver. They asked to be relieved of their duties, but Marcos refused; he said he needed them. Behind the conflict was the contest for succession with Imelda Marcos and Ver. Everyone knew that Mrs. Marcos wanted the post, and Enrile was a likely rival. In 1984, Enrile said he might run for president if Marcos did not seek to stay in office.

Military officers since about 1983 had begun talking informally about Ver's corruption of the armed forces and the resulting demoralization of the troops and the weakening of their ability to deal with the Communist insurgency. In early 1985, a group of colonels set up the Reform Armed Forces Movement (RAM), which would gather some 700 members and many more sympathizers out of the military's 15,000 officers. They began to circulate documents outlining their complaints about favoritism, corruption, the lack of training and discipline among the troops, the failure to supply soldiers with adequate equipment or welfare support. The army, as an independent, nonpolitical institution had been destroyed by Marcos. Top generals, many past the age of retirement, owed their jobs to Marcos and Ver. Many military commanders in the provinces had made alliances with local political and economic powers, some of whom were virtual warlords themselves, with thousands of men in private armies. The colonels were encouraged by some retired generals, but the military's senior officers criticized them as troublemakers.

The movement became public in March 1985 at the Philippine Military Academy (PMA) graduation, when officers wearing T-shirts that said, "We belong . . . ," ("We belong to the 'Reform the Armed Forces of the Philippines Movement,'") unfurled banners calling for an end to corruption and human rights abuses in the military. In August 1985, Enrile and a core group of officers started planning a coup. The idea was first suggested to Enrile by Honasan, 38, and Lieutenant Colonel Eduardo "Red" Kapunan, 38, chief of the MND Special Operations Group, both members of the PMA class of 1971 who would play key roles in the plotting that would continue through the next year. Enrile said he was with them. Other key RAM people involved were Navy captains Felix Turingan, 43, chief of MND information management, and Rex Robles, 43, Enrile's assistant for plans and programs and the RAM spokesman.

RAM was used to establish a network of officers who would support the coup. They began *sorties* around the country, and, using their RAM connections, began talking informally among the younger officers. The idea was not to remove Marcos but his *cordon sanitaire*, General Ver and the cronies Marcos had promoted to high positions. The conspirators gathered the support of colonels, majors, and captains who were prepared to carry out the coup. They met during September and set the coup date for Christmas or New Year's Day. Enrile funded the preparations and the purchase of 1,000 weapons, mostly Israeli assault rifles and machine guns. The strategy was to capture Malacañang. They would set up a junta for two to five years until presidential elections could be held. Marcos would remain as a figurehead.

Lieutenant General Ramos sympathized with the Reformists, but opposed suggestions for a coup, though some of his aides were involved. "Stop pushing the president; this could be the last straw," he told them. He warned that their plan might make Marcos angry and told one officer, "Don't exacerbate the situation. It's enough I'm already tolerating you." Ramos had always been a cautious man, a safe player. He put up with ridicule by Marcos, tolerated abuses by his constabulary, and had not done anything to reform the army during the time of Ver's trial when he was in power. He claimed his hands were tied by Marcos.

When the snap elections were announced in November, the coup plans were shelved. But the Reformists found an organizing advantage in the campaign. In January, they launched Kamalayan, or consciousness, '86, a program of prayer meetings at military camps to urge the officers and soldiers to support fair elections. "It gave us a way to test the mood of the armed forces, to organize and to make contacts and get some funds from businessmen, religious, political and civic organizations," said a military man who was involved. Leading Aquino backers such as Ongpin gave them money. Some promised them sanctuary or jobs if they got into trouble. The project was also a way of emboldening the public by letting them know that elements in the military opposed a fradulent election.

In January, the Reformists met with Pentagon official Colonel William Weiss, who told them the Americans did not want them to do anything unconstitutional, "No bloodshed or violence, but you can move to defend yourselves."

The plotters asked Cory if she would support the coup. She knew they needed her because she was nationally recognized and accepted. "We have to go through elections," she said she told them. "I don't want to be a puppet of anybody." She thought, "If I did not have the elections, what kind of power could I possibly refer to as being my own?" However, her brother Peping remembered another conversation. When RAM leaders, Honasan, Kapunan, and Colonel Vic Batac of PC Intelligence told him they were planning a coup and asked if Cory would support them, he recalled that he said yes. They did not tell him when they were planning to move. Peping told Cory about the plans, and she said, "You take care of that." "They needed Cory, that's what they were always saying; Cory had to be the leader," he would explain later. "We never got into the planning. I didn't ask them. The less I knew, the better." Some representatives of sectoral and social action groups—including the teachers and Bandila—also met with the Reformists and hinted broadly that one of the options open to them was to move against the president.

The RAM boys, as they had come to be known, had been calling the American Embassy to say they were going to act and to ask how the U.S. would react. The Embassy policy was to be unresponsive to requests for assistance. A week before the election, one of the colonels called a CIA contact and asked for anti-tank weapons. The officer had to say why he wanted them. The plotters did not get the weapons, but the U.S. learned of their plans. The Reformist officers would later believe that the Americans briefed Marcos.

Ver had also learned of plotting through one of the officers in the Presidential Security Guard, who Honasan thought supported the coup. At the same time, the Reformists were intercepting the palace's radio communications. "We knew something was in store for us. It had to be preempted," one said. Enrile and the colonels met the weekend of February 15, the same days the National Assembly proclaimed Marcos and Tolentino president and vice president and that Cory held her mass rally. The military men decided to carry out the coup the following Sunday, February 23, at 2 a.m.

Philip Habib arrived in Manila Monday, February 17, and the U.S. moved to intervene. The CIA station chief, Norbert Garrett, told Ver to strengthen the palace defenses but not to act against the RAM officers. The U.S. assistant Army attaché, Major Vic Raphael, believed by local observers to be the Defense Intelligence Agency's officer, told Kapunan that Washington would not look kindly on unconstitutional moves by RAM, that it had told Marcos not to persecute RAM, and that the U.S would understand moves made for self-defense. The colonels decided that the Americans were playing both sides.

Ver, was kept apprised of the conspiracy by his informant, called a meeting of his trusted generals and told them of the plan. Rather than round up the plotters, because of the U.S. warning, he planned to turn the palace into a trap when they approached. He established a contingency "Oplan Everlasting," which would include the arrest and assassination of opposition political leaders and Enrile, Ramos, and the RAM officers—supposedly by the Communists—and a declaration of martial law. "Everlasting" meant it would make the regime last forever. Enrile learned about the meeting of the generals and the contingency plan.

General Ver was an investigator and intelligence man but had never gained staff experience or commanded combat troops. His appointment was an insult to experienced generals and particularly grated on Fidel "Eddie" Ramos, a West Point graduate, a veteran of the Korean War, and a respected professional, who had been passed over for the job. Ramos, 58, a slight man with slicked-back hair, aviator glasses, and a mild look and manner, was a second cousin to Marcos, but that no longer seemed to help him. After Ver's acquittal, Marcos had said that the armed forces chief would be retired, then vacillated and made it known he would retain him until after the elections. It was a great let-down for Ramos. On Wednesday, February 19, Ramos went to the palace to protest the retention of Ver and the "overstaying" generals who had been kept beyond retirement age. Marcos replied that Ver would retire in good time and that Ramos had no claim to the job. Ramos left, pessimistic about his future.

Enrile's troops departed Cagayan province for Manila to be ready for the assault on the palace, and Enrile's plane "Cristina," named after his wife, followed with a shipment of arms.

On Thursday, Robles and Turingan talked with Peping. They discussed Cory's plans to go to rallies in Cebu and Davao. "Don't let her go to Davao," the officers told him. Something might happen, and they could protect her better in Manila. "We have intelligence that armed groups there might cause her harm," Robles warned. But Cory flew to Cebu on Friday. "There's no way I can back out now," she said. Cancelling the rallies would demoralize the people who had organized them.

At midnight on Friday, February 21, a meeting took place in Enrile's home in the expensive, walled, Dasmariñas Village in Makati. His press secretary Silvestre Afable, Captain Turingan, and two other officers went over a speech Enrile would read thirty-six hours later over national radio and television. After the planned assault on Malacañang at 2 a.m., February 23, when Marcos would be captured or killed, he would proclaim himself head of the "National Reconciliation Council." Cory, Ramos, Cardinal Sin, and several technocrats, such as Marcos's Prime Minister Cesar Virata, would be invited to join the junta.

The rebellious officers were aware of a military build-up around the palace that had begun a few days before. When the meeting broke up at 3 a.m., Honasan and Kapunan took a swing around the palace and found a battalion of marines at the site of the planned attack. They knew their plan had been betrayed. At 10 a.m., they began calling their supporters to halt the attack plans. Then they sped to Enrile's house.

That morning, Enrile had been having coffee with some newsmen and politicians in the Atrium Coffeeshop, a favorite gathering place in Makati. He got a phone call from Trade and Industry Minister Roberto Ongpin—Jimmy's brother—that nineteen of Ongpin's security men had been arrested by marines during night exercises at Fort Bonifacio. They had been undergoing training by some of Enrile's men and Ver thought they were part of the coup plot. Enrile called some of his aides and learned about troop movements into the city.

He returned home for lunch; Honasan, his aide Major Noe Wong, and Kapunan, arrived soon after to tell him Marcos was ordering the arrest of Enrile, Ramos, RAM officers, and some opposition leaders. Intelligence officers in Malacañang said they had uncovered a RAM plot to assassinate Marcos and take over the palace. "Oplan Everlasting" was being put into effect.

Lieutenant General Ramos was at that time home, busy with a group of Cory's Crusaders—friends and neighbors who threatened to picket his house with placards that said "Ramos Resign" and "Investigate the Antique [Evelio Javier] Murder." He asked if they would not just talk with him. A newspaper publisher called his wife to say Enrile was about to be arrested. Informed of the fact, Ramos said, "Maybe I will be next." But he turned back to dealing with Cory's Crusaders.

Enrile telephoned Ramos shortly after: "Eddie, we are about to be rounded up. Will you join us?"

Ramos answered, "Don't use the phone, sir, this is not a clear phone. But I am with you all the way."

"If that is the case, then join me at Camp Aguinaldo," Enrile replied.

"I will join you, sir, but I still have to dialogue with some people right here," and—apparently determined to finish the discussion of his neighbors' complaints—he went back to talk to Cory's Crusaders.

There was another call. He answered it, "Sir, I will join you as soon as possible." He left the protestors and went to Camp Aguinaldo.

Enrile asked his wife to call Cardinal Sin; then he took his favorite Uzi submachine gun and left for Camp Aguinaldo, where he and Ramos began calling commanders around the country for their support. He had then only about 300 troops. Enrile also telephoned Bosworth and the Japanese ambassador.

Mrs. Enrile reached Cardinal Sin, and he contacted the contemplative nuns—the Poor Claire Sisters, the Pink Sisters, and the Carmelites—and told them, "Go to the chapel and stretch out your arms and pray and fast and don't eat solidly until I tell you." He explained, "We are in battle and you are the powerhouses. And the moment we do not win the battle, you will have to fast until the end of your life."

Mrs. Enrile also phoned the press: "Go to Camp Aguinaldo. Minister Enrile's life is in danger."

At about 4 p.m., soldiers began barricading the four-story, white concrete Ministry of Defense building inside Camp Aguinaldo.

Meanwhile, Cory in Cebu met that morning with local opposition

111

leaders, then held a noon press conference at the Sacred Heart Center. She said there were no immediate plans to set up a parallel government, but that she would appoint committees whose heads eventually would be appointed to her cabinet. She said the opposition would adopt radical protest actions if three months of the present strategy did not convince Marcos to turn over power. In the afternoon, she led a parade of her supporters to Fuente Osmeña, the town plaza, a circular park with a fountain in the middle, named after the former president. She asked local opposition leader Tony Cuenco for a list of Cebu firms she should add to the national boycott list. The rally started at 5 p.m., and she began her speech half an hour later.

Afterward, Cory, Peping, and her daughter Kris, went to the house of a personal friend, a local businessman's wife, where they were staying. Journalist Belinda Olivares, who had heard the rumor of Enrile's arrest a few hours earlier, chose instead to tell Cory about how the wife of Cory's cousin Danding had gone to a wedding a few nights before and become furious because Coca Cola, bottled by her husband's company, San Miguel, was being boycotted. She ordered someone to fetch a large bottle and put it on the table. Cory was amused and shocked.

Opposition leader and former member of parliament, Ramon "Monching" Mitra arrived, and Olivares interrupted her story to whisper to him, "Did you hear about what happened in Manila?"

"Did you tell Cory?" he asked.

"No, not yet," she replied.

"Well, what are you waiting for?"

She turned to Cory. "I've news for you. Enrile has been arrested."

"Oh, really?" Cory replied. Olivares thought she looked worried for a second, but then she went on to ask more about the wedding. About a half hour later, somebody turned on the television and saw Enrile holding his press conference. They realized he had not been taken prisoner, but was holed up in Camp Aguinaldo.

In the capital, Enrile and Ramos were on the third floor in the social hall of the Ministry of National Defense. The lights were out throughout the building, and heavily armed solidiers were deployed on all floors and on the roof. Five helicopters arrived with more armed troops from Cagayan; they thought they had come to carry out a coup.

The press conference began at 6:30 p.m. Enrile wore a long-sleeved fatigue jacket over a bullet-proof vest, blue jeans, and sneakers. Ramos had on a gray bush jacket and pants, and was, as usual, smoking a thick cigar. Enrile did not mention the coup. He said, "I was informed by my boys that there is to be an effort to arrest all members of the Reformist movement. So, this afternoon, some of my boys came to my house and asked me to move to the camp."

He said, "As of now, I cannot in good conscience recognize the president as the commander in chief of the armed forces. I believe that the mandate of the people does not belong to the present regime, and I know for a fact that there had been some anomalies committed during the elections. I searched my conscience and I felt that I could not serve a government that is not expressive of the sovereign will." He declared, "Personally, I think Marcos did not really win this election."

He also mentioned his personal gripes. He told the reporters that promotions had been made without consulting him or Ramos, that the MND had become a decoration, a deodorant.

"Our loyalty is to the Constitution and to the Filipino people, to our country, and I'm calling on all decent elements in the cabinet, decent elements in the government, decent Filipinos and decent soldiers and officers of the AFP [Armed Forces of the Philippines] who are trained to respect the constitution and to protect the welfare of this nation and its people to wake up and support the movement," he said.

Ramos declared that Marcos had pressured the military to issue arms to his followers to carry out political terrorism and fraud. He also revealed the details of the palace plans to arrest the opposition leaders and military reformists.

Enrile, who said he had not had any contact with Cory, at first hedged about whether he would support her. Would he accept her authority as president?

"I am not making any conclusion," he replied. "Whoever is considered by the Filipino people to be the representative of their will must be respected."

Was he willing to talk with her about the situation?

"I suppose at this point that anybody who would support us is welcome," he said.

Would he serve under Cory if she were installed as president?

"I am talking of a country and people and not of men to whom we owe loyalty." He declared, "I am not interested in power or position in the government. I am not doing this because I want glory or wealth or power. I am doing this as a matter of duty and obligation to our people."

But the journalists pressed him. If he believed Cory was duly elected, would he support her?

He was pushed to the wall. "I am morally convinced that it was Mrs. Aquino who was elected by the Filipino people. Yes, we are comitted to support her."

Would he agree to join her government? "I have not made up my mind," Enrile said.

After the broadcast, Cory and the opposition leaders sat down for dinner before discussing what they would do. Everyone else was pensive and tense, but she was smiling, talking and laughing. Then they turned on Radio Veritas to get the news from Manila.

Cory stayed with the wives eating and talking, while the men moved out to the terrace. They included Peping, Cuenco, Mitra, Aquilino "Nene" Pimentel, Neptali Gonzales, and Homobono Adaza. Although Laurel had been in town for the rally, he could not be reached. He had not been invited to the dinner because Sonny Osmeña, Cory's local political leader, was feuding with him. When he found out about the rebellion, he chose not to contact them and simply returned to Manila in his own plane the next morning.

The opposition leaders began to become concerned about Cory's safety. Ironically, the house was in a cul-de-sac, back-to-back with an army camp. They decided to move her out and, to throw off anyone who would be snooping, to keep her son-in-law and others who normally accompanied her visible in the garden. They asked Nancy Cuenco to find a secure place for Cory. She would call the Carmelite nuns, who were friends.

Cory called Manila to tell her daughter Ballsy to go to a safe house. When she got off the phone, she said, "Guess who's trying to get hold of me? Johnny [Enrile]." The phone rang minutes later. It was their first conversation since Ninoy's assassination.

She asked Enrile the purpose of his actions. He said Marcos did not have the people's mandate and that she should assume the presidency. He also told her that Marcos had planned to arrest her. She asked what she could do for him and the rebel troops. "Madam, there's nothing much you can do for us right now except to pray," he replied.

"We are very much with you and we'll keep praying for you," she said.

The American consul in Cebu, Blaine Porter, arrived at the house and told Cory that a U.S. submarine tender was at the dock and at her disposal. She declined the offer.

In Manila, after the press conference, Ramos went to Camp Crame to set up a defensive position. The rebels still had only 300 troops and 1,000 light arms. They were ranged against Marcos's Presidential Security Guard of 8,000 men, with tanks and helicopter gunships. But the Presidential Guards were led by an incompetent, General Fabian Ver.

Ver expected the coup at 2 a.m. the next morning and spent Sunday afternoon at a wedding. He rushed back to the palace at 5 p.m., then called Enrile, who consented to speak with him after the press conference. Ver begged, "You must tell your men not to attack the palace." Enrile asked Ver not to attack Crame that night; they would discuss the matter the next morning. They agreed to hold their fire. The campaign was waged on the telephone, as Ramos and Enrile called military commanders all over the country to seek their support. They would win over the key officers, including the air force and helicopter command.

At 9 p.m. Cory, Peping, Kris, and the Cuencos got into a new white Ford sedan borrowed from Lito Osmeña, a member of the local political dynasty. Peping told the security men not to follow them. As they drove off, Mrs. Cuenco told her husband, "We are going to the Carmelite Monastery." Cory was very calm. It was a three-mile drive, but they took a roundabout way, doubling back through the streets. "Why are we turning and turning?" Kris asked. "Tony is trying to avoid whoever is following us," her mother replied. They thought they were being trailed by a motorcycle. The gate of the high-walled monastery was padlocked, and Cuenco sounded the horn. A nun opened the gate, and they drove up to the large concrete building. Cory went to bed while Peping and Cuenco stayed up to listen to radio reports. She slept "magnificently"—although without a mattress. The nuns had told her they were ready to die to defend her.

At 9 p.m., in Manila, Cardinal Sin went on Radio Veritas: "I am deeply concerned about the situation of General Ramos and Minister Enrile. I am calling on our people to support our two good friends. Go to Camp Aguinaldo and show your solidarity with them in this crucial period. Bring them food," he added. "They have nothing to eat." Cory would later comment that he had been hesitant to issue the call but had been pressed by a number of church laymen. In the beginning, only a handful of people heeded him.

At 10:30 p.m., Marcos called a televised press conference to expose the aborted coup and to display some of the arrested officers. He said Honasan, Kapunan, and others had planned to attack the palace and capture him and his wife. Colonel Marcelo Malajacan, an infantry battalion commander admitted that the plan had been to seize Marcos, force him to resign or go into exile, and invite some credible people to lead the country. Captain Ricardo Morales, another prisoner, said they would have set up a multisectoral council, with such members as Cory, former Prime Minister Cesar Virata, General Ramos, and Cardinal Sin, to govern until a constitution was drafted and elections were held.

"I feel sad," Marcos said. "I did not know Enrile and Ramos could reach this height of treason and rebellion." Marcos's charge was widely disbelieved. Ramos called it a figment of Marcos's imagination; Enrile dismissed it as "a lot of bull."

Cecilia Muñoz Palma called Radio Veritas to express support for Enrile and Ramos. Butz called her and asked, "Justice, is it true that we are supporting Enrile and Ramos?"

She told him, yes, but to be careful.

Butz promptly went to see Enrile to tell him, "I came to help you." Enrile replied, "We need all the support we can get."

Butz phoned members of Bandila and also went on Radio Veritas to call people to march with him to Camp Aguinaldo. By 10:30 p.m. only six people had shown up at the rendezvous site, but by midnight, there were 10,000. They marched to the camp; soon there were 20,000 to 30,000 in the streets around the compound and on Epifanio de los Santos, the big boulevard between Camp Aguinaldo and Camp Crame, called by the initials EDSA.

Other commanders joined the mutiny. Marcos called on one of his generals to disperse the crowd, which had dipped to a few thousand before dawn, but the general stalled him; he had gone over to the rebels. Finally, hours later, he told Marcos the crowd was too big to remove. Marcos sought to silence Radio Veritas, but the commander ignored his order. By then there were 50,000 people in the streets surrounding the camps. They were leaning on car horns, chanting, singing nationalist songs, strolling, buying food from the sidewalk vendors who had quickly come on the scene. Banners of local student clubs and activist groups were hung from the camp gates. There was a carnival atmosphere. But, by early Sunday morning, the crowds that had numbered 50,000 at EDSA had shrunk to 500.

In Washington at 4 a.m. Manila time, the White House released a statement that noted the resignations of Enrile and Ramos, and said their charges of election fraud "strongly reinforce our concerns that the recent elections were marred by fraud, perpetuated overwhelmingly by the ruling party, so extreme as to undermine the credibility and legitimacy of the election and impair the capacity of the government of the Philippines to cope with a growing insurgency and troubled economy."

In Cebu, Cory met reporters in the morning for a pre-scheduled press conference at the Magellan Hotel. She told them she had been taken by surprise. Jubilant, she urged the country to give its full support to Enrile and Ramos. She again called on Marcos to step down. She also said she was happy with Reagan's statement. Somebody asked why she had not issued a statement the night before. "Nobody woke me up," she answered.

After the press conference, she drove to the airport. She was cheered by the employees and passengers on the tarmac before she took a private Cessna to Manila. It flew low to avoid jets Marcos might send after her. She had remained unruffled since discovery of the rebellion, but she said a lot of rosaries on the plane.

At noon, Enrile and his men joined Ramos across the street at Camp Crame to consolidate the rebel forces there.

Cory arrived in Manila at 2:20 p.m., went to the home of her sister Josephine Reyes in Wack Wack, an expensive walled community. She called Cardinal Sin and said she was worried. "There is a big problem. There is a third force."

He said, "No, they are staging this because they want you to be the president. Go there and thank them. Without this, you could be demonstrating every day and you will still not be president. But now you will be. You can see the hand of God. This is the answer to our prayers."

She talked with Enrile by phone. Opposition leaders had met that morning, and several went to see him to assess the situation.

Ramos broadcast an appeal for more people to protect the camp. There was word of an impending attack. He said, "An overwhelming

117

force has been assembled and directed to move against us." Enrile called Bosworth and said a tank column and two marine battalions were on the way and that if they attacked, they would kill many people, including journalists, some of whom were Americans. The message was meant to be passed on to Malacañang. Enrile also called Ver to tell him that he and Marcos would go down in history as butchers if they attacked. Ver agreed to hold the tanks.

Marcos, nevertheless, was determined to fight, but his troops delayed for hours. When the tanks and armored transports and 3,000 soldiers finally arrived on the roads leading to the camps, they were stopped by human barricades. Nuns knelt in front of the tanks and recited the rosary. There were over half a million people around the camps; they would grow to a million that day and at the height, reach several million.

Cory's aides and supporters made frequent visits to the camp to see Enrile and Ramos. On Sunday, Tañada expressed fears of a military takeover, but Enrile assured him that he and Ramos "will deliver everything to Mrs. Corazon C. Aquino." Peping promised Enrile and Ramos to bring out more people to protect the camp. Enrile told opposition leaders that it would be advisable for Cory to announce formation of her government not later than Tuesday, the day of Marcos's planned inauguration. He declared that he recognized Cory as the "duly elected president" and was prepared to serve under her administration with "absolutely no preconditions."

In the evening, Cory went on the radio to call on people to go to EDSA to protect Enrile, Ramos, and their rebel forces. She said she had been surprised by their decision to quit the government and urged decent Marcos officials to do the same.

In the early hours of Monday morning, there were few people left at EDSA. The rebels, monitoring the palace communications, heard the orders to attack at dawn. June Keithly, the chief broadcaster on Radio Veritas, called on people to come out to protect the camps. At 4:30 a.m., four trucks with heavily armed soldiers approached the camp. An hour later, riot troops dispersed crowds with truncheons and tear gas, and broke into Camp Aguinaldo.

Across the street at Camp Crame, the soldiers heard mass, were given absolution, played the Philippine Military Academy anthem and bade each other good-bye. They believed they were going to die. Shortly after dawn, at about 6 a.m., they heard the helicopters as they appeared to dive toward the camp. "That's it; this is going to be bloody," the officers thought. But the gunships, that were to support the loyalist assault troops, pulled out of their dives, climbed and then returned to land one by one at Camp Crame. Cheers erupted. The defectors embraced the rebels. Three other choppers flew to Manila's Villamor Air Base, controlled by loyalists, and destroyed six helicopters that were on the ground. Then they proceded to Clark Air Base, a half hour to the north, and were armed and refueled by U.S. military authorities. The commander of the navy also defected and sent a ship to turn its guns on the palace.

In Washington, Manila's night was daytime, Sunday. Key White House advisors met with Secretary of State George Shultz at his house in the morning and talked to President Reagan in the afternoon. They decided that Marcos was finished. At 6:30 a.m. Manila time, the White House issued a statement that any attempt to resolve the situation by force would cause bloodshed, polarize the country, and cause untold damage to relations with the U.S. It was very specific: "We cannot continue our existing military assistance if the government uses that aid against other elements of the Philippine military which enjoy substantial popular backing." Reagan sent a private message to Marcos saying he and his family were welcome to live in the U.S.

On Monday morning, after a false report that Marcos had fled, Cory went on radio to thank the people for supporting Enrile and Ramos and asked them to continue protecting them. Cory and opposition leaders met in the house of Doy Laurel. Homobono Adaza and Luis Villafuerte were sent to talk to Enrile and Ramos to make an assessment of the situation.

Cory had been pressing to go to EDSA, but her security officers and many of her supporters were against it. General Ramos, also opposed, said there might be snipers. She insisted and was about to leave when security told her there were loyalist troops on the way to the site. She went on to another meeting with opposition leaders at Laurel's house.

Villafuerte and others who had been to see Enrile reported back to Cory and the coalition. Villafuerte said he wanted to go back to Enrile to see if they could get some guns so that if the camp were hit by Marcos, they could take military action outside. Cory was vague about her position on securing arms, but the others favored the idea. After the meeting, Cory insisted on going to EDSA. "I am responsible for those people at EDSA; I must show myself to them."

She told her security, "If you do not take me there, I am going by myself." People had been clamoring for Cory's presence at the military camps, and she and Laurel finally appeared at 3 p.m., speaking alongside of Enrile and Ramos from a makeshift platform on the steps of the Philippine Overseas Employment Agency. She told the crowd, "For the first time in the history of the world, a civilian population has been called to defend the military." She declared, "I am proud of you" and urged them to continue their vigilance.

Villafuerte returned with several others to find out whether they could secure arms. Enrile told him that the armory was at the other camp under control of the Marcos loyalists, and he had only enough weapons for his own men.

Enrile urged them to tell Cory and Laurel to take their oaths of office even if Marcos stayed. He said they should appoint five cabinet members. "You tell Cory and Doy to organize a civilian government. You take care of the civilian operations, we take care of the military operations."

Marcos went on television to belie the rumors of his departure, but the broadcast over the government's Channel 4 was cut off midway. The station had been taken over by the rebels. Later, one of the defecting helicopters flew over the palace and fired six rockets, terrifying Marcos.

In the afternoon, military security men phoned Cory at her house on Times Street and told her to move out because there was going to be a firefight at a television station little more than a block away. While they were talking to her, live radio at her house broadcast the bursts of gunfire that had already erupted.

The White House wanted Cardinal Sin to go to Malacañang to negotiate with Marcos, but Sin responded, "It should be the president of the United States who insists that he should leave the country." The U.S. also arranged a phone call to Sin from José Azcona, the president of Honduras, where he hoped Marcos could go into exile. President Azcona told the cardinal, "We have decided not to accept him, but if you ask, we will do it." Sin declined the suggestion.

Marcos ordered his fighters to bomb Camp Crame, but they refused. Washington knew of Marcos's orders for a direct assault, but did not act. U.S. representatives continued collecting information on which units had gone over to the rebels. The Reformist officers felt let down by the U.S. "We felt the Americans did not do anything. They refused even to refuel our helicopters until after we were already winning," said one. Another added, "Till 85 percent swung over to the Enrile-Ramos side."

Monday afternoon, Ver decided on a final "suicide assault" on the rebels, but Washington learned of it, and finally, in a statement issued by his spokesman, Reagan publicly called on Marcos to resign. He said, "Attempts to prolong the life of the present regime by violence are futile. A solution to this crisis can only be achieved through a peaceful transition to a new government." Bosworth read the message to Marcos and offered him an aircraft to use to leave the country. Habib would return to help arrange the transfer of power. Ver was already on the phone giving his orders to fire, but the commander had gone over to the other side. Cory's spokesman, Rene Saguisag, told the press that the statement constituted Washington's "functional recognition" of the Aquino government.

In the evening, Marcos went on television to say his family was "cowering in terror in Malacañang because of the threat of bombing by helicopter," but that he would not leave the country. He showed a dated newspaper to dispel rumors that he had fled. At 3 a.m., Marcos put through a call to U.S. Senator Paul Laxalt. He promised a compromise with Cory and asked the help of the White House. Laxalt consulted Reagan and his top foreign policymakers. When he called Marcos back a few hours later, he told him to "cut and cut cleanly."

"I am so very, very disappointed," replied the fallen dictator.

Cory decided to hold the inauguration at Club Filipino, which she said was a neutral and public place. It also had a history as a meeting place of early Philippine nationalists and later of the anti-Marcos opposition. Enrile had pressed Cory to hold the ceremony at Camp Crame on the grounds that Club Filipino was not defensible, but she refused. "No way am I going to be installed in a military camp for my proclamation, because that would just give everybody the wrong impression," she told her advisers at her Times Street home early Tuesday morning. "First of all, we must remember what Crame means to me and to the people. Camp Crame was the first place where Ninoy, where every political detainee was brought," she said. "Today it may be a place of heroism, but unfortunately, a lot of tortures, executions and summary detentions took place there in the past." She concluded, "I have decided against being inaugurated in a military establishment. I am a civilian president." She also did not want it to appear that she had taken office through a military coup.

General Ramos recommended strongly that she go to the site by helicopter, but she "absolutely refused." She said, "I wouldn't want to be trapped in a place where I can be brought anywhere the pilot might want to bring me."

As she was getting ready to leave Times Street, the sound of machine-gun and rifle fire reached the house. Reformists were attempting to capture the nearby television station. A sniper on one of the towers could be seen through the picture window.

That morning, Marcos called Enrile and asked if he could cancel the election and stay until 1988 as honorary president while Enrile headed a provisional government. "I just want a graceful exit," he said. "I would like to leave politics in a clean and orderly manner." Enrile told him, "We are not really interested in power. Our mission was not to establish a military junta or a military government." Besides, he said, "It's too late, because we've already committed ourselves to support Mrs. Aquino."

Enrile and Ramos flew in separate helicopters the four blocks from Camp Crame to Club Filipino. There were about 800 people jammed into the hall. They were the city's upper class, the ones who lived in the exclusive walled communities where armed guards sat at the gates to monitor visitors, the ones who had made the decisions about the people power revolt. With a few exceptions, the men and women seated on the platform also represented the country's elite. Outside, several thousand ordinary members of the people power brigades pressed their faces against a wall of windows, or waited to listen to the ceremony over loudspeakers.

Cory arrived shortly after 10 a.m. in the white Chevrolet van she had used during her campaign. Wearing a trademark yellow dress, she took her oath on a Bible held by Doña Aurora. "I would like to appeal to everybody to work for national reconciliation, which is what Ninoy came home for," she said in her brief inaugural address. She said she was magnanimous in victory and called on those who were not her supporters to join her to rebuild the country. Then they sang the Lord's Prayer, the nationalist hymn, "Bayan Ko," and the national anthem, raising their hands in the Laban sign.

Cory named Laurel prime minister and minister of foreign affairs, Enrile minister of national defense, and Ramos chief of staff of the New Armed Forces of the Philippines, with a promotion to general.

When Marcos took his oath at noon, his vice-presidential partner, Arturo Tolentino, did not show up. The diplomatic corps was not invited, and most reporters were barred from the ceremony. That afternoon, Marcos phoned Enrile again and asked him to contact Bosworth to provide security for his departure. Bosworth arranged for the U.S. Military Assistance Group to do the job, then called Cory at her sister Josephine's house to tell her Marcos would leave for Clark Air Base, and he would notify her when he arrived.

It was after dark when two U.S. Sikorsky helicopters landed on the palace golf course. Marcos and his family boarded one; Ver and his sons took the other. They lifted off at 9 p.m. and reached Clark half an hour later. Bosworth phoned Cory and, relaying a message from Washington, asked if Marcos could remain for a few days in Ilocos Norte. Her initial reaction was to let him stay in a spirit of humanitarianism. She asked Bosworth if Marcos was about to die. He answered, no.

Her advisors told her that Marcos's presence would be a rallying point that could lead to bloodshed. Cory refused the request. "Tell Marcos to continue his trip to the United States. It is in the interests of the Filipino people that he immediately leave the country."

When the helicopters took off, people began gathering at Malacañang. By midnight, sure Marcos was gone, thousands stormed the palace. Some looted the rooms they could break into, burning and defacing Marcos's papers, pictures, and property. They also stole weapons, including 1,100 Galils, Uzis, Armalite rifles made in the Philippines, and handguns. Someone drew a moustache on a painting of Imelda Marcos. Troops arrived after a few hours to restore order and protect the palace.

Cory cleared the names of those that would leave with Marcos, including her cousin, Danding. However, she did not know they had packed millions of dollars in cash, gold, jewelry, furs, stocks, property deeds and certificates of deposit. Officials at Clark made Marcos leave $3 million in U.S. currency in the Philippines, but he was allowed to take the rest.

Ever cognizant of the worth of things, Marcos had left his phony war medals in the palace.

The Presidency

CORY was a phenomenon. A charismatic leader who spoke in a monotone, she aroused trust, love, even adulation among the masses. She was not simply Catholic, but spiritual to the core. She did not attend daily mass, but prayed often and referred to God in her private conversations as well as public speeches. She believed that God moved her, that if there was something she had to do in the world, God would take care of her. She was also a fatalist. Death would come at the appointed time. Those who tried to scare her should have realized that her faith and fatalism would make her a willing martyr.

Those closest to her said her most trusted advisor was not any of her aides, but her husband. A picture of Ninoy taken in the plane moments before his death had a place of honor in Cory's Malacañang office. She said that when the difficulties of her office overwhelmed her, she turned to the picture and said, "What would you do? How would you handle this?"

Cory was a polite, courteous, upper class lady. But underneath the smile, lay a strong character and personality. During Ninoy's imprisonment, his family called her "wonder woman" and "woman of steel." One of her ministers once remarked, "The whole world is going into a panic, but you don't see it in her face." She was known for what some called moral resolve and others said was a stubborn streak.

Years in America had made her frank and blunt in her speech. She had, she said, a long memory for those who had helped her and a longer memory for those who had stood in her way. She said, "It takes me a long time to get really angry, but it takes me equally long to forget." Referring to her husband's death, she remarked, "I try not to think about those people who are responsible for the assassination of Ninoy, but I continue to pray that God will give me grace to forgive them."

Yet, in a society of macho politicians, she was not concerned about looking strong. She did not display anger frequently in dealing with the opposition. She did not practice a confrontational style of government. She felt that as a woman she had something unique to offer her country. "Women are less liable to resort to violence than men," she said, "and at this time in my country's history, what is really needed is a man or woman of peace." Singapore's Prime Minister Lee Kuan Yew would call her "gentle, softspoken, unpretentious, sincere, not wanting to impress, wanting to do what is right, with an abiding sense of her responsibility and her duty to her people."

Sometimes her personal sense of what was right had to take second place to her responsibility as president. Before she received the South Korean foreign minister, her advisors reminded her that she should not mention opposition leader Kim Dae Jung, who was her friend. "I always have to consciously remind myself, okay, your personal life is a thing of the past. You now represent the Filipino people. I will not do anything to upset Philippine-Korean relations," she would remark later. When an emissary from Kim asked if she would invite him to visit, she thought to herself, "I'm no longer my own boss."

Cory was controlled. She would not be rushed. She looked at each dot and comma in the speeches her aides drafted. She was orderly; the objects around her were carefully arranged. It was a fastidiousness that extended to smoking, which was banned or discouraged in the palace building that housed the presidential offices.

She had always lived simply, and her style would not become ceremonial. Protocol chief Miguel Perez-Rubio asked her the day after the inauguration if he should call her Madam President or Mrs. President.

"Oh, Miguel," she said, "why don't you call me Cory as you have till now?"

He insisted.

She said, "Mrs. President. If there's a Mr. Reagan and a Monsieur Mitterrand, what's wrong with Mrs. President?"

He asked if he should send a memo to the ministries stating her preference.

"No, Miguel," she replied. "I just happen to like Mrs. President more."

She wanted to cut down on the extravagance and extravaganzas of the previous administration. Marcos, presiding over cabinet meetings or dinners, used a higher, "imperial-style" chair. Cory insisted that she sit level with everyone else. She would be taken aback by the pomp and ceremony that greeted her in her travels. After she returned from Indonesia and Singapore, she told relatives, "Now I know why people so desperately want to become president. When you visit a foreign country, you are lionized." "I guess I'm still not used to all the power," she told an interviewer. "Although I have to admit, my goodness, nothing to worry about as far as traffic is concerned now, especially since my security won't stop at red lights."

A more stirring reminder of her change in status came when she visited Camp Aguinaldo. "Before, I used to be so afraid every time I went there," she said. "I had to get my ID and wait before, finally, I was allowed to see Minister Enrile. Now, all of a sudden, it's different."

Cory spent the first day as president still in her penthouse office in the Cojuangco building in Makati. Troops were sweeping the palace and grounds for booby traps and cleaning up the debris left by the thousands of looters. However, as she had promised during the campaign, she would not live in the palace, a beautiful, sprawling white concrete colonial Spanish-style building set in a park and elegantly furnished with antiques. She maintained her campaign declaration that it was inappropriate for the leader of an impoverished nation to live in such luxury.

Her first task was to assemble her cabinet. It was done hurriedly. "One day, we were on the barricades, and the next we were in power," recalled her aide Saguisag. "During the revolution, the observation was made that power abhors a vacuum," he said. "There was a sense of urgency in putting together a Cory government."

The key people helping her were Saguisag, her brother Peping,

Jimmy Ongpin, Joker Arroyo, and Ateneo University President Father Joaquin Bernas. Quick consultations were made with groups and individuals. There was no luxury of a transition period to ruminate over candidates.

But Cory knew whom she wanted. Some opposition leaders who met in a "crisis committee" to help her choose the ministers, discovered that she already had a list of seven appointees. The cabinet was picked mostly from among the people who had worked with her and with Ninoy since the time of Marcos. She wanted people she knew and trusted. Some were members of what came to be known as the Catholic Church-Ateneo University mafia that one wag dubbed the "Council of Trent." Enrile would later complain that the military had not been consulted on cabinet appointments.

She immediately chose Arroyo to be her executive secretary and chief aide. Jose "Joe" Concepcion, who had headed NAMFREL and ran a food and flour manufacturing company, and who was close to the Church, was made minister of trade and industry. Ongpin, also of "the council," and Cory's chief economic advisor now as before the election, was named finance minister. His appointment raised some flak when it was discovered that he knew that Imelda Marcos's brother, Kokoy, secretly owned 60 percent of the Benguet Mining Corporation that Ongpin had run for sixteen years. Another controversial cabinet member appointed shortly was Marcos's holdover Jose "Jobo" Fernandez, who kept his job as head of the Central Bank. Solita "Winnie" Monsod, an economics professor at the University of the Philippines, was selected as head of the National Economic Development Authority and took some UP economics department people along with her.

Diokno would be made head of the Presidential Commission on Human Rights, and Salonga would be charged with recovering the stolen wealth of Marcos and his cronies. It was difficult to find acceptable nominees for the controversial labor and agrarian reform ministries and those appointments were delayed. Cory later explained that she had been sure she could get fifty honest and qualified men and women to help her run the government, but it turned out not to be so easy. As a result, she had had to take some people who had been connected with Marcos. "How many can be like Ninoy or Pepe Diokno or Salonga?" she asked.

Justice Palma, who had suggested to Cory that there ought to be more women in the cabinet, was in the president's Cojuangco building office the day the first list of ministers was to be announced.

"You said we should have women in the cabinet," said Cory. "Here is the ministry of education. Can you think of a woman to fill this position?"

Palma suggested Lourdes Quisumbing, president of Maryknoll College, a Catholic girls school. Cory did not know her. "She has an exemplary family life, is a good Catholic, and has administered the school," Palma told her. Palma served on Maryknoll College's board of trustees. Education is a crucial area for the Church, and the education ministry is traditionally given to someone from the private Catholic sector of education.

On that basis, Cory said, "All right, contact her." Quisumbing was not reached until the afternoon, but quickly accepted, and her name was on the list of cabinet members Cory announced to the press at the Mondragon building later that day.

Nene Pimentel, the head of PDP-Laban, who had run the 1978 ticket that Ninoy headed and been elected to the Assembly in 1984, was made minister of local government, charged with weeding out the Marcos men from municipal to national office. Monching Mitra, a wealthy cattle rancher who had been elected to the Senate in 1971 and the Assembly in 1984, became minister of agriculture. Ernesto Maceda, one of Ninoy's aides and lawyers during his exile, was given the ministry of natural resources. Neptali Gonzales, dean of the law school of the Far Eastern University, was awarded the justice portfolio.

They and other members of the cabinet represented the middle and business class that had put Cory in power. Gone were the members of the old families of the landed and commercial oligarchy and their representatives. Marcos's selective land reform of rice and sugar plantations and his establishment of marketing monopolies over sugar and coconuts had broken their economic power. These were the new rich. When Cory reported her net worth, about $885,000, and asked her cabinet ministers to do the same, almost all of them listed six-figure incomes. There were no people of working class or peasant origins, though the labor and agrarian-reform ministers appointed later would be acceptable to worker and farmer groups.

Cory finally "took power" in Malacañang two weeks after her inauguration. She moved into a converted bedroom of the whitewashed guest house, a long and narrow two-story building with a glass facade, with upper rooms set off a balcony over a two-story "sala" that ran the length of the house. Furniture was moved out of some rooms to make space for office desks, but the white bamboo chairs and couches with greenish-blue flowered cushions were left in the new lobby. A picture book called *People Power,* about the February revolution, would later lay on the coffee table. Malacañang was opened to the public as a museum, a reminder of the Marcoses' excesses. Cory asked her cabinet ministers to follow simple and austere lifestyles.

Cabinet meetings were held in the ornate state dining room where ministers sat on chairs of white and gold painted carved wood covered in red velvet. Light wood paneling edged the hexagonal mirrors on the ceiling; and the long room was lit by crystal chandeliers and wall sconces. At one end was a mural of peasants at a fiesta; another picture showed them harvesting rice.

Cory encouraged discussion and debate in the cabinet so she could hear different views before making her own decisions. She did not pretend to know everything, but she could not be easily swayed or forced to come up with a quick answer. She would sit and listen. When she reached a decision and said, "This is what I feel," the discussion stopped. In most cases, she delegated decision-making to the ministries. When ministers asked her to press a colleague to go along with a certain policy, she told them, "Work it out among yourselves." She did not like being pressured. Once, annoyed at all the people who presumed to tell her what to do, she declared that she did not like "unsolicited advice." Cory would get involved immediately when there was a question of personalities rather than issues and try to smooth over the conflicts.

The revolution that made her president had been supported by a wide spectrum of groups and interests, across classes, ideologies and parties. The differences that had been pushed aside before now came out, particularly in the weekly cabinet meetings that were used as a quasi-parliamentary sounding board in the absence of a legislature. The elegant surroundings were sometimes the venue of inelegant bickering. The pro-worker minister of labor, Augusto "Bobbit" Sanchez, battled the pro-business ministers of trade and finance. "The need of the country is investment, and here we are with a labor minister talking about profit-sharing," protested Ongpin. Pimentel backed up Sanchez, saying, "There is a need to address mass poverty. We have to give labor a fair shake." At that point, Cory got exasperated, and declared, "I'm the one who makes the decisions."

Some of the cabinet appointees also fought over turf. Half of them were hoping to be elected to the new parliament and sought to establish political strength. At one meeting where cabinet members were splitting hairs, she declared, "I've had it. I just have to remind you I'm the president, and if you cannot respect me, there's no way we can work together." They froze and later related the story, in astonishment, to reporters waiting outside.

One consolation through all the conflict was that she was not beholden to the radical Left, and they were not in her government. "Thank God, they didn't help. Now I don't owe them anything," she told her aides.

The first major issue for the government was what to do with the Marcos institutions. Cory and her advisors feared they would be stymied by a legislature dominated by Marcos loyalists. They began immediately to discuss the need to abolish the constitution and proclaim a revolutionary government.

The members of Marcos's KBL, trying to keep their hold on whatever they could, promised they would legitimate Cory's government in the parliament if she kept the old constitution and Batasan. In a committee set up to consider the issue, Laurel and Enrile suggested that the parliament be retained on condition the MPs agree to ratify certain democratizing amendments and to formally proclaim Cory and Laurel president and vice president, respectively. But compromising with the Marcos loyalists was out of the question. Cory said that it was necessary to cut through red tape and push through political and economic reforms. She feared being trapped by a KBL majority that might make promises in order to stay in power but not abide by them. Then, they could be removed only by charges proved in individual cases. Cory declared that the parliament was a "cancer in our political system which must be cut out." She said, "Just as cronies pillaged our economy, so the KBL Batasan majority debased our politics." A month after she took her oath, she abolished the constitution and the Batasan.

She proclaimed a provisional Freedom Constitution, written by Father Bernas, that included a bill of rights and other safeguards of liberty. Otherwise, the president had blanket authority to pass or change all laws, reorganize the government, revoke or alter agreements on the use of natural resources made by Marcos, and select or remove all elected or appointed officials. She would have to convene a commission within sixty days to draft a new constitution. She would not call her transitional rule a revolutionary government;

she did not like the word "revolutionary" and took it out of the proclamation, though everyone recognized the government was, in fact, revolutionary.

Her new powers did not dismay most people. The head of the Chamber of Commerce and Industry called the new provisional government democratic in character and essential to bring about a democratic government. He said the government had to respond to the needs of the people without being hampered by legal obstacles based on the 1973 constitution which the peoples revolution had dismantled.

A few of her advisors, such as Palma and Pimentel, opposed the abolition of the constitution and parliament.

Palma told Cory, "We have to preserve the institutions, while we do not like the people who are there, if we will abide by our promise to the people that we will effect reforms through the constitutional legal process in place. We could do it." Cory replied that she had to abolish the legal body, because that is what the people wanted her to do.

The Marcos opposition had a field day, charging that she was installing a new dictatorship and threatening street demonstrations. Marcos labor minister Blas Ople said she had "opened the floodgates of abuse and refuted her own claims to being a champion of Philippine democracy." People took such charges by the ousted Marcos officials with a grain of salt.

Some in the Unido branch of the coalition were also at odds with the president. Its general secretary, Rene Espina, called her government "dictatorial" and said it was making decisions without consulting its allies. At a press conference, Espina said the Freedom Constitution was authoritarian. He said a radical wing was gaining dominance in the government and that the Unido members of the legislature might join the reconvening of a rebel Batasan in defiance of the Aquino government.

The fragile election coalition was beginning to fall apart. The underlying reason for Unido's hostility was its leaders' view that its members had been cut out of appointments. They got only a few cabinet jobs and, even more important for the health of its base, felt they had not gotten enough middle-level and lower posts in the national administration and local government. Perhaps more to the point, Rene Espina had been left out.

The Marcos appointees clearly had to go, and under the revolutionary government, Cory did not recognize the legitimacy of the elected KBL officials. She decided to replace nearly all of them with Officers in Charge, OICs. Elected officials' terms expired March 2, and a law passed by the old Batasan had extended them through June on the assumption there would be an election in May. Cory decided it was too soon for another contest.

Local government minister Pimentel proposed that the incumbents be replaced, and the massive job was begun, with the posts awarded on the basis of consultation with the groups that had supported Cory in the election. Local bishops and priests also wielded important influence. "They were political positions, and the opinions of the recognized political leaders of an area had to be given much weight," said Pimentel.

The wholesale firing of more than seventy provincial governors, 1,600 mayors and more than 10,000 council members set off a storm of bitter protests that would continue through the year. In the end, 90 percent of local officials—elected on tickets supported by Marcos—would be replaced. But the conflicts that were engendered in the first few months when Cory was just learning the job would severely weaken her government and her reputation as a presidential manager.

The first to clamor were the fired officials. They said they had been elected and should be allowed to serve until the next balloting. Cory had called for reconciliation rather than revenge, and some of the Marcos holdovers mistook her attitude for weakness and decided to take advantage of it. Some officials, including justices of the Supreme Court, refused to resign on the grounds that their terms were protected under the constitution. Many appointments provoked protest rallies and other demonstrations organized by ousted job holders, who occasionally barricaded themselves in their offices. In some cases, the military had to persuade recalcitrant mayors to give up their posts.

The appointment of OICs was rushed in the beginning out of fear that the incumbents might destroy important records and loot whatever was left of their treasuries. There was not much screening of either them or their replacements. Pimentel, who picked the new officials, explained to Cory that he gave out jobs to people he knew and in whom he had confidence. But he was the leader of PDP-Laban, and it seemed to many others that he had a simple test for the OICs: membership in his party and loyalty to his ambitions. Everyone knew that control of local officials would be the basis of the political machine that could sweep the coming national and local elections. To try to reduce their political advantage, Cory ruled that critics of OICs would have to resign 90 days before elections if they wanted to run. But many months later, she would rescind that order, explaining that it would be too difficult to find replacements for them all.

Pimentel did not know the local situations; he simply wanted to replace the officials as quickly as possible. In some areas, he was acting on the instructions of Peping, whose interest was in building a political machine. The Marcos elections may not have been fair, but the party tried to get popular candidates to stand for office. Some of the mayors probably would have won honest votes. Their demise not only raised the ire of many communities but also destroyed the machinery Cory needed to put her programs into effect.

There were also widespread stories of job-buying and favoritism. On the island of Sulu, the OIC governor, Indanan Anni, got his wife, son, two brothers, a brother-in-law, and two nephews-in-law mayoral or other appointments. In his home province, Pimentel appointed a governor who had been a Marcos mayor but changed affiliation a year or two earlier. He allowed him to pick most of the new mayors, who turned out to be his old friends—the Marcos mayors who had bought and intimidated voters in the February election.

Pimentel protested that his party had gotten a minority of the posts. A Unido governor, Leandro Verceles, explained, "The early appointees of governors and mayors were PDP. That created an impression that never was removed." He acknowledged there were some "really bad" PDP people. He noted that though some appointees had left Unido to join PDP—in the tradition of Philippine politics—Unido eventually had gotten its share. He called the debacle a question of mismanagement. And perceptions. No matter what their parties, appointees owed their jobs to Pimentel. "Laurel thought Nene was building a base for PDP in 1992," he said.

Her supporters urged her to get involved with the OIC question to try to prevent it from blowing up. Of the hundreds of letters and telegrams she received every day, half were from people complaining about appointments. The cabinet meetings became the venue for raging disputes between Laurel and Pimentel over the matter. She named Pimentel, Laurel, and Political Affairs Minister Tony Cuenco to an arbitration board to purge the incompetents and undesirables.

But each of the men had his own political agenda, and the conflict festered. Occasionally, she got involved as a court of last resort and removed or changed officials. She would reinstate twenty-four KBL mayors in Ilocos Sur, Marcos territory, because they had strong local support. In another case, where Pimentel refused to appoint the supporters of Evelio Javier to positions in Antique, she sent a hand-written note to him ordering him to do so in twenty-four hours.

After the controversy had gone on for several months, she commented that critics of OICs' lack of experience were unreasonable. "I beg you to consider," she told an audience in Davao, "that if they had too much experience they would have been the men of Marcos, who has been in power for the past twenty years. I had no experience. If I had had experience, it would have been in Marcos politics, and I would not have led you to freedom."

The bottom line was that Cory trusted Pimentel. He had an excellent opposition record: he had been imprisoned by Marcos and he had been Ninoy's friend for years. And it was a job guaranteed to sandbag any administrator. Every post had multiple aspirants, and all but the winner would promptly raise hell. Cory's aides argued that only the bad appointments made the papers and that leaving the KBL structure intact would have undermined the government. But her management of the OIC problem was widely viewed as the worst mistake of her domestic policy. When the crisis blew up, she did not deal with it.

But she tried not to repeat the mistake. Cory asked the Supreme Court justices to resign, but she said she would not carry out wholesale replacement of judges and justices. She also pulled back on an initial intention to carry out an extensive purge of the civil service. However, selective firings in the bureaucracy had some government agencies in an uproar as people sought to protect their turf.

In the spring, Cory moved to the government guest house at 1514 Arlegui Street. It was a white concrete, two-story, Spanish-style mansion with a red tile roof and second-floor balconies with balustrades. Set between the 14-room house and the wrought iron fence that shut it off from the street were several young Narra trees. Symbolic of what Filipinos wanted their president to be, the Narra was the national tree, admired because its wood was strong and durable. The house was just minutes' drive from the palace; it answered the appeals from the public and security officers worried about the dangers of her daily twenty-five minute commute from Times Street.

Cory allowed no police cars with sirens and flashing lights to guide her bullet-proof Range Rover swiftly through Manila's infamous traffic jams. At her insistence, the five-car convoy stopped at every light.

But she was learning that she would have to accept some isolation from the public. In the beginning of her presidency, she had told rally audiences: "If there are any problems, please let your government know." After a while, she told her advisors, "Let's cut this thing about coming to me with their problems. The extent of people power is leaving me quite exhausted. When I get home at night and expect to be able to relax, I see hordes of people in front of my house with problems they want to share." Now, military guards and barricades blocked off the entrances to her street.

In May, Cory appointed forty-four members of the Constitutional Commission, including the head of the Farmers Movement of the Philippines and another leftist, leaving five vacancies for the opposition to fill and one for the Iglesia ni Kristo, a fundamentalist sect with one million members which had backed Marcos. The Church declined the offer. Some critics said the commission should have been elected, but Cory disagreed. She and her aides believed that the politicians who would run would address immediate concerns, but that "wise people," who would not be inclined to contest an election, would think about longer-term problems. And the lawyers in the cabinet told Cory that what counted was the ratification which would be by public referendum.

Key issues for the delegates were the nationalists' demands to legislate against U.S. bases and restrict foreign economic privileges, the adoption of a bicameral or unicameral legislature, and the extent of land reform. The commission would also have to deal with issues close to the Catholic Church, such as abortion, and women's rights. Enrile and others who saw themselves being passed over for power wanted a parliamentary system with a strong prime minister that would make Cory more of a figurehead.

Cory's presidential style was beginning to emerge. She would be a very visible president, making frequent speeches and appearances before civic and professional organizations and later would add trips to other islands to meet local labor, church, farm, and business leaders in well stage-managed and publicized "consultations." Some of her aides thought that since she was the only institution of government, people should see her. Other advisors and cabinet members thought she gave too many speeches and should be more selective.

They wished she would cut down on her public schedule to have more time for reflection and discussion of policy.

She selected a few priority issues and delegated other matters to her ministers. Those priorities were the constitution, the military and the insurgencies, and political democratization. But she appeared to ignore other problems of her government. Stories of corruption involving two of her ministers—Ernesto Maceda in Natural Resources, and Rogaciano Mercado in Public Works—and lower-level officials in national agencies and local posts hounded her administration almost from the start. "There were rumors, but no one came up with anything remotely approaching evidence," said Saguisag, but others pointed out that bribery was difficult to prove since those involved would be unlikely to step forward. And everyone seemed to know a story about government malfeasance involving those ministers and others. Admittedly, that had been the style of the Marcos years, and the private sector had learned it was the way to do business and survive.

In an effort to counter the rumored corruption in her public works ministry, Cory required Maceda to send contracts to her office for review. But the situation did not improve. People were disappointed that Cory did not make the eradication of corruption a main goal of her program, a moral crusade. They saw local and national politicians building war chests, and wondered if the Aquino administration was going to sink into the familiar political swamp. She seemed to overlook charges against high-ranking officials who had been loyal to her and Ninoy. Nor did she appear to understand that the national and local bureaucracies which were crippled by ineptness, corruption, power struggles, and disputes over patronage would keep her programs from taking off.

Cory had promised to close the gambling casinos, but she changed her mind, saying the government needed the revenue. The move called forth disappointment from Cardinal Sin and more criticism from the press and public which pointed out that three of the casinos' top officials, including one with questionable associations, were friends of her brother, Peping. Though there was no evidence that he had profited, people felt uneasy.

Critics also targeted her inner circle of human rights lawyers, especially Arroyo, for lack of administrative talents. Draft decrees from the cabinet ministers regularly disappeared in the mounds of paper on his desk. In a conversation, the likes of which had happened dozens of times before, Salonga, charged with recouping Marcos's stolen millions, talked to Arroyo on the phone. "You lost it?" Salonga said in an incredulous voice. He listened for a moment, then promised to send over another draft of the document in question. After he hung up the phone, he shook his head and grumbled in a mixture of astonishment and disgust. Draft decrees for implementation of government reorganization, action on an anti-insurgency plan, and changes in the labor law also got buried in Arroyo's office as he insisted on clearing all policy decrees and appointments.

Cory was criticized by erstwhile supporters for not asserting her leadership or giving direction, for not ending the divisiveness in her cabinet, for her failure to take charge. They said she was weak, drifting, ineffectual, indecisive. When a problem came up, she often hesitated instead of taking resolute action. People blamed her personality and her advisors. She resorted to so much consulting, even her supporters got impatient.

Saguisag pointed out that the critics of her weakness seemed to forget that at the start of her term they were condemning her for being too bold and taking steps deemed too strong. "You release all detainees [which the military and many businessmen didn't like], you're too harsh. You abolish congress, you're too harsh. You go revolutionary, you're too harsh. You can't win. People in a macho society can't accept a woman really leading them."

A trip to Indonesia and Singapore in August helped boost her confidence. At a time when she was wondering whether some of her critics might be right in saying she was too slow or not forceful enough, President Suharto of Indonesia and Prime Minister Lee Kuan Yew of Singapore could advise her. As she recalled, they told her, "Okay, everybody has problems in the beginning. Nobody is expecting you to solve all these problems in six months. What is important is that you choose your priorities and that you just devote all your energies to these priorities." When she returned from her trip, she was determined to visit and learn from other world leaders.

The draft constitution was finally delivered in October. It established a presidential system with a bicameral legislature restoring the political structure the U.S. had established for the Philippines at independence forty years earlier, set mild restrictions on foreign investment in deference to nationalist feelings and local self-interest (limiting foreign participation in natural resources exploitation to 40 percent), and required a two-thirds Senate vote to approve treaties, including the extension of U.S. bases, which could be put, on decision of congress, to a referendum.

The nationalists had pressed for a one-house legislature on the grounds that a bicameral system would give a veto to the elite; only the very rich could afford the estimated $600,000 needed to run for the Senate, which was elected on a nationwide basis. Stalemates by special interests in the old two-house congress was one reason why some people had favored its abolition under martial law.

The most controversial element in the document was an extension of the terms of the current president and vice president to 1992. The opposition, charging that no one knew who had won the February balloting, demanded a new vote.

Under the new constitution, the president's relatives to the fourth degree were forbidden from holding high posts in government or government-controlled corporations. Neither could active military officers hold civilian posts in the government or its firms. The document guaranteed women equality before the law, but banned abortion by protecting the life of the unborn from the time of conception. It put strict limits on the president's power to suspend habeas corpus or declare martial law, and prohibited secret detention, solitary confinement, holding prisoners incommunicado or subjecting them to intimidation, violence or torture. The constitution declared for land reform, but left implementation to the congress.

Cory was gratified at the outcome and determined to play a major role in the ratification campaign.

Confronting the
Military & the Rebels

IF CORY HAD ONE PRIORITY, it was ending the seventeen years of guerrilla war that had divided the country, killed tens of thousands of Filipinos and threatened the reconstruction she sought to begin.

The New People's Army had grown from 300 soldiers in 1969 to 16,000 or as many as 23,000, according to various accounts, and claimed the support of some ten million people, nearly a fifth of the population. The Communist Party had some 30,000 members. The military acknowledged that the guerrillas controlled one-fifth of the country, with a presence in sixty-three of the seventy-three provinces. The NPA controlled most of the island of Samar and large areas of Mindanao, Negros, and Panay. In those peasant villages, the National Democratic Front (NDF)—which grouped the NPA and all the civilian underground organizations that supported it—had set up alternative governments, collecting taxes and meting out justice. In Mindanao, the remnants of a Muslim separatist movement existed although they were quiescent, and renegades who had turned to banditry posed a more serious problem. She would deal with the Muslims, too, but they were a minor irritant compared to the NPA. Cory would also find that she had to confront not only the rebels, but a military that had been nearly destroyed by factionalism and corruption. The revolution had not automatically abolished those problems.

Days after her inauguration, Cory made it clear in her public statements that she was ready to speak with the NPA. "I have had several private contacts," she said. "Not everything can be told to the whole world." Saguisag hinted that the government had already offered the guerrillas a cease-fire and proposed a peaceful solution to the conflict.

The National Democratic Front called Cory's election "a significant victory in the Filipino people's struggle for genuine democracy and national independence," but it warned that Enrile and Ramos, who had defected from Marcos only at the eleventh hour, threatened those gains.

Cory had promised to release all political prisoners, and she ordered thirty-nine freed February 27, then announced the next day that the government would release "without exception, all political detainees." The military objected to the freeing of four top communist leaders, including Joma Sison and Bernabe Buscayno— "Commander Dante." There were also pressures from business groups, afraid the released radicals could start agitation that might destabilize the economic situation.

The crowd at the thanksgiving mass at Rizal Park March 2 was bigger than Cory's pre-election rally and the one that had launched the civil disobedience campaign. She announced the restoration of the writ of habeas corpus and said she would retire the overstaying generals that had been the base of Ver's power. Repeating her promise, she told the military that the release of Sison, Dante and other top rebel leaders was essential if a dialogue with them was to succeed.

Forty-eight generals got their walking papers three days later. She was left with fifty-three, nine of them extendees. That same day, Cory freed the Communist leaders along with other detainees that brought the total of those liberated to 517. Commander Dante was released to the custody of Doña Aurora. Cory's mother-in-law did not know Dante; she had only seen him at Ninoy's trial in 1976 when prosecutors accused Ninoy of ordering the murder of a local peasant leader. Dante testified in court that he had been offered a million pesos (then about $135,000) to say the Huks had done the killing on Ninoy's order. Doña Aurora was touched. She told Cory, "That man is brave at this time of times, when they can do anything to one, to say he was being offered one million pesos." She thought Cory must have remembered that. Doña Aurora found out about her appointment from friends who heard it announced on the radio. When she asked Joker Arroyo about her responsibilities in the job, he laughed and told her there were none. It was good public relations. For the same reason, Cory invited Sison and Dante to her office and the three chatted and smiled for news photographers.

The RAM officers now claimed they wanted to be actively involved in helping the country and gave Cory a draft proposal that called for a cease-fire in place.

A government spokesman predicted that peace was at hand, that the rebels would come down from the hills. But two weeks after Cory took power, the first encounter between the NPA and military troops occurred in Bicol, one of the NPA's strongest regions, in the southern section of the main island of Luzon, 340 miles south of Manila. The NPA regional commander issued a statement: "Marcos is not the only problem." He said there were still social problems that the government needed to solve. Other raids and ambushes occurred throughout the country.

In March, she set up the Presidential Commission on Human Rights. In addition to chairman Pepe Diokno, its members included Sister Marianni Dimaranan, the head of Task Force Detainees, the chief nation-wide Church-backed human rights group that had spent years documenting abuses committed by the military and paramilitary groups. Other members also had strong human rights records. The commission was charged with investigating disappearances, kidnappings, killings, tortures, hamletting (refusing to let residents of suspected NPA villages leave their towns), and food blockades (refusing to allow the shipment of food to such towns). The military did not like the establishment of this committee, either.

Diokno was told not to investigate Enrile's connection to rights abuses although it was widely told that he had ordered killings in his personal interest, as well as presided over a policy of military violence. But Cory's power was not consolidated, the army remained a question mark, and she wanted Enrile in the government and on her side.

Seeking to show the rebels her good intentions in a dramatic way, Cory ordered a unilateral cease-fire in central Mindanao, stopping all military operations against the NPA and the Muslim forces. Troops would turn their attention to the paramilitary and recover the illegal arms that had been issued to hundreds of Marcos supporters during the election. The regional commander, Brigadier General Rodrigo Gutang, said he would work with church and civic leaders to convince the guerrillas to agree to peace talks. But the cease-fire would not last, and the military did not pursue the paramilitary or the illegal arms.

Also addressing herself to the military, Cory appeared before some 2,000 people at the Philippine Military Academy graduation ceremony March 22. The 700 PMA students had defected to her at the height of the rebellion and reacted enthusiastically to her presence. The moment she got out of her car in front of the grandstand, she saluted, and they went wild, cheering and applauding. Later, every cadet got a handshake and a salute. The first woman commander in chief told them that human rights abuses would be dealt with. "Only by exposing the wrong-doing can we start the rebuilding," she said. "Only through an honest explanation of the past can a clean start be made for the future. Past abuses will be investigated, and any officers and men found guilty of crimes or serious misconduct will be dealt with appropriately."

She appealed in her speech to the rebels, whom she called "our brothers and sisters in the hills." "You waged war against Mr. Marcos, because he was the embodiment of the worst injustice, greed and cruelty. I fought Marcos for the same reasons." She urged them to make peace: "I shall soon call on you to come out and rejoin your people in rebuilding our country. There should be no more reason to continue fighting." But, she warned, if they did not, she would prosecute the war and they would face a "reformed and reinvigorated fighting force dedicated to the protection of democracy and the honor of our country."

There were already hints that some elements in the military wanted to keep their options open for future military action. RAM had had an underground as well as an above-ground component, and it continued its network, looking toward a time when the president and the defense minister might part ways. A RAM officer who was loyal to Cory wondered whether the hopes some had invested in their failed coup might have lingered in their minds.

"The coup rumors started because of a disagreement between the military and defense and the Cory government on the release of Joma Sison, Commander Dante, and the other hardcore Communists," declared Renato "Rene" Cayetano, Enrile's former law partner and leader of the Nacionalista party which would become home to many former members of Marcos's KBL. Aquino admitted, "Of course, there are those who are still loyal to Marcos. We cannot avoid that. . . . He was there for twenty years. I constantly ask the military for advice, and I think that most of them support me."

But NPA leaders, a month after her inauguration, were cautious. They said they would not lay down their arms in response to her call for a cease-fire, but that reconciliation was not impossible. In a statement, they assured Cory that her appeal for an end to fighting "has not fallen on deaf ears." They emphasized that they expected "more than just a cease-fire." They wanted to see "more substantial change made in the economic, political, and military spheres."

On March 24, more than 1,000 Communist cadres, some with their weapons, surrendered to military authorities on Negros. It was the first mass surrender of rebels since the revolution. Two weeks later, Cory appointed an emissary to make contact with the NDF to prepare ground rules for negotiations.

Cory was seeking aid from the World Bank for a rebel rehabilitation program, but it would be about five months before a cabinet committee was set up to review proposals from the various ministries and another five before the cabinet got around to dealing with the matter seriously. It was a major failure in her effort to urge massive defections by the NPA troops in the hills. The government was not offering them land, jobs, or homes if they complied. In some places, churches and community groups filled the gap and organized aid for returnees.

Tony Cuenco speaking at surrender ceremonies of fifty NPA rebels in Cebu, cited another obstacle to peace when he said the government would not achieve national reconciliation if the warlords were not eliminated and their empires dismantled. There were several hundred private armies. But no steps were taken to achieve this. The military did not want to fight on two fronts at once, and Cory could not move against the military.

She kept offering peace, but stressed her readiness to prosecute the war. In a speech in April at the University of the Philippines, chosen because it was the stomping grounds of the Left and a hotbed of nationalism, Cory encouraged the communities directly affected by the insurgency to take the initiative and "reach out to their brothers and sisters who were not as patient for peaceful change as they were."

She said the armed forces had been honoring a unilateral cease-fire, but the insurgents continued to strike. "I shall interpret this kindly to mean that the message of peace has not filtered down to all combatants. But I will not allow this state of affairs to continue for long."

She continued, "I know that the roots of insurgency are in the economic conditions of the people and the social structures that oppress them. I am not asking the Communists to give up their stern vision of a just society. I am asking them only to give our people a chance to work out their own version of a just and progressive society in peace." But she added that, "The soldiers of the Republic are under my wing. I have obligations to the security of the people, the stability of their new democracy, and the honor of the army, and I will not renege on any." Many officers were enthusiastic over the speech.

But there was a great amount of mistrust by the NPA national leadership, part of it the result of Enrile's membership in the cabinet. Cory encouraged regional cease-fires in the hope that autonomy and divisions within the insurgent forces would lead to accords. In a number of cases it worked. Other times agreements were shattered, with each side blaming the other for provoking an attack. At the same time, Enrile was saying publicly that government must not sacrifice national security in the pursuit of reconciliation. He announced that the army was breaking its post-revolution self-imposed cease-fire. He said also that the investigation of human rights abuses by the armed forces and the replacement of local officials should be done slowly and selectively. The cabinet was increasingly suspicious of him and the military.

Rumors of coups had begun as early as April. The loyalist opposition began to challenge the government by threatening to proclaim itself the legitimate power. A group of KBL Batasan members applauded the proposal of naming former speaker Nicanor Yñiguez as interim president. They planned to hold a rump session in April, and Cory said they would not be arrested. "Let them reconvene. That's their problem. People are free to listen to them. They are free to do anything they want," she said. But they would become increasingly a thorn in her side.

Laurel, appearing to back up the growing criticism by Enrile, warned in a speech to UP alumni that a military coup could take place if the government did not respond to the country's problems and failed to bring political and economic stability.

In May, Cory gave Communist leaders six months to respond to her offer to hold cease-fire talks. She felt that without a deadline, the NPA would drag out the discussions interminably.

Cory and Enrile were in conflict again when he said he would not allow Amnesty International, "an outside force," to carry out a human rights mission in the country. General Ramos backed Cory's decision to allow the Amnesty visit.

Cory saw Enrile becoming more and more vocal against her policies. Some of her cabinet members responded to his attacks in kind. She reacted by trying to win him over, but she also commented to a friend, "Nene [Pimentel] has been valuable, because he's the only one who stands up to him." Locsin and Arroyo advised her, "In this period in your presidency, you're facing a challenge from Enrile. What you are looking for is not brains, but guts, because it's going to come down to a fight. Value people like Pimentel. You can put a lot of smart people around you, but at the first whiff of a coup, they're all in Hong Kong or New York."

On a visit to Davao City, Cory pressed her efforts at reconciliation. At a convent she spent twenty-five minutes with 168 rebel returnees. She offered them amnesty, but four of their representatives told Cory they wanted assurances of safety and aid in leading new lives. She replied, "If I were to promise you that I will give you jobs, then you know that I will not be telling you the truth." She said the chief of the Southern Command would protect them. They would get some help through a rehabilitation program set up by local church and civic leaders. Under the arrangement with the military, the rebels had surrendered their arms to a reconciliation committee, not to the military, with the understanding that they would retrieve them if they were dissatisfied. One of the fighters was eighteen and pregnant. "I have grown tired and weary in the hills, carrying a gun and being continually on the run on an empty stomach," she said to explain her surrender.

Later in the day, Cory declared in a speech that she was struck by "the extreme youth of these former insurgents and their obvious bravery and acute sense of justice." She said, "It is tragic that such youth and virtue have been wasted in fighting that could be harnessed for the greater good of our country." And she noted that as poverty was a major cause of the insurgency, the returnees needed a chance for a new life to convince them to return. She said she would consider the feasibility of an "arms exchange" program—guns in return for rehabilitation and skills training. She noted that there were 33,000 hectares of military reservation in the area that could be subjected to land reform.

She also promised to deal with a major complaint of people in Mindanao—the depredations of warlords (of which former provincial governor Ali Dimaporo was the most legendary) and the abuses of the paramilitary Civilian Home Defense Forces that had been organized in all barrios suspected of being infiltrated by the NPA. They had no military training or discipline, and they often served as the troops of powerful political figures and landlords or carried out independent attacks on the populations they were supposed to protect. Harassment, extortion, intimidation and murder were common. During her visit, she held discussions with Mindanao citizens who complained about CHDF abuses. Human Rights Commission Chairman Diokno had asked her to dismantle the service because its members were guilty of most human rights violations in the countryside.

She responded, "I direct the minister of defense and the chief of staff to prepare and immediately implement a disarmament campaign against the warlords in the countryside and the criminal syndicates in the cities. I will not accept as an assumption that the CHDF are a necessary component of rural security in Mindanao and expect the chief of staff to submit to me a justification for its continued existence."

However, the military balked at confronting the warlords and abolishing the CHDF. At Marine Camp Malagos, where Cory spoke before a brigade of marines and top military officials, Brigadier General Gutang said the military had pushed back to June 15 a deadline for Dimaporo to surrender arms issued to him by Marcos during the election campaign. He had given up only sixty-eight firearms and still had about 1,700. He also ran two training camps for his troops, the "Barracudas." The extension was granted because of the observance of the Moslem Ramadan, which would end June 10. If he did not give up the weapons, the military would go after him. But when he failed to comply, they did nothing.

Ramos told her it would be difficult to fix a deadline for disarming the warlords. He would first try a policy of persuasion; if that did not work, he would take police action. Ramos feared an action against Dimaporo could be turned into a rallying point for Muslims against the Christians and erupt into violent conflict. Enrile opposed disarming warlords who were his allies in the north. Some of Cory's ministers complained that the defense ministry was ignoring her orders. She told them she knew it.

Military officials at the camp also opposed the plan to dismantle the CHDF because, they assured Cory, they were needed to protect the citizens and a stricter recruitment system would prevent abuses. Ramos agreed to support a reform by reducing the term of service from a year to three months so officials could speed up the turnover and select better members.

As Cory sought to consolidate her hold on the military, however, the warlords and CHDF became secondary to her attempts to secure a cease-fire. She told the military she wanted an agreement for a definite and inextendable period during which there would be negotiations she hoped would lead to an honorable and lasting peace. But should she fail, her administration would wage war against the rebels till victory.

Cory said in her speech at Camp Malagos that she would consult with Enrile on the feasibility of an immediate regional sixty-day cease-fire in the area during which regional leaders could establish contact and negotiate with the insurgents in a particular region. Cory felt the National NDF leaders were taking too long to respond to her call for a cease-fire. Individual Communists had sent out informal feelers, the Communist party operations were decentralized, allowing regional commanders relative autonomy, and she believed her policy could divide the insurgent leadership.

The RAM officers attacked her cease-fire proposals as naive. "They tell her, this is the way to do things, you need a cease-fire in place; the next day they change their tune," said Locsin. "Cory just wrote them off." Enrile would say later that regional cease-fires were never worked out with the military, that there was never a policy on them. "The only policy Mrs. Aquino initiated was a policy of reconciliation."

One reason for the standstill was the Communists' "rectification" process. They had discovered some "deep penetration agents" in their midst and were about to carry out a party purge. The military would later find graves of dozens of victims. With the threat of the possibility of regional cease-fires that would split their ranks, the

NDF responded by appointing an emissary to negotiate with the government. Speaking through their official organ, the Communists said they would consider a cease-fire, but would not surrender their weapons because, while she was liberal, her government was a "fragile coalition of conflicting forces." They believed her hold on power was precarious because she lacked her own bloc in the armed forces.

Cory acknowledged she was uneasy with Enrile and Ramos. "It would have been impossible for us to work together right away," she said. "You know what our past relationship was. I mean he [Enrile] was in charge of Ninoy [in prison] before, but I'm working on a better relationship with Johnny and Eddie, who have really gone out of their way also to work not only with me but with the rest of the civilian government. It just takes time, like everything else, to adjust to each other."

But there was more to it than that. There were already rumors of coup plots reported in the press.

Cory knew she lacked control over the military. She said that not all loyalist military men had cut their ties with Fabian Ver.

The Communists, meanwhile, were pressing the clearly unacceptable demand that the military remain in the barracks. Antonio Maria "Tony" Zumel, chairman of the NDF, told the press in June that the guerrillas had been fighting because the military had not changed its offensive posture. "The military is not agreeable to a cease-fire," said another rebel statement. "The president may be sincere, but we are awaiting as to whose view will finally prevail."

The insurgents also protested that more than 400 political prisoners remained in detention.

A few weeks later, Cory and Ramos met in Malacañang with representatives of Task Force Detainees, which sought the freedom of more political prisoners. TFD chair Sister Dimaranan said some people remained confined even after Cory had ordered their release. "The problem is that the big people have been released while the small ones are still in jail." Cory was surprised to learn that there were still so many locked up, many charged or convicted of common crimes. "It is unsettling that in four months, the list of political prisoners has not been whittled down and more names cropped up," Cory told them. They agreed to set up a committee to study how the government could facilitate the release of more than 500 political detainees.

Human rights violations in the countryside had decreased, but hadn't stopped. Cory saw a delegation from Mindanao that included labor leaders, former political prisoners, and officials of Bayan who told her that summary executions, massacres, hamletting, and forced evacuation of villagers continued in their region.

Enrile's criticism was growing. He expressed pessimism about the outcome of talks between the government and insurgents and doubted the sincerity of the NPA in seeking peace. He also said the Communists had infiltrated some government offices. A palace official called his charge "irresponsible" and aimed at blocking the peace efforts. Cory denied rumors of a rift with Enrile or a threatened coup.

But the perceptions of a rift grew. A newspaper reported that Cory was planning to announce Enrile's ouster from the cabinet, and he claimed he was ready to go if the president chose to remove him. He had left the previous week's cabinet meeting early; speculation mounted he had had a disagreement with the president or her supporters. After the rumors, hundreds of Marcos loyalists had camped out in front of Camp Aguinaldo.

Cory tried to reassure the country. "I'm not one who just abandons friends or who thinks ill of anybody," she said. She added that he left the cabinet meeting for a speaking engagement with the National Council of Churches. That same day, Enrile gave a speech in which he disagreed with Cory's stand on the U.S. bases, saying the country could not afford to lose them.

At a press conference, she said coup rumors were false and all was well between the civilian government and the military. She added, "If things are not okay, maybe I will not be here anymore." She was not worried by pledges of support to Enrile by Marcos loyalists. "They can pledge loyalty to anybody they want to. I don't expect them to pledge their loyalty to me." She said they were trying to sow intrigue to destabilize the government. She also admitted that warlords remained a problem. That same day, loyalists in Marcos's home province of Ilocos Norte declared their support for Enrile.

The rebels, continuing their pronouncements to the public, gave mixed reviews to Cory. NDF leader Tony Zumel praised her as a "populist president," but said the air of democratic freedom existed only in the cities; there were still military abuses in the countryside. And he lauded the government's reforms, but criticized its failure to draw up a land-reform program.

Reports increased about conflicts in the cabinet between the "human rights faction" and the military over policies regarding peace talks with the NPA and human rights. Meanwhile, the RAM officers committed to Enrile were building their network. It did not include all the RAM members, many of whom were loyal to the government and said they feared creating the conditions for "a banana republic." But the Enrile RAM faction extended now to former Marcos loyalist officers. An officer who had been involved in RAM's reform activities wondered how such a discredited group could be incorporated into a supposedly noble undertaking.

The Manila Hotel
Incident

BY APRIL, the Marcos loyalists were holding weekly Sunday rallies at the Luneta. From 5,000 to 7,000 people would show up, wearing their old Marcos T-shirts, waving red, white, and blue banners [Marcos's campaign colors], shouting the campaign cheer, "Marcos again," and claiming that Marcos's vice-presidential running mate, Arturo "Turing" Tolentino, was the acting president.

The 75-year-old Tolentino was threatening to take his oath as vice president. He had visited Enrile in late April and told him that Marcos had instructed him to take the oath. Enrile said he told him he should not allow himself to be used by Marcos and reported the meeting to Cory.

In early June, taking stock of the first one hundred days of her government, Cory said, "I'm not really afraid of the loyalists, because I see them as being disunited, which was also our problem before when we were opposing Mr. Marcos." On Tolentino's repeated assertion he would be sworn in, she said, "I think it's a joke. It doesn't bother me."

A few days later, thousands of loyalists tried to march on the palace. Dozens were injured in battles with the police. The plan had been designed by former military intelligence chief Brigadier General Rolando Abadilla, a distant nephew of Marcos. His Metrocom Intelligence and Security Group had been linked to several killings of anti-Marcos activists before Cory took office. The goal of this plan had been to storm the palace and hold Cory hostage. Tolentino would wait to see if the plotted military coup aroused a popular anti-Cory "people power" rebellion. If it did, he would signal Marcos's warlords to seize control of local governments in several provinces. The plotters wanted to stir up a crisis that would force Enrile to take over the government and restore order.

The palace learned of the plan from a foreign intelligence source. Locsin confronted a member of the military who told him, "Yes, we were going to tell you."

"The officer admitted he was scared because of Abadilla," Locsin explained later. "Most of his men were Abadilla men."

A loyalist rally was dispersed by the military two weeks later.

The standoff between the new president and the loyalists would come to a head in July.

Tolentino continued to announce that he would take his oath of office—"before August 15," he told the Manila Jaycees. That would end the six-month period within which, under the 1973 constitution, he would have to be sworn in or forfeit his office. Marcos loyalists continued to meet every Tuesday afternoon to plot their moves. They considered courting arrest by holding rallies without permits. Then, Tolentino and Marcos decided to act. Abadilla again had designed a plan.

On July 5, Tolentino and some of his supporters checked into the Manila Hotel under false names. Built by Americans in 1912, then restored after it was burned during World War II, it was the finest hotel in the city, rated a few months earlier as one of the seven best in the Orient. The eighteen-floor, 570-room, white California mission-style structure sat at the edge of Rizal Park looking out over Manila Bay and was the favorite stopping place of foreign journalists from rich news organizations, business travelers and visiting diplomats and was owned by the government.

On July 6, Cory and Ramos went to Cagayan de Oro City in Mindanao to meet with sectoral groups. On that same day, some 500 soldiers left Camp Olivas in Pampanga, north of the capital, and made their way to Manila. The Defense Ministry had been told about plans to install Tolentino as president at the Manila Hotel, but officials later said they had heard similar rumors twice in the past few months and did not take them seriously. Armed Forces General Headquarters received reports of troop movement about noon.

Enrile said he got word Sunday afternoon. He was on the seventeenth hole of the Villamor Golf Course and was informed that some soldiers at the Luneta were wearing black arm bands. "When they started to put on black bands, we knew something was afoot," he said later. "We wanted to see what it was all about. Even some people in the rally did not know the entire situation." Afterward, he said he assumed the troops were crowd control units. Enrile called Armed Forces vice chief of staff Major General Salvador Mison who informed him that the troop movement had been discovered that morning and the information sent to Ramos at noon.

Police cars spotted loyalist soldiers at 2:30 p.m. while they were moving through a provincial town, but allowed them to proceed, authorities said, for fear of "untoward violence."

In fact, military intelligence reports later would say that Enrile's boys encouraged the action and participated in its planning. The idea was to generate a "people power" reaction a million strong, said a high-ranking military official. He added that there was no direct evidence that Enrile was involved, just speculation.

Marcos supporters started to gather at Rizal Park shortly after lunch. Their leaders had secured a rally permit for 1 to 5 p.m. About 300 anti-riot police were deployed nearby at the Army and Navy Club next to the U.S. Embassy.

When the rally got underway, there were some 3,000 Marcos supporters there. Most of them seemed poor; they wore Marcos T-shirts and rubber shoes. About 200 heavily armed troops arrived in fifteen army trucks and jeeps; they carried Armalite rifles, Uzis, and machine guns and wore black and red head bands with the word "Guardians," an acronym for Gentlemen United Association, Reality, Dauntless, Ingenuous, Advocator Nation Society. Their name plates were covered with stickers. Most of them were soldiers and CHDF forces from Ilocos (Marcos's bailiwick), Cagayan (Enrile's stronghold), Bataan and Pampanga. They strutted about flashing Marcos's "V" sign. The anti-riot police were pulled out and returned to headquarters. After reports that the loyalists would move to the palace, the military secured that area.

At about 3 p.m., the loyalists moved over to the Manila Hotel and stormed the building, sending people in the lobby scattering to safety. They took over the $800-a-night MacArthur suite as their command post. The soldiers mixed with the 5,000 Marcos supporters. Some carried guns tied with red, white, and blue ribbons. The atmosphere at the hotel was festive. People shouted, "Marcos again!" and "Viva Tolentino!" Loyalist soldiers inside manned .50 caliber machine guns and spread out along the two staircases. Some of them jumped into the swimming pool. The ever-present vendors sold red, white, and blue Marcos-Tolentino T-shirts.

On the hotel driveway, Tolentino read a letter from Marcos: "I hereby order that in view of inadvertent and unavoidable absence from the Philippines, I authorize Tolentino to be the legitimate head of the country until such time that I return to the Philippines."

He was sworn in by former Supreme Court Justice Serafin Cuevas. Others at his side were former KBL leaders and some loyalist generals. One of them, Brigadier General Jose Zumel, was the brother of NDF chief Tony Zumel. Another was retired Major General Prospero Olivas, former Manila police commander and one of the twenty-five officers acquitted of Ninoy's murder. Brigadier General Jaime Echeverria, ex-regional commander of the Davao area, was also present. Former Marcos officials, including former MP Rafael Recto, Marcos's lawyer, were there with their supporters.

Inside the hotel, Tolentino talked by phone at 5 p.m. with Marcos in Honolulu, who suggested Tolentino use the hotel as his operations center. Marcos would make six more calls to the loyalists; all would be transcribed at the instruction of hotel officials by a telephone operator who had recognized his voice.

In another call, the deposed dictator told Tolentino to continue to hold out in the hotel. "Dimaporo is coming in late tonight. Just coordinate with him," Marcos instructed. "I have three men in the hotel observing things." Later, Marcos told Recto to exercise maximum tolerance and not to march on Malacañang. In yet another call, he said, "Just in case you feel that the military is going to strike, I do not want civilians hurt. Keep the civilians away from the firing." Marcos also instructed Recto, "Tell Turing to draft a resolution and send it to Reagan at the White House stating you want me back there."

At a press conference on the fourteenth floor, Tolentino appealed for support for his government. He announced his appointment of Enrile as minister of defense and named four other cabinet heads.

More than 300 paying guests moved out of the hotel. Foreign news organizations, including the U.S. television networks, kept their regular, sumptuous headquarters, and room service continued. Tolentino's troops and supporters lounged in the lobby and hallways, but were otherwise inactive.

Cory and Ramos learned of the events shortly after the hotel takeover. She was holding meetings with sectoral groups who were gathered in classrooms at a local school. Ramos sent out a red alert informing commanders that the 300 military men who had joined the Tolentino action were "misguided Marcos diehards," and that the action was "not a coup, repeat, not a coup." He said the defense and military leadership was supporting President Aquino, that she was safe and in command of the armed forces. Then he met with Cory and the cabinet ministers on hand to brief them, concluding, "The situation is under control."

Ramos ordered anti-riot troops and police to block the roads leading to Malacañang with military vehicles, fire trucks, and barbed-wire barricades. Police were sent to protect public utilities. Other troops loyal to Cory ringed the hotel, setting up a virtual war zone within a half-mile radius. Inside that zone, loyalist supporters burned some tires. Cory continued with her Cagayan de Oro program as planned.

Enrile ordered the military not to engage soldiers loyal to Marcos, "because if we do, there is going to be a carnage. . . . It is better to leave them alone for the moment." Colonel Honasan, later backing up the decision not to attack the rebels, seemed less concerned with bloodshed than with lashing out at the wrong enemy. "How do we assault a group that advocates anti-communism?" he said. "And when they said they were fighting for Enrile and Ramos, how could we attack them?"

In the evening, Cory held a press conference. She said she would order the justice minister and solicitor general to file sedition charges against Tolentino for having "illegally installed" himself as acting president of the country. She also ordered the capital command of the Philippine Constabulary to arrest the 300 armed soldiers supporting Tolentino "once they start violence." "I have always been for maximum tolerance in dealing with Marcos loyalists, but now that they have exceeded, I have no other recourse but to order necessary action," she said.

At a press conference at Camp Aguinaldo at 10 p.m. Enrile declined the Tolentino cabinet offer and said, "We have only one government in the Philippines, and that's the government of Cory Aquino." He declared, "I am not looking for another job. There is no need to panic." He said Tolentino would have to answer for his actions.

In Honolulu, Marcos's spokesman said, "President Marcos is awaiting further spontaneous developments."

Several hundred troops surrendered at dawn. Troops from Pampanga said they had been misled, that they had received a telegram that called on them to go to the hotel to support Enrile and Ramos who were alleged to have defected to Tolentino's shadow government. It was a believable ploy. Enrile, in visits to Marcos strongholds, did nothing to contradict their heroic vision of the deposed dictator and made it easy for them to transfer their support to him.

In the morning, authorities cut the hotel's telephone service.

Cory arrived back in Manila at 10 a.m., then met with Enrile, Ramos, and other top military officials at Malacañang. She asked Enrile how long it would take to settle the problem. "Maybe seventy-two hours, then we will have to do something," he replied. But Saguisag suggested they be given only twenty-four hours during which no charges would be filed, and she agreed.

Later, she stood on the steps of the palace guest house and, smiling and unruffled, told news reporters, "I want to reassure the public that the situation is fully under our control and we can all go about our usual business." She said, "The military involvement in this sorry adventure is confined to a small number of men and officers with special loyalties to the previous government and who were largely misguided by a disinformation campaign launched by the loyalists and instigated by Mr. Marcos." She declared, "The law will not be violated with impunity. While moderation will remain the yardstick of our response, let me state now, however, that an incident like this will not be allowed to happen again. There will be close monitoring of die-hards and other similarly subversive activities from here on."

Learning that her followers were threatening to march on the hotel and crush the uprising, she said, "This is not an occasion for a demonstration of people power. The incident is small, and there is no threat to their democracy. Please try to keep a cool head."

She formally accepted the surrender of 220 soldiers who had defected to the Tolentino group. They apologized to her and said they had been hoodwinked. Cory ordered Ramos to investigate the extent of the military's involvement and he ordered his commanders to comply. "I don't know what possessed Tolentino," she declared.

Following her instructions, Enrile gave military personnel twenty-four hours to return to their units without facing charges. He told news reporters, "Let us not use the word surrender, because we do not want to embarrass anybody, and we want to protect a unified military command. We will be exercising maximum leniency to prevent embarrassing them." Colonel Honasan was dispatched to head a surrender committee at the park grandstand.

Enrile temporarily closed a radio station that Tolentino and his group had used to spread disinformation and call for support for their attempted coup, and military authorities later shut down several others that were similarly engaged.

Holed up in the hallway of the hotel, Tolentino told a reporter he had been swept along by events. "There has been a lot of pressure on me to take my oath of office at these rallies. They rally, they shout, 'Take your oath, take your oath.' This is the people. And so I took my oath in obedience to the clamor of the people."

"We did not take over the hotel. We checked in here, that's different," he told another journalist.

The hotel cut power and stopped room service.

At 5:30 p.m. Tolentino finally climbed down the hotel fire escape and rode in a gray car to the Army and Navy Club across the Luneta to meet with Deputy Defense Minister Rafael Ileto and other government representatives. Recto and Echeverria accompanied him, and some soldiers went along in other cars. Then Tolentino went home.

Marcos, keeping in touch with the events, told the press he had nothing to do with it all. He said the letter authorizing Tolentino to take over leadership was written a long time ago, just after he left the country.

Enrile told the rebel troops remaining at the hotel that he would welcome back without punishment those who returned to military authority. After six hours of negotiations, the last troops left the site early in the morning and went to Fort Bonifacio in Makati. The officers were given permission to leave the hotel with their guns and assured safe conduct to join their units "as though nothing had happened."

When they arrived at the military camp after 6 a.m., Ramos greeted them: "We welcome you back to our fold." He said, "We understand the pressure and the reason and possibly even the misinformation that they gave you to make you join Tolentino two days ago at the Manila Hotel." He stressed the importance of the military maintaining its capacity to confront the Communists.

"We are not going to humiliate, punish or embarrass any one of you," Enrile told them. "I stand on this even to the point of gambling my own honor, my own life and my own position to see to it that what we have promised you will be fulfilled."

Ramos ordered them to do thirty push-ups—and joined them in the exercise. Then they all went to eat breakfast. "The push-ups were done mainly to relieve the tension, establish rapport among all the AFP members present, and emphasize unity among those in uniform," he explained afterward.

The remnants of civilian loyalists finally left in the morning when a loyalist movie star told them to go home.

The corridors of the hotel were littered with cigarette butts and ashes, leftover food, containers of juice, plastic bags, empty bottles of beer and cheap liquor. It was time to mop up, both literally and politically.

The hotel management estimated the cost at half a million dollars in damages, stolen cash and tableware, food and champagne consumed, and loss of revenue.

There was a clamor to punish the rebels. "My supporters want me to show firmness and arrest people like those who fight me," said Cory, in a meeting with a visiting delegation from West Germany. "But my feeling is that I should not go after followers but should look at the motives of the leaders."

The cabinet was divided between those who wanted to make an example of the perpetrators and those who favored dropping the matter. Enrile had promised the troops clemency; he said that all he did was restate Cory's policy. "It's easy for you to talk," he told the others who wanted to get tough on the soldiers. He suggested that the fraternal organization to which many of the military rebels belonged had clout. "If you only knew how extensive is the Guardians brotherhood, you wouldn't find it so easy."

"You're telling me this is not a professional army, but an army of gangsters," shot back Locsin.

"How come everybody blames the army," inquired Ramos. He added that administrative actions such as demotion or removal from a command might be applied. "They shouldn't be charged. It wasn't a coup," interjected Laurel. Others argued that trials could give the loyalists a platform. Cory tried to calm them down: "Okay, okay, okay, everybody quiet." She said, "We don't want to make a martyr out of Tolentino." There was fear his arrest would be a focus for new demonstrations.

Some in the cabinet wondered why Enrile had not learned of the plot in time to warn the president. But nobody thought he was involved in it.

Two days after the revolt ended, Cory announced that no criminal charges would be filed against the loyalist leaders, including eleven military officers, provided they took an oath of allegiance to the Freedom Constitution. "I am glad that the incident ended without bloodshed," she said. "This was my chief concern when I said that if the loyalists were to quit the hotel in twenty-four hours, this circumstance would be considered greatly in their favor. Let us put this matter behind us."

The Catholic bishops commended her stance. Others protested the kid-glove treatment of the rebellious troops and civilian loyalists. "Any group within the armed forces or even any other force outside it, as long as it espouses an anti-communist line, is free to mount a rebellion or a revolt and, if it meets with failure, all the vanquished group's leaders have to do is wait for the victor to negotiate with them and, without any punishment waiting for them, be embraced by the government with open arms," protested *Business Day* columnist Niñez Cacho-Olivares.

Cory declared she would prohibit rallies designed to promote rebellion against the government; later, Arroyo said the government would not ban demonstrations but would not allow any more mini-revolts. Cory elaborated on her semi-weekly television talk show that if loyalists gathered in significant numbers, they would be dispersed. Further military involvement in such acts would be severely punished.

She also protested against criticism that she had been too lenient. She told a meeting of the Bishop's–Businessmen's Conference, "When you think of it, the results show it pays to be kind. We did not lose a single life."

She created a board of inquiry headed by Health Minister Alfredo Bengzon to look into the extent of military involvement in the incident. Ramos also set up an investigating committee. Cory expressed concern about the failure of military intelligence in the matter: "I was really a little bothered by that, and I could not imagine that here we are in control of the military and not knowing ahead of time that there was something going on."

General Ramos sent a notice to his commanders saying that the Manila Hotel incident had showed that the chain of command in some units was not functioning well, that those commanders had loose control over their officers and men, and that "the blatant disregard of the authority of the chain of command" had enabled some troops to move to Manila without knowledge of their chiefs. He said their actions had been prompted by an "incorrect perception or appreciation of the policies of the government on counterinsurgency." He called on the commanders to strengthen their control over their units and to begin a troop information and education drive about government policies. He included for their use excerpts of speeches by the president.

President Reagan said he had seen no evidence that Marcos was involved in the attempted coup, which would be a violation of the U.S. Neutrality Act that bans activities aimed at destabilizing a government with which the U.S. is at peace. A month later, when reports of the Marcos phone conversations hit the newspapers, the White House announced it would have to review Marcos's status if he were shown to be involved in partisan political activities in the Philippines. A congressional committee began an investigation into the matter.

Reagan, ignoring Marcos's unsuccessful attempts to call down raids on the people power redoubt at EDSA, said "I can't put out of my mind the fact that—and nor should any of us—his leaving the island was preceded by his denial of permission to the military . . . to take action. The one thing he did not want was bloodshed or civil strife . . . and so he left rather than permit that."

Showing little appreciation of Cory's leniency, Tolentino and the others refused to swear allegiance to the constitution on grounds the document was illegal because it had never been ratified. Several weeks of shadow-boxing ensued. Enrile said that the government could not be harsh on Tolentino while it was "soft" on known Communists. He said all Tolentino had done at the Manila Hotel was drink a few bottles of whisky and brandy. Tolentino and some forty leaders of the coup attempt were given a deadline to take the oath; when it lapsed, they were given another. Still, they refused. Critics said Cory was indecisive and weak, that she should prove she was in charge. Those who had flouted the law were being protected.

As she was being criticized for letting Tolentino walk all over her, she told an Indian visitor that she was inspired by Mahatma Gandhi's policy of nonviolence. She told him, "I too felt that my job is primarily to save human lives, and I don't mind being accused of being too soft on the perpetrators of the Manila Hotel incident."

The sense that the activities of Tolentino and his followers had been really only comic opera was broken July 27 when a twenty-four-year-old man wearing a yellow T-shirt was beaten to death by loyalists who had gathered at Rizal Park.

Finally, the government filed charges of rebellion against Tolentino and his accomplices, including former speaker Nicanor Yñiguez, several former MPs, four generals, and other military officers and former government officials. But Cory still promised them amnesty if they took the oath. They would have to pledge allegiance to the republic, recognize the existence of the present government under the Freedom Constitution and renounce the use of force and violence to overthrow it. That same day, most of them complied.

Tolentino was facing a minimum jail term of twenty-four years to life under a Marcos decree that imposed stiff penalties for crimes against the state and which Cory had not repealed. Arroyo, who fought the decree during the Marcos regime, called its application "poetic justice."

Cory was still offering clemency, but was not very sanguine. On her television program, she stated, "I hoped to see concrete proof that they are sorry, but there was none of this." But, she said, "I don't see any positive act of sincerity or desire to cooperate with us. We cannot allow them to keep fooling us. We are also entitled to justice."

Tolentino continued to protest that he should not be charged because he had not signed his oath of office and none of his followers had accepted appointments. He said swearing allegiance would be a "public humiliation." Finally, he took an oath of allegiance to the government but not the Freedom Constitution, which the government dropped from the pledge because it did not intend to humiliate the coup participants. Later, at a press conference, Tolentino said, "I still consider myself part of the Marcos government, but we are only dormant."

The Manila Hotel pressed its claim for $800,000 in unpaid bills and damages. Tolentino refused to pay, saying the hotel had more than made up for the loss by free advertising in the international press that had made the hotel a tourist attraction. The hotel filed a $900,000 damage suit.

Some said the one-and-a-half day coup attempt had been a ludicrous joke; a newsmagazine titled its story, "A room with a coup." But others said the government should not have dismissed the event so readily when it presaged real danger. They wondered why the Defense Ministry, which had to know there were troops coming from Central Luzon, did not stop them. The conclusion some reached was that this represented the flowering of an alliance between the loyalists and Enrile forces. The RAM boys were integrating the loyalists into their ranks, and the Manila Hotel incident had been a trial balloon. If masses of people had responded, the loyalists, RAM officers and their military backers would have marched on Malacañang.

It was chastening for Cory's side to realize that some officers and men were ready to fight the government in the belief that Enrile and Ramos were spearheading a rebellion. They feared that this display of support, and the gratitude for his defense of the erring soldiers, had strengthened Enrile's position inside the armed forces. The Bengzon Report, which was never made public, did not say Enrile was involved, but Minister Jose Concepcion commented, "Based on the testimony, it looks difficult for the military not to have known."

Peace Talks

WHILE THE TOLENTINO DRAMA WAS ABOUT TO UNFOLD in Manila, Cory arrived in Cagayan de Oro City on the north coast of Mindanao. It was a region where there had been repeated clashes between the NPA and soldiers and paramilitary groups, one of which, Tadtad, was composed of religious fanatics notorious for chopping up their victims' bodies. Thousands of people waving yellow streamers and banners met Cory in the street and at an open-air stadium.

More than a dozen rebels surrendered to Cory and told her about their hard lives in the hills. They took an oath of allegiance to the republic. She thanked them for answering her call for reconciliation. According to one account, they had surrendered in December, but the government gathered them again for the photo opportunity. Both sides were playing a propaganda game. The NPA said some of the returnees were "deep penetration agents" who had been found out. General Ramos showed reporters a common grave where he said rebel victims were buried. The NPA would acknowledge that it had carried out a purge of adherents deemed to be "dpa's" or spies.

Community leaders who had been invited to meet with Cory reported that CHDF forces had enforced a food blockade on one village suspected of aiding the NPA. A hundred residents of another town had fled to the provincial capital to escape the CHDF.

While the conflict showed no signs of letting up in the south, at the other end of the country, moves toward an end to the violence were taking place. Father Conrado Balweg, a forty-two year-old priest had led his tribal parishioners into a seven-year alliance with the NPA to fight Marcos, who had awarded much of the tribe's ancestral land to timber firms. They were also combatting efforts to build four dams on the Chico River that would inundate other large portions of land. But in April, saying his demands were not national but only related to the Cordillera Mountain region, Balweg cut his ties to the NPA and set up his own armed group. It sought an autonomous state for the five provinces of the Cordillera Mountains, an end to the military presence, and a halt to the Chico River dams and to the operations of the Cellophil Resources Corporation and Cellulose, two private logging companies owned by Marcos cronies.

Cory called Butz one early June afternoon and asked him to come to her office. "Your friends have been complaining that you have not been appointed to anything, so I have decided to appoint you to something."

"What?" inquired Butz.

"To talk to Father Balweg, to be my personal emissary."

"Okay, I'll talk to him," replied Butz. "First thing I have to do is find him."

Cory laughed. She had information that Balweg was ready to talk. "Find out what he wants," she said.

Balweg had been suspended from the priesthood and had married a local villager, Corazon Cortel, who had been detained by the military in 1984 and imprisoned until Cory came to power. Through a newspaperman and leftist activist, Butz got in touch with Balweg's wife, who invited him to the Cordilleras. Butz talked with Balweg's people for three days. He told them Cory wanted peace in the area. They had heard a lot of rumors about her, and they seemed to trust her because she had also been a victim of the Marcos regime.

The next week, Butz met Balweg, accompanied by 400 supporters and troops. At that meeting and a second one, Butz heard their grievances and demands. They also argued among themselves about what was to be done. Finally, Balweg agreed to come down from the hills and meet Cory to present the demands of the Cordillera Peoples Liberation Army. Butz returned to ask Cory if she was prepared to meet the CPLA.

"Yes, immediately," she replied. "Invite him here."

"No way will he agree," said Butz. "It will look too much like a surrender. If he loses face and credibility, he will no longer be an effective leader. We don't want to do that, especially now that he's ready to talk to the government."

Cory's security guards wanted the talks to take place in the palace. The military wanted the talks in an area they controlled. Balweg wanted Abra province, his home ground. He wanted Cory to see the people's poverty.

Meanwhile, rumors of coup plans by the RAM boys were becoming stronger. The palace was also getting reports of arms shipments to the Ministry of National Defense. Some crates checked by customs officials at the Manila airport were marked "Jusis," fabric used for the traditional Filipino men's shirt, but the contents were Uzi submachine guns. Some crates also held the fabric. "What are they running, a tailoring shop?" Cory asked her aide, Teddy Locsin.

In Lanao del Sur province in Mindanao, where Ali Dimaporo held sway, ten Carmelite nuns and a Protestant pastor, Brian Lawrence, a member of International Mission, Inc, a New Jersey-based Baptist medical mission, were kidnapped. Armed men had broken into the nuns' hilltop convent and a day later had also dragged Lawrence from his apartment in Marawi City, the provincial capital. His wife escaped by hiding in a closet. The kidnappers demanded a ransom of $100,000. Enrile told Cory the assailants were believed to be linked to Dimaporo, that his nephew Ismael was one of the leaders of the band made up of the warlord's armed "Barracudas" and a renegade group of Muslim rebels.

A month earlier, a French priest, Father Michel Gigord, chaplain of Mindanao State University in Marawi, had been seized by armed men also identified with Dimaporo and released unharmed after three weeks. Two weeks later, a Swiss tourist, Hans Kunzli, was kidnapped from a beach in Zamboanga, in Mindanao.

Cory ordered the military to act decisively and settle "once and for all" the problems raised by warlords and the paramilitary in the area. She promised the public that the military would soon stop tolerating the warlords and bandits there. But government ministers admitted that the military would not move.

The division between Cory and Enrile was becoming more public, and she was annoyed by the talk about it. She would call him to say, "Johnny, we have to work together." He would urge her to ignore the press reports. "Madame, I hope you will not believe these things," he told her. But he would continue to contradict her publicly. She repeated on her television program in July that she had asked the military to take a defensive position. Enrile said there had been no Malacañang guidelines to govern the day-to-day military operations against the rebels.

The Communist organ, *The Nation*, said people were becoming disillusioned with Cory's failure to address fundamental problems in the country. Moving to a tougher, more critical view, the Communists said her government was reactionary.

In August, Cory ordered army commander General Rodolfo Canieso to explain reports that military operations against the NPA in a northern Mindanao province had dislocated more than 1,000 families.

Cory took a direct hand in the peace negotiations which proceeded, albeit at a snail's pace. Saturnino Ocampo and Tony Zumel, representing the NDF, had asked for freedom of movement to test the government's sincerity, and she ordered it granted. The safe conduct passes would be effective until talks were completed. But after the first meeting on August 5, talks seemed to bog down over ground rules; the Communists demanded to be given the status of belligerents.

While the negotiations with the Communists were going nowhere, Cory would attempt peace talks with another adversary, the head of an organization of Muslim rebels in the south.

Decades of migration by Christian settlers from the north and the intrusion of Filipino and foreign corporations—all seeking wealth from gold, logging, and agriculture—had displaced hundreds of thousands of Muslims in Mindanao. When Marcos came to power, he began to sell off what was left of their lands and resources to cronies and foreign firms. In 1913, Muslims were 98 percent of the island's population; by 1976, they were only 40 percent and owned just 17 percent of the land.

In the late 1960s, there was widespread terrorism against Muslims by paramilitary groups, financed, many suspected, by individuals and companies who wanted their remaining lands. Getting no protection from the Christian governors and mayors, the Muslims organized resistance and in 1968, founded the Muslim Independence Movement. A year later, Nur Misuari, then a twenty-seven year-old political science professor at the University of the Philippines, organized the Moro National Liberation Front (MNLF).

Insurrection finally broke out when martial law was declared. Estimates of war deaths ranged from 50,000 to 100,000. More than a quarter of a million refugees fled to Malaysia. Misuari went into exile in the Middle East in 1976. A cease-fire negotiated in Tripoli that year under the sponsorship of the Organization of the Islamic Conference gave autonomy to thirteen provinces, with power over local administration, finances, Sharia law courts, and education. But Marcos reneged on the agreement, and Misuari's MNLF returned to its original goal of independence.

There were two other Muslim factions as well: Hashim Salamat, who had been Misuari's number two, headed the Moro Islamic Liberation Front, and Dimas Pundato led the MNLF Reformist Faction. Although the smaller groups advocated autonomy, not secession, the divisions were largely tribal, with each leader's strength in different provinces. The total Muslim military force was about 20,000 troops. There was no cooperation with the NPA, and for some time there had been only sporadic fighting with the military. The focus had shifted to political organizing.

Muslim politicians had traditionally used the autonomy issue to get votes, but many people, especially the middle class, were not interested in continuing the conflict. Moderate countries such as Saudi Arabia had also pressed Misuari to drop his secessionist demands, and Muammar Qaddafi, an important backer, had reduced his financial support.

Ninoy had met Misuari in Jeddah in 1981 and had proposed a return to the Tripoli Agreement and withdrawal of all Christian troops from Mindanao. Cory herself had not developed a policy to deal with the Muslim problem. She set up a task force on regional autonomous government, but it could not function without a policy.

In the summer, Butz received word that Misuari was in Jeddah and wanted to resume talks. When Butz went to see him, Misuari said that the MNLF would "try autonomy" for the thirteen Muslim provinces. Butz announced on August 24 that Misuari would meet with Cory the following month.

Cease-fire talks with the Communists proceeded slowly, still bogged down on matters of procedure. NDF negotiators rejected as inadequate the guidelines on safe conduct passes issued by the army. A day later, Ramos reassured them that the passes had no time or geographical limits. Cory issued another call for peace talks to the NDF officials.

Meanwhile, the seed of another element in the melodrama was being planted. Lieutenant Victor Corpus, now 42, had been a bright young cadet and then teacher at the Philippine Military Academy when he became outraged over the military's assassinations of political and activist leaders; he had deserted the army in 1970 to join the NPA. Six years later, newspapers headlined his capture. He spent ten years in prison, not to be released until a week after Cory came to power.

In August, Corpus had written to Pete Lacaba, a screenwriter who was scripting the movie of his life. He wanted the story to be told accurately. "My conscience is bothered no end, especially that portion where you depicted my capture," he told Lacaba. "I must confess that I lied to you regarding this matter. The truth is: I surrendered." He said he had surrendered because of his disillusionment with the NPA, the killings done for "flimsy and dubious reasons," and particularly the killing of innocent civilians at Plaza Miranda. "I kept this fact from you for fear of destroying my public image; but more so, for fear of outright liquidation." He said he would rather risk liquidation and a shattered public image now than be hailed as a fake hero. He asked for revisions in the script.

Corpus declared that the Plaza Miranda bombing in August 1971 had not been carried out on orders of Marcos or Ver, as people had supposed, but by the Communist party. He said he had been present when Joma Sison and other party leaders plotted the attack. He also said he had been disillusioned by the rich lifestyles of Communist leaders, who lived in cities, "leading the revolution in the countryside by remote control," while their troops existed on $2.50 a month. He recalled a time when he and his fighters had to survive on coconuts.

Corpus would later explain that the Communists set off the explosion "to heighten the contradictions within the ruling class which would make them fight each other, weaken the ruling class and facilitate our takeover of power." The bombing would also "force Marcos to adopt repressive measures which would isolate the ruling regime and push the middle forces over to our side. The moderates would realize that the parliamentary struggle is useless." The Communists, who had less than one hundred armed members, would then get troops to carry the guns they were expecting from China.

Lacaba returned the letter as "too hot to handle." Lacaba had been a political prisoner and Corpus, fearing a slip to his contacts among the Communists, gave the letter to some friends to serve "as a death statement" in case something happened to him.

It would become public sooner than he expected.

When Cory arrived home from Singapore at the end of August, Butz asked her if she was prepared to meet Misuari and where. Misuari wanted her to go to Jolo, the historic center of the Muslims, on Sulu, midway between Mindanao and Malaysia, which was almost 50 percent under his control. It had been bombed by the army during the height of the secessionist war. No Philippine president had ever gone there. Cory thought for a few seconds and then said, "Yes. If it will help bring about peace, I'm prepared to go to Jolo." She would take Ramos and Enrile.

Military officials did not want her to meet Misuari in Jolo. They argued that it would give his group a legal status. They said he should come to Manila. They also wanted Cory to meet with Christian and other Muslim leaders of the region. Rival Muslims wanted Cory to see Misuari at the palace so she would not appear to be favoring his Tausug tribe. Cory told her advisers, "Misuari does not know me, and I have to show him that I am sincere by setting aside these objections and flying to Jolo, to show him that in the search for peace I will disregard protocol."

Misuari agreed to a meeting on September 5. There would be a congress of the MNLF on Sulu, September 2-4.

Government troops were dispatched to Jolo for security; forces were deployed along all the roads to Maimung, the town eight miles from Jolo where Misuari and some 10,000 followers—several thousand armed with automatic rifles or grenade launchers—were holding their congress and where the talks were expected to be. Navy ships were deployed off shore.

The night before she arrived, Cory held a dinner in Malacañang for other Muslim and Christian leaders of Mindanao. They were worried about what she would concede to Misuari. They did not want secession or an autonomous Muslim republic. She reassured them there would be no separate Muslim state.

Misuari arrived on a Malaysian gunboat. He held his first press conference in the country in ten years. "Our struggle is not a question of dismemberment [of the republic]," he said. "We have never been part of the Philippines." He told his Moro congress, "We have been a nation and we shall remain a nation forever, separate from all nations in the world, including the Philippines." But his words had been similar before he signed the Tripoli Agreement.

The congress was attended by representatives from his two rivals, which confirmed his influence, though the two other leaders would protest that they would not adhere to any agreement they had no part in reaching.

Cory arrived aboard a military plane at 8:45 a.m. and was met by Ramos and Enrile and thousands of Tausugs in brightly colored ethnic costumes. They welcomed her with MNLF flags and yellow banners that said, "May Allah bless you on your mission." She saw the region's top military officials, then went on to the conference site kept secret—until the last minute—the Carmelite Convent of Notre Dame College in downtown Jolo half a mile from the Marine Brigade headquarters. The paint was peeling off the walls of the building which was surrounded by contingents of the military and MNLF.

The talks began at 10 a.m. in an anteroom of the convent. When Misuari came in, he said, "Do we really need the security?"

"No," replied Cory, dismissing her guards. They talked alone. Almost. Because there was no air-conditioning, the jalousied windows on two walls had been left open at a height of eight feet. About thirty people from both sides pressed against the building to hear the conversation. Butz noticed that seemed to ease the tension. "Everybody forgot his rifle and tried to listen."

Cory did all the talking for the first fifteen minutes. "I came here against the advice and pronouncements of a lot of people close to my office," she told Misuari. "I wouldn't have attempted this gesture if I wasn't sure we could do something together to help further the cause of peace in this part of the country. Faith has brought me where I am today. My reason for being here is to reach out to our Muslim brothers to attain peace." Their common enemy was Marcos who was now gone. It was time to find out how they could have peace.

Cory felt his eyes focused on her. She thought he was trying to outstare her or size her up. She told him, "It must be very difficult for you, because my husband always told me that Muslims consider women as second-class citizens." She said, "Even if I am a woman, I am very determined as far as my search for peace is concerned."

Misuari said he appreciated deeply her "bold and sincere" gesture, but he noted that he had also taken some risks. "I had to get the permission of many of my Muslim brothers to come here. In fact, my being here violates a legacy or tradition which has governed our people for over 400 years. We've always believed that our leader never meets the leader of our enemy. But I violated this legacy for the sake of peace and for our people."

They moved to talk about a cease-fire. Cory hoped he could lead the way to an agreement for Mindanao. He approved the idea, but said he would have to visit the provinces to consult with the other Muslim groups.

Cory was furious. She thought the meeting would cement Muslim-Christian amity, that it would mean the end of hostilities, not more bargaining sessions. "I am the leader of my people, and I was led to believe you were the leader of the Muslims," she told him. "I am the leader of my people, and I never consult." She cut the meeting short and called in Butz, Enrile, Ramos, and the other generals and ministers; Misuari brought in his advisors. They discussed the cease-fire and agreed on language for a communiqué that said both sides would "support the continued cessation of hostilities." They did not deal with the issues of autonomy or secession.

"Let's just go back to Manila," Cory told her aides, still fuming.

Enrile said the military made no recommendations, "because there was no time. Mrs. Aquino was in a hurry. After a while, photos were taken, and that was it." General Ramos was left behind to write a press release and the agreement with Misuari which was signed by Butz Aquino. At the end, they agreed to set up panels to continue the dialogue. Misuari and his leaders had been impressed by Cory's sincerity and courage in coming to Jolo, but they wondered whether the military would respect any agreement she would sign.

After the meeting with Cory, Misuari's stock went up. He created a furor by traveling around Mindanao with his armed troops, "consulting" with Muslim communities and frightening a lot of Christians. The other Muslim factions sought to emphasize their presence. After the meeting, one of them attacked a Catholic church and killed eight people.

"I knew we were going to have problems again," Enrile said. "You are resuscitating the ghost of the Moro National Liberation Front."

But Cory kept on with the peace process. The next dramatic moment came a week later when she met Father Balweg. Discussions on the venue had led to a compromise. They agreed to talk at the government-owned Mount Data Lodge, in the Cordillera Mountains 160 miles north of Manila, empty now because of the conflict in the region.

Butz fetched Balweg by helicopter. When they reached the lodge, it was surrounded by two battalions of troops. Balweg had more than a hundred supporters; they were asked to leave their weapons at the door. Cory also arrived by helicopter at 10 a.m. with her ministers. They entered the large dining room, and ten representatives from each side sat at a long table. Most of the Cordillera leaders sat and squatted on the floor. Some of them wore loincloths under their coats.

Before the talks began they sipped wine—California Chablis provided by the hotel—in a glass with a peso coin in it, a symbol of unity. Balweg explained, "It has been our custom here to start talks between warring groups with a ceremonial toast aimed at bringing about unity between our forces."

Cory began to speak. She had come, she said, to offer "my friendship and the sincerity of the government to help solve your problems so that we could develop and progress together as brothers and sisters."

"I understand that the long neglect suffered by you during the previous regime and the exploitation of your natural resources have brought about your struggle for justice." She said, "The key to a just and lasting peace in our whole country may be in the Cordilleras. The efforts that we have made here are becoming a show window. . . . If we are successful here, the implication is nationwide."

Balweg told her the struggle of the Cordillera people was provoked by the unnecessary government and multinational projects that threatened to destroy their natural resources and cultural heritage without giving any benefit to the tribes. "We have a common objective, which is peace, freedom, unity, and justice. That is why we try to reach out for a solution in order to solve the useless loss of lives," he said.

All of the Cordillera representatives spoke, thanking Cory for coming and telling her of the problems of their people and the abuses they had suffered at the hands of the military. Their demands for government assistance were minimal—footbridges rather than highways.

Enrile and Natural Resources Minister Ernesto Maceda did most of the government's talking, because they spoke the local dialect, Ilocano. Balweg, who was fluent in English, also deferred to the tribal leaders for whom he translated. Enrile felt better about this meeting than the one with Misuari. "We could work out some kind of autonomy for the Cordilleras that would prevent the Communist elements from making use of the area as a sanctuary," he explained later.

Cory had gone there with a draft based on the talks Butz had held, a general agreement to stop violence between the two sides, remove the $10,000 price on Balweg's head, and recognize his people's desire for self-determination and demilitarization of the area. Balweg also wanted the tribes to be consulted on any other government projects in the region.

Cory told them the projects they objected to would be stopped. The licenses of the logging companies had already been revoked, and the dam project would also be canceled. Negotiating panels would be set up to address the details of their demands. Balweg agreed to ask the NPA to keep its troops out of the mountains. He said his people would not interfere with local government authorities or regular police work, and would allow the completion of existing government projects. The military pledged not to interfere with CPLA members consulting with their leaders in the provinces.

Then Balweg suggested an exchange of gifts as part of the traditional native peace ritual. The Cordillera people wanted to give Cory a spear and have her return a weapon as a sign that both sides were prepared to protect each other. The security men felt the president should not handle a spear, so it was handed to Enrile; Ramos got a wooden shield and a head axe. The tribal leaders wanted an Uzi in exchange, but Enrile demurred and ordered they be given a M-16 Armalite rifle tied with a yellow ribbon. Cory also gave Balweg a rosary and Bible.

After an hour and a half, Cory left in her helicopter to avoid the clouds that would close in at late morning and make flight dangerous. Balweg drove off in Butz's car to see a screening of "Father Balweg—Rebel Priest," which was scheduled to open in Manila the next week.

Cory would prepare for her visit to the United States. She hoped her two peace-talk victories had bolstered her image.

Economy

CORY'S INTEREST IN THE U.S. was largely economic—she wanted to spur American aid and business investments.

She had taken power in a country saddled with unemployment that had reached 20 percent, with underemployment at 40 percent. The minimum wage was less than $3 a day, and the law was barely enforced: only four in ten workers actually got it. Teachers earned $75 a month. Wages for skilled workers were less. Sixty percent of the population lived below the poverty line, figured at an income of $120 a month for a family of six. Seventy percent of children were malnourished.

The government was nearly bankrupt, with a deficit of $250 million for the first quarter. With $26 billion owed, the Philippines was the fifth largest debtor in the world.

Cory had made commitments to urban workers, peasants, and business leaders to promote the economy and share its benefits, to seek an end to poverty and repression, and to free business from having the state as its "silent partner." Sometimes the promises would conflict.

She did not start out with a well-developed economic philosophy. She later would declare herself a Christian Socialist like Ninoy, by which she meant she advocated capitalism with some state intervention to aid the poor. She believed that the government's role was to provide an environment where the private sector could flourish. It should not be interventionist or organize enterprises in areas best left to the private sector.

Cory set about to establish economic priorities. She asked the economic ministers to get together and come up with a recovery program. She told them to refer to the basic principles she had enunciated during her campaign—efficiency, less government, and alleviation of poverty. Her chief goals were to help the poor by creating jobs and reviving the depressed countryside, a strategy that also aimed to combat the insurgency.

She approved broad policies, but did not deal with the details of programs or the general week-to-week discussion on economic policy. There was no council of economic advisers; decisions were often made by phone among the ministers.

Cory began by almost immediately dismantling the sugar and coconut trading monopolies. It was to be the only economic policy that was clearly and swiftly carried out.

Her most visible task was to promote foreign investment. The message of her trips to Singapore, Indonesia, the U.S., and Japan was, "Invest here." In Manhattan, she told members of the Economic Club of New York and the Philippine-American Chamber of Commerce, "Invest in the Philippines, not because we need your money, although we do. . . . Invest in the Philippines, because it is to our mutual advantage." She touted the country's English-speaking, educated, cost-efficient labor force, its natural resources, agricultural abundance and idle or under-utilized productive capacity. She would make the pitch again and again.

Cory's first big decision was whether to honor the Marcos government debts. Finance Minister Jimmy Ongpin and Central Bank President Jobo Fernandez, with longtime commitments to the international financial community, wanted to pay them all. National Economic Development Authority Minister Winnie Monsod advocated selective repudiation of foreign loans that Marcos had made in collusion with foreign suppliers for overpriced goods.

In a cabinet discussion, some of her ministers said repudiation of the debt would frighten creditors.

"My heart bleeds," argued Monsod. "But my constituency is the Filipino people, and if they have to pay for a loan arrived at through collusion, it's unfair to the Filipino people."

Cory said, "That's right; I agree with Winnie. Let us pay according to our capacity to pay."

Nevertheless, based on a discussion of the country's international credit standing and considerations of attracting foreign investors, Cory finally chose to honor all the debts except the nuclear power plant loan. The government continued to negotiate with creditors in the hope of getting better terms on time and interest.

Cory's comments on the issue at home contradicted what her ministers did abroad. In December, she told Anthony Spaeth of *The Asian Wall Street Journal* that the country had to have an agreement that allowed it to cut its debt payments when economic growth fell. Ongpin and Fernandez had just returned from a meeting with creditors in which they had not pushed for that at all. "Her rhetoric has nothing to do with reality," Spaeth concluded.

There was no improvement in minimum wages after Cory came to power. The pay floor, less than $3 in cities and under $2 on farms—not enough to pay for a family's food ration—was still largely ignored. Conservatives, led by Ongpin, said higher wages for labor would discourage investment. Monsod explained, "The government is prepared to be flexible as long as there is an agreement between labor and management, even if there is no union." That simply meant the government would continue not to enforce the law. Increases were never a possibility.

Three months into her term, Cory announced on her TV program a plan to create a million sub-minimum wage jobs in eighteen months. Called Agenda for a People-Powered Development, it was the centerpiece of a six-year agriculture-based, employment-oriented, economic development plan would produce a million temporary jobs a year for the construction of schools, irrigation and water supply facilities, roads, and reforestation projects. The strategy was to give a short-term boost to the economy by improving the demand for goods and reduce poverty from nearly 60 percent of the population to 45 percent. She asked her ministers to submit proposals for the program's implementation.

But nothing happened; the jobs program never got off the ground. The bureaucracy continued the habits it had developed during the Marcos years. There were no well-organized programs to carry out the ideas, no way to distribute the money efficiently at the level of the local bureaucracy without it being dissipated or stolen. The money that was spent was simply used to build patronage. After providing only about 107,000 jobs, the program was suspended in December because of the constant delays in funds coming from the national treasury.

The bureaucracy also blocked her policy to privatize the hundreds of government corporations—banks, resorts, industries—that were listed, albeit overvalued, at $7 billion, and instead of producing profits, ate up a substantial part of the national budget. Sometimes, the new managers did not want to give up their fiefdoms; in other cases, they moved too slowly to implement sales.

There were some hopeful economic signs during Cory's first year. Interest rates were cut from 30 percent to 15 percent because more money was available: capital flight had dropped and some money came back from abroad. Inflation fell to 3 or 4 percent from 33 percent in 1985, and 60 percent in 1984, largely because of austerity measures adopted under the International Monetary Fund pressures during the Marcos government and because the lack of money in the economy reduced purchasing power. But economic growth that was expected to be 1.6 percent was only .16 percent for 1986. Investors were still uncertain about the future. They saw political drift. The government published its economic goals and targets, but had no plans to realize them. Cory seemed to lack a handle on economic policy. She offered no economic vision or leadership to match her boldness on the political side. Payoffs were still the way of doing business, but now investors were not even sure whom to pay off. Wary, they held on to their money. Investment from January to August was down 38 percent.

Business also was unnerved by an increase in strikes which proliferated—up nearly 60 percent from the year before. They were a result of a finally freed labor force seeking to push up the prevalent miserable wages. Of the more than 500 strikes by mid-October, only twenty-one were against multinational firms, which tended to pay better. Many business leaders thought that Labor Minister Bobbit Sanchez, an outspoken advocate of workers' rights, was to blame for the strikes and sought his ouster. He responded that most disputes had been resolved and their length was shorter than in past years.

The union movement was feeling its oats. The Trade Union Congress of the Philippines, supported by the AFL-CIO, had been the only labor federation recognized by the Marcos regime. It claimed 1.3 million members. The leftist May 1st Movement (KMU) was founded in 1980, and it listed 600,000 members. Several other federations existed as well, though organized labor was only a tenth of the workforce.

Labor Day in Manila was something out of the ordinary. On May 1, Cory Aquino was the guest of honor at a mass rally at the Luneta grandstand before a joint assembly of all the labor federations, which had never gotten together before. Communist leaders Joma Sison and Commander Dante sat with union officials and dignitaries on the grandstand. A street theater group sang "The Internationale." If Cory felt uncomfortable, she did not show it.

In her speech, she pledged an "economic revolution that will lift us from poverty, underdevelopment, and economic injustice." She promised to end the laws that repressed workers' rights and to ensure that labor shared fairly in development. "I have also come to plead for your patience, understanding, and support for specific policies and programs which may not immediately benefit your sector but will in the long run give us a country and an economy strong enough to fulfill the cherished dreams of labor," she told them.

She announced a series of measures that enhanced workers' rights to organize and strike. And she promised to appoint union representatives to policy-making bodies. She said the ministry of labor would call a conference of labor, business, and government representatives where she hoped they would explore the mechanisms for profit sharing in line with her policy of seeking equitable distribution of wealth. She asked them to work hard to increase productivity and to exercise restraint in using their right to strike.

"Make me prouder, my workers, of this second revolution to make our country free, not only of a tyrant in the palace but of tyranny everywhere: the tyranny of poverty and underdevelopment, as well as the tyranny of political power."

The workers were delighted.

Business people were appalled.

Cory sought to explain her program to the country's business leaders. The audience of the Philippine Chamber of Commerce and Industry booed Sanchez but gave Cory a standing ovation when she arrived to address them in July. They would not like what she said.

"Business wants to think of itself as the engine of the economy," she told them. "But it looks to me like this engine wants to be pushed until it finds a gentle downward slope where it can coast along without effort. Well, for your information, we are at the foot of a steep mountain, and the flood waters are rising."

"In my view, the militancy of Philippine labor is the inevitable result of years of economic plunder and mismanagement, from which you all suffered, but from which labor suffered even more," she declared. "Surely we can once again blame Marcos and his cronies and technocrats, but should we not also look at ourselves? What did we do during those years to protect the interests of our workers? Is it any wonder that they now aspire to protect themselves?"

"Whatever its roots," she said, "the militancy of labor is now a fact of life that we can neither reverse nor suppress. Instead, we should respond constructively to the legitimate grievances of labor."

She did not get a standing ovation when she finished, nor did her speech have much impact. Stability, not exhortations, would be needed to make investors put their money back into the country.

The next month, Cory told Sanchez to stop being lenient with illegal wildcat strikes and to find a more forceful way of dealing with the problem. It was a political gesture and sign to Sanchez as much as anything else. Filipinos ignore court orders, because the legal enforcement system does not work. It is one of the reasons people have private armies and goons. But Sanchez did issue rulings against workers in several walkouts.

The country's peasants represented an even more intractable problem. They were 70 percent of the population, and their poverty and oppression under near feudalism had been the fuel that fired the insurgency. They no longer wanted simply to improve the tenancy system; their demand was for land reform.

Less than 20 percent of farmers owned the land they tilled.

Sugar workers who lived in the wood and grass huts on Hacienda Camili, not far from Bacolod City on Negros, rose before daybreak to walk three miles to a neighboring plantation to cut cane for less than a dollar a day. They said the owner of Hacienda Camili refused to give them work even at the same low wages because he opposed their membership in the sugar workers union and called them subversives. Their living conditions were miserable. They had no electricity or running water: the community well, bathhouse, laundry, and toilet was the river. They ate only rice, camote, casava, or bananas. The children got diarrhea from eating wild grass. They wanted the right to farm small plots where they could grow vegetables. They were the people who supported the NPA. "They will take the land of the rich people," a peasant explained. "For the poor people, that's a good idea." But Cory said little about the land problem. It did not appear to be a top priority for her. She told Agrarian Reform Minister Heherson "Sonny" Alvarez, "Do what you think is good, and let's carry it out." His policy was to proceed with the Marcos program which was limited to distribution of lands that were planted with rice and corn. Most advocates of land reform thought that was not enough.

Peasant members of the radical Farmers' Movement of the Philippines (KMP) spoke with Cory in July and proposed that she return peasants' land that had been seized by Marcos and also distribute lands that were nonproductive or were government lands not in use.

In October, on National Peasants' Day, the group organized a four-day march of several thousand people to the palace to press Cory to implement land reform. They said there had been no clear stand taken regarding peasants' demands for eight months and that the government still had not decided what kind of agrarian reform it wanted to carry out. They were alarmed by the apparent policy not to go beyond Marcos's program.

Cory explained to a reporter that the government would not take any private property beyond rice and corn land. "You can't take land away without just compensation," she said. "We just don't have the money."

One of her cabinet ministers said later, "Land reform was a dilemma because of the possible misinterpretation that taking away land from the landed and giving it to the poor could be misconstrued as veering toward the Left. Most businessmen sprung from the landed gentry and are tied to land or real estate. There was worry that would upset the business community." Alvarez confirmed that: "At this stage, she's trying to balance off the investment climate with the social justice program. She is careful not to send unwanted signals."

Farmers' groups protested that even the existing program was being blocked. In some cases, people in government had pressured local officials to protect the lands of their constituents from being included in land reform. In South Cotabato, Mindanao, twenty-five

corn-growing tenants who had gotten land on an estate were harassed, one shot to death, another injured, and ten ejected forcibly
by armed goons hired by the owner. Witnesses identified the killers,
but no arrests were made, nor did the government attempt to
reinstate or protect the tenants.

The perception was that Cory had no interest or commitment to
land reform. Luis Taruc, the old Huk "supremo," who now headed
an alliance of moderate farmers' organizations, worried that the government was moving too slowly, that all the agrarian reform agency
was doing was preparing documents for people who had already
occupied land. The question of distributing other lands would be
left to the congress, which Taruc predicted would be dominated, as
it had always been, by businessmen and landowners.

Finally, Hacienda Luisita remained a microcosm of the country's
problems and a symbol to many of Cory's attitude toward land
reform. There was severe unemployment; only a minority of the
30,000 people who lived there had permanent jobs. Others were
seasonal workers employed during the milling period. The rest of
the time they worked two to three days a week at for a few dollars
a day. The workers and their families lived in villages of grass-roofed
huts or concrete block houses on the hacienda grounds Some of
them had electricity when the mill was running.

The Cojuangcos continued to fight the judicial decision to distribute the land to tenants, filing an appeal to the appellate court in
December 1986.

Alvarez was questioned about Hacienda Luisita at the journalists'
breakfast roundtable at the Manila Hotel. "Converting Hacienda
Luisita into a model for land reform was an election promise of
President Aquino. What is keeping her from fulfilling this promise?"
a reporter asked.

He replied, "This is a very democratic president. She will have
to talk to her brothers and sisters There is a ticklish problem of
family and interpersonal relations there."

"Let's wait for the policy to be implemented nationwide," he said.

The Game of Politics

ONCE DURING THE CAMPAIGN, when Cory's aides were joking about what jobs they would get when she won, she told them disapprovingly that her government would be "a moral crusade." She had seen the kind of political horse-trading that went on in politics during her years with Ninoy, and she did not like it. In fact, she did not much like politics. It was divisive, and she was the president of all the Filipinos. She had made it clear she would not seek reelection and thought that allowed her to stay out of the political arena.

But political realities said otherwise. Under the new constitution, voters would choose 250 members of the lower house—200 by district and fifty by national party lists on the European proportional representation model. They would elect twenty-four people to the Senate at large and would choose thousands of provincial and local officials. Unless Cory controlled the legislature and a goodly share of local offices, her administration could be stalemated.

To elect office holders and keep them in the fold, one had to make alliances based on the currency of political power, which was patronage and the pork barrel, spoils in the traditional competition between political factions and elites. Most of her cabinet members had played the game before martial law, and they took up where they had left off. The opposition would compete for its share. Cory's closest advisors worried that politics could defeat her unless she learned how to play the game.

The parties of the post-Marcos era were not much different from those before his reign. They had a patina of ideology—the leftist party, Partido ng Bayan (People's Party), was indeed based on ideology—but most of them were still collections of people who lined up behind a leader, with local leaders supporting national leaders, "a pyramid culminating in the head honcho," as one government official put it.

The fall-out from political rivalries was weakening her government. Cory acknowledged the conflicts in her cabinet and pointed out that though all had been opponents of Marcos, it would be asking for a miracle to expect them to agree now. She said after elections, the government would shake down. But she did not deal with the political reasons for the instability in her coalition.

Meanwhile, the opposition was getting itself together. Enrile's ally Rene Cayetano reorganized the Nacionalista party, and Enrile said he considered himself a member of the organization under whose banner he had run for office several times. He added that he had resigned from the KBL. The Philippine Nacionalista party was formed by Blas Ople and younger, former KBL leaders. The parties opposing Cory were expected to organize a coalition that would include the Nacionalistas, the PNP, the KBL, and the Liberal party wing led by Eva Estrada Kalaw. It would probably include some elements of Unido.

There would have to be a coalition of the forces supporting Cory in order to win seats for members of parliament and local officials to carry out her program. But Cory declined to deal with the problem of putting it together. She left political tasks to her brother Peping, her brother-in-law Paul Aquino, and her cousin, Ding Tanjuatco, who worked with some of her close supporters in the cabinet. At first, they made attempts to merge PDP-Laban, Unido, and the Liberal parties, but they failed. Pimentel and Salonga opposed the idea on grounds that the groups had different ideologies and platforms and would lose their identities. They also had their own political ambitions; both wanted to run for president.

Cory's relatives, aides, and many of her ministers thought there ought to be a "Cory party," and Peping broached it to her.

"I don't think I should be involved in any one party," she told him.

"She doesn't think of herself as a politician," Peping explained. "She thinks of herself as a person with a mission."

"She wants to maintain being above it all so she can continue to be the unifying factor," said Tanjuatco. "She thinks that once one joins a party, there is a danger the others will be polarized."

Faced with her refusal, her relatives and supporters began thinking about setting up a coalition of members of pro-Aquino political parties. Its main components would be people from PDP-Laban, Unido, and the Salonga Liberals. It was called an "umbrella"; members would not have to leave their old parties. Those behind the idea hoped it would be converted into a formal political party after ratification of the constitution and before the selection of candidates for the May 11 parliamentary elections.

Peping discussed the political question with Cory in August. She told him to wait; it was not the appropriate time. But in New York a month later, she told the Asia Society that she would not join a party, but would play a role in picking candidates.

Cory met with Peping and one of her ministers, Luis Villafuerte, in Malacañang just after her return from the United States. She was still cold to the idea of forming a political party or designating one as her own. Peping posed the other option. "Many of the ministers would like to form some kind of movement to bring people together," he said. "They want an umbrella, a coalition of some kind." She nodded silently; Peping took that for "no objection," and went ahead. Cory knew that once the election came, her endorsement would be valuable. "Definitely I will have a hand in the selection of candidates," she said publicly. "Maybe I will just call them Cory candidates."

"We still want her to have her own party," said Apeng Yap. "The other elements of the coalition would be forced to join because of her popularity. But she doesn't want to be involved."

Her relatives and close supporters worried that unless Cory established a strong party, the members of her coalition would turn against each other in the fight for political power. Her problems would not end with the expected government victory in legislative elections. "There is no question that there will be a pro-Cory majority," said Yap. "The question is that they will quarrel for spoils and position.

Who will be the speaker, the floor leaders, the chairmen of committees?" He said such disunity could mean the rise again of the old system of groups working to protect vested interests through political deals.

In October, the word spread that Cory's top advisors would launch a "political movement," the first stage of forming her own political party. It would be called Lakas ng Bansa, loosely translated as People's Power, with the old acronym, Laban, or "fight." It would be an expanded version of the Cory Aquino for President Movement, the umbrella campaign organization.

Laban would accept members of various parties. The idea was to woo KBL and Unido political leaders. Enrile had been invited, but said he would not join the Aquino party or any other. Laurel had also been asked to join, but he declined. Lakas ng Bansa was announced October 8.

At her press conference in Bacolod City a week later, Cory was asked whether she would head the new movement. "I am not in favor of creating a new political party," she repeated. "There are enough political parties now. I would like to take a direct hand in the selection of candidates. I would like for all the different parties and organizations to get together, the same coalition that got us where we are now."

But much as she wanted things to remain the same, the parties and political alignments were changing. A week after the Lakas ng Bansa announcement, Laurel held a press conference at Club Filipino and said he would run for election again if the constitution was turned down, as that would signify a rejection of the nation's leadership. He also announced that Unido would field its own candidates in legislative and local elections.

There were rumors that Unido might join the opposition. It had been weakened by defections and by differences over the Aquino government. Of thirty-five Unido MPs elected in the 1984 elections, less than ten were with the party and recognized Laurel's leadership. Unido Secretary General Rene Espina favored a split from the PDP-Laban coalition, and Jose B. Laurel Jr., who was head of a Nacionalista faction, held talks with Rene Cayetano on reunifying the Nacionalista party which had been strengthened by the advent of many ex-KBL leaders.

In October, Peping consolidated his hold over PDP-Laban with his election as president. Some commentators saw it as the ascendency of the traditional politicians over those on the Left identified with Pimentel. With the change in leadership, PDP-Laban also began taking in members of the KBL.

Lakas ng Bansa was launched officially November 8 with almost the entire cabinet present. Political Affairs Minister Cuenco said it would be the "party of the future."

That same month, Lakas announced that fifty prominent political opposition leaders would join, including members of the KBL and Nacionalista parties identified with Marcos. Some members of the umbrella group objected.

"They are not all vicious and crooks and killers," said Tanjuatco defending the decision. "A number of them happen to be in the wrong party. And they still have political clout. You have to balance these things." Yap said, "They are being taken on a case by case basis in consultation with local people and if they are not so notorious."

Unido was also maintaining an "open door policy" toward KBL members who had shown a "clean record" of public service and were not "heavily identified" with Marcos, said party spokesman Manuel Malvar. Politicians of all stripes were seeking to "broaden" their appeal to increase their chances for victory.

Enrile declined the presidency of the Nacionalista party, but everyone knew he had become the unofficial leader and prospective standard bearer for the opposition. People suspected that Laurel had made a secret alliance with Enrile, but with his penchant for opportunism, no one knew on which side he would end up, and many in his own party would not follow him.

Cory, despite her protests, would have to deal with the political questions raised by the realignments when candidates for the spring elections besieged her, trying to get her endorsement. She would have to make hard choices and learn how to bargain.

For Cory's advisors, another big question was whether her popularity would be translated into victory for the candidates she endorsed at the local level where political power was based on family alliances and patronage.

Once the congress was elected, Cory's problems would take on a new dimension. The strategy of the opposition was not to contend with her in the race for Senate, whose members needed a majority of the national vote, but to attempt to capture the House to stalemate her program in the bicameral legislature.

The Game of Politics

Many of her supporters who won seats would have their own agendas. Even those whom she had endorsed would sometimes take independent stands. She would have to learn how to hold the hands of politicians, even how to pacify them by using the patronage and pork barrel system which she opposed. She could try to change politics, but if she insisted on staying away from it, her ability to govern the country would be at risk.

The Hot Fall

THE FALL BEGAN auspiciously for Cory. After the victories of the cease-fires and the beginning of peace negotiations with the two rebel groups, she prepared to leave for the United States where government officials and the public, who had watched the February revolution on their television screens in astonishment, were ready to give a heroine's welcome to the woman who had toppled a dictator.

But there were a few sour notes. One was a message from unnamed U.S. officials, issued before she arrived, telling her she ought to get tough with the Communists. She replied that Marcos had needed the Americans to prop him up, so he allowed them to interfere in Philippine affairs. She would not.

Another was increasing criticism by Enrile along the same lines. U.S. Embassy people were telling Enrile and his allies that he was right to press for a stronger military policy against the Communists. "Johnny is on the right track in advising the Filipinos of the danger of communism and in briefing the government of the dangers of the projected cease-fire," they repeated to Rene Cayetano.

Enrile and his MND aides were chafing at what they considered exclusion from key decisions, including discussions and policies on the insurgency and the cease-fire negotiations. He saw his powers reduced by Cory as they had been by Marcos. She had even been putting her own men in place as military officers. Whereas in the beginning, Enrile and Ramos had determined promotions, with Cory giving her automatic approval, she had now become directly involved in the decisions. Malacañang officials were also talking openly about investigating the wealth Enrile had amassed during the Marcos years and of prosecuting his "RAM boys" for violations of human rights.

And the peace talks were bogged down after the government demanded that the National Democratic Front agree to an unconditional and immediate thirty-day cease-fire. The NDF representatives said it was not possible; it could not be enforced, and they asked the government to consider the proposal they had submitted for immunity and security guarantees for the negotiators and other personnel involved in the talks.

Finally, there were rumors of a military coup during Cory's absence. The RAM boys were proclaiming their dissatisfaction with Cory and hinting "coup" broadly to journalists, diplomats, and anyone who would listen. It was part of a psychological warfare campaign—they referred to it casually in military jargon as "psy war"—that aimed to get influence for Enrile and his boys in the cabinet.

The military was divided into factions loyal to Cory, Ramos, Enrile, and Marcos, with the latter two having compatible interests. By then, Cory had appointed more than half the generals, whom she began to call in one by one to take the measure of their loyalties. However, she was still not sure of her support. She did not want to make an issue of Enrile's attacks. She admitted on television that she could not move effectively against Enrile and his group because she did not have complete control of the military. "When I do move, I fight to win," she declared.

Ramos would begin to take an active role to attempt to mediate the conflict. He feared the RAM officers might do something reckless. He did not want soldiers shooting each other.

Enrile was like a foreign presence in the cabinet. Everyone was acutely aware that he was one of the architects of martial law and had been the jailor of half a dozen of them.

Villafuerte told Cory as much when she was trying to determine how to deal with Enrile and seemed puzzled about his attitude.

Every time she talked to him he was amiable and said he had nothing against her personally; then he would go out and harshly criticize the government. As Villafuerte had known him at law school, she asked his assessment. Villafuerte replied, "Consciously or subconsciously, he feels he does not belong, he's not part of the team."

Some of the ministers began to call for Enrile's resignation, and in a talk before military officers, he in turn declared that if they kept that up, he might become difficult. "Maybe these people are not aware that when I lose my patience I am like Rambo." He said later he was joking, and Cory ignored the incident.

She had a sense of humor, too. Just before she left for America, CBS-TV aired a "60 Minutes" broadcast in which correspondent Diane Sawyer asked her if she trusted her defense minister. Cory looked off camera. "Are we on . . . ?" Enrile did not find that funny.

Cory's advisers urged her not to go to the United States. They said there were too many problems at home—including the possibility of a coup. She brushed aside their worries and arrived in Washington on September 15 for a ten-day trip.

Although she was a heroine to the public, the administration's view was somewhat mixed. Reagan and his advisers did not like what they viewed as Cory's uncertain attitude toward the insurgency, the American bases, and the foreign debt. On her part, Cory distrusted Reagan's friendship with Marcos and the delay in U.S. economic aid. But her meeting with Reagan went well; she felt they had hit it off. The pre-lunch conversation that was supposed to last ten or twenty minutes went on for nearly an hour. Reagan told her how he had fought the Communists in the actors' union in the late forties and early fifties. Afterward, at lunch, he regaled everyone with jokes about Mikhail Gorbachev and other world leaders.

As she drove up to the Capitol, she could not help thinking about the last time she had been there. Ninoy was scheduled to appear before a congressional committee. They drove from Boston, Ninoy and Ballsy taking turns at the wheel. It was difficult to find a parking space, and she and Ballsy circled the Capitol while Ninoy went inside. "At that time I was not getting all of the fringe benefits that go with the presidency. This is something that I never experienced before," she would remark later. "Now, I guess parking is no longer a problem. I am just so sorry that Ninoy never had a chance to enjoy this."

Normally she felt nervous before giving a speech, but standing in front of the House of Representatives she was completely calm, even buoyant. Her aides did not feel so good. She had firmly turned down five or six speech proposals and finally jotted down her own thoughts for a draft. Her supporters complained, "There's no foreign policy, no economic policy; it's not sufficiently statesmanlike."

"This is what I want to say," she told them. "It's as simple as that."

She talked about Ninoy's arrest, his imprisonment in Laur, his hunger strike. She talked about their faith in democracy, and she told them of his murder and her loss. "But his death was my country's resurrection in the courage and faith by which alone [people] could be free again," she declared. "And so began the revolution that has brought me to democracy's most famous home, the Congress of the United States."

Some of the listeners had worn yellow articles of clothing, and many pinned on the yellow flowers that had been given out by Cory's supporters. She told them of the stolen election, the massive outpouring of the Filipino people, and her efforts now to make peace with the insurgents. She asked them to, "Join us, America, as we build a new home for democracy, another haven for the oppressed." When she stepped down from the podium, Republican majority leader Senator Robert Dole told her, "Cory, you hit a home run!" "I hope the bases were loaded," she replied.

A few days later, in her speech at the United Nations, she ignored the advice of her ambassador and attacked the international body for its hypocrisy on human rights.

There had been an agreement with her critics at home that they would be silent while she was away, but after her speech in Congress, Enrile and Laurel renewed their attacks. While Cory was in New York, meeting with business leaders and talking to creditors, Enrile spoke to 100,000 people at a rightist rally in Bacolod City, Negros. He condemned the Communists and pledged to wipe out the guerrillas. "The military organization is ready to confront the enemy, if Madam Cory will give us the order to do so," he declared. He appeared on television to say Cory had a duty to deal with the insurgency, that she was responsible for the people threatened by the NPA and for the soldiers "who are dying and getting wounded in mounting atrocities."

The rebels were taking advantage of government reconciliation efforts, he said. Their attacks were designed to gain better leverage in cease-fire talks and to acquire more arms. While the NPA hit military, police and civilian targets, the army was only on active defense and could not seek out its assailants.

A day later, Laurel echoed, "I am not happy about the way the insurgency problem is being addressed. I think it should be dealt with more decisively."

The legal Left was not altogether happy with Cory's performance, either. Rolando Olalia, leader of the KMU labor federation and the leftist Partido ng Bayan, criticized the policies outlined to foreign investors. He said labor could not be "coopted in any economic program designed to serve foreign interests," that "an economic program based mainly on attracting foreign investments requires, among other things, cheap labor and corollary to this, the repression of trade union rights." He reflected the views of economic national- ists who charged multinationals with being exploitive of both labor and the country's national resources and wanted to build up native capitalist enterprises through protectionism and other government restrictions.

Back from the U.S., Cory responded to reporters' questions about the suggestions by Enrile, Laurel and others that there be new pres- idential elections. She said the February revolution had legitimized her government. Also fearing the mileage Enrile might gain from his anti-communism, she privately told some of her ministers to speak out more strongly against communism themselves.

The government and NDF were now about to sign a thirty-day temporary cease-fire when Rodolfo Salas, reportedly head of the Communist Party's military commission and thus the top NPA com- mander, was captured by military intelligence officers along with his wife and driver-security aide as they left Manila's Philippine General Hospital where Salas had gone for a checkup after minor surgery. The military had been tailing him for months and picked him up, one military source explained, to show they could capture one of the Communists' top men. But many people thought the goal was to throw a monkey wrench into the peace talks. "You don't bag Salas without checking with higher-ups," a local journalist said.

Cory met with her advisors and Ramos after the capture to discuss her response. The meeting lasted into the night. They agreed she should commend the military. "I have to issue a statement," she said. "I am the president of all the Filipinos." Cory praised the armed forces for the capture. Her stand calmed some military fears, but the peace talks collapsed.

One of the stumbling blocs to the talks was the government's insistance that an agreement granting immunity and safety guarantees for the NDF negotiators would have to include an accord for an immediate cease-fire. The NDF panel said there were not yet adequate guidelines, mechanics, and structures for implementing and monitoring such a cease-fire.

On October 8, the cabinet declared its support for General Ramos's six-point counter-insurgency program presented in a fifty-minute briefing. Enrile attended the meeting but did not state his views and would not answer questions posed by other cabinet members. Relations between him and the rest of the cabinet were fast deteriorating. A day later at a conference of travel executives, he spoke in response to news reports that the cabinet had adopted a national counterinsurgency plan. He said it did not have a plan at all, just a call for a plan, and blamed the failure on the lack of "consistent national policies" and the "ambivalence of some people" in government. He said that unless the government laid down consistent policies, the Philippines would become like Nicaragua or El Salvador. Enrile also told an audience that the first two years of martial law had been good. "There was order and liberty, except for those who violated the law." It had turned sour later.

There were, in fact, elements of a counterinsurgency program, but there was no machinery to implement it. Cory had ordered her ministers to work on their components of a plan. She expressed no annoyance at Enrile's comments to her aides. Critics, especially news columnists, wondered why Cory was not telling Enrile to shut up.

It was reported that schools in Bacolod City and some parts of Mindanao were being used as evacuation centers for families displaced by hamletting. Ramos's spokesman, defending the practice, told the press that it occurred to prevent civilians from being caught in the crossfire between government and rebel troops. However, Ramos invited the National Democratic Front to supply members to take part in investigations of reported hamlettings. He also accused Nur Misuari of violating his agreement with the government by using his consultation trips around Mindanao to call for secession. Misuari and 1,000 armed "bodyguards" were prevented by the military from entering Zamboanga City until they agreed to check their guns outside town. However, Ramos added days later that the military was in favor of dialogue to work the problem out.

In spite of these difficulties, Cory was upbeat publicly. "When I started, I had no generals, but ever since I became president, I think the number has gone up," she said in a speech to business organizations. Since taking power, she had appointed twenty-one new generals and promoted seven generals to key commands out of a total of sixty-nine. A coup was, therefore, not likely. "I am more confident now," she said. "I hope I have impressed upon the military my sincerity in not only trying to improve their lives, but also in the matter of getting both civilian and military sectors to finally unite."

Cory enjoyed a brief sweet victory when the U.S. Senate finally approved the $200 million supplemental economic aid that it had rejected twice during the week. "You can't imagine how much heartache that $200 million has given me," she said a few days later. "When it was first defeated in the Senate, all of a sudden, my entire U.S. trip was being judged on the basis of the $200 million, which I did not even ask for. . . . I was so depressed when people said all Cory got was applause and no cash."

But the coup rumors continued, along with Enrile's attacks. He charged that Cory "forfeited her mandate, repudiated it, threw it away by creating a revolutionary government and issuing a freedom constitution. He said she had to submit to new elections. It was an open challenge of her right to govern. "Why can't Enrile wait if he wants to be president?" Cory said to a small group of advisors.

RAM officers spread stories that the palace was training a "yellow army" at Hacienda Luisita to counter hostility from the military and Marcos loyalists. The exercises turned out to be by members of the Presidential Security Guard being trained by American advisors. The Enrile boys were also telling people that an unspecified event relating to the Plaza Miranda would be a signal for some action. They had gotten hold of Corpus's letter and planned its release to be the signal for a coup.

Cory moved to bolster her position in the military. She increased the hazard pay of soldiers from $7.50 a month to $10 a month, still absurdly low, and invited junior and senior military officers to the palace to interview them for promotions. Enrile's boys made a fuss about it to foment discontent, and officers resented her prying into their personal lives. "I've heard you have two wives," she would say. She also brought up allegations of ill-gotten wealth and human rights violations.

Enrile pressed the demand that Cory fire ministers he deemed corrupt or too far to the left. He also virtually dared Cory to fire him. "I'm expendable; I don't mind being sacked," he told officers and men at Camp Aguinaldo after the flag-raising ceremony. "All we want is to be recognized for our little contribution to the revolution." He said the military was shackled in its fight against the insurgents.

Rising criticism of corruption in the government added to Cory's problems. The word out of Malacañang was that she would not fire any ministers, though she would urge some of them to run in the coming elections.

Enrile skipped the next cabinet meeting in mid-October which focused on a compromise agreement between the government and the NDF on the jailing of Sales, his wife, and security aide. The wife and aide were ordered released by the Supreme Court that day. Cory stated that the release underscored the government's efforts to exhaust all peaceful means to arrive at a negotiated accord with the insurgents. During the cabinet meeting, Enrile was giving a speech at a dentists' conference. He said cabinet meetings were "a waste of people's money if there is nothing concerning my ministry which will be discussed."

The Constitutional Commission's approval of the proposed charter on October 15 pushed those seeking to destabilize Cory's government to move faster. Once the constitution was ratified, her legitimacy could not be assailed. Laurel announced he would submit to new elections if the constitution were not approved. Commentators began to speculate about an Enrile-Laurel alliance. Relations between Cory and Laurel were tense.

Enrile appeared to give a speech every day to business groups, professional organizations, and military gatherings in which he accused the government of being soft on communism and not effective in fighting the rebels. He claimed there was no anti-insurgency policy. The government was ineffectual, unstable; it could not make decisions. Newspaper columnists were calling her weak and indecisive for her failure to confront Enrile, but she did not want to fire him and make him a political martyr. She did not think she could remove him while he could make an issue that he had been fired because of his opposition to communism. Conscious of Filipino cultural values that attach great importance to gratitude, she also was weighing how to draw the line between the gratitude owed Enrile for his role in the revolution and the need to assert the prerogatives of the presidency.

And finally, she was not quite sure what power he had over the military and where their loyalty lay. She never said a word of public criticism. Later, she would explain, "I always believe that it takes two to fight . . . I was not in a fighting mood, so it didn't occur to me that this was something really so delicate and so sensitive . . . I always keep in mind that the higher goal is the greater interests of the Filipino people, and whatever I believe will work in attaining that goal will guide me in my actions."

Some ministers were continuing to demand Enrile's ouster. Cory told them to cool down; she did not want to provoke Enrile or give him cause to think she was asking her aides to attack him, which might make the situation worse. Cory thought she understood him, that his behavior stemmed from his insecurity. She phoned him, trying to win him over, asking, "Why is it we cannot work together? Can't you see the rationale of getting together for the good of the country?" She told a friend, "In all my fifty-three years, I've never tried to woo a man that way." Her closest advisors thought she was treating Enrile with too much importance while the man was insulting her every day.

At that time, Cory went to Bacolod City to meet with sectoral groups—teachers, workers, businessmen, clergy, peasants, and sugar planters—and to kick off the beginning of her campaign for the new constitution.

Bishop Antonio Fortich, a seventy-two-year-old clergyman who had promoted the organization of the sugar workers union in 1971, was on the plane bringing the press from Manila the eve of the visit. About ten reporters trooped over to the bishop's house that evening and drank beer and tea and nibbled chocolate cake that the Bishop joked he had baked himself. A lively man with black slicked-back hair and gold-rimmed glasses, Fortich had had contacts with the NPA for years. "The head of the Negros NPA, Commander Eco, was our student here," he said. "There are three ex-priests in the NPA, but they are no longer in the institutional church."

He had seen NPA leaders in June, and they had indicated their interest in talking with Cory. Two weeks later, the military shelled NPA territory for two weeks. After a lull, a local colonel asked Fortich to initiate another dialogue.

"Colonel, this is not the proper time. The wounds are still open," said the bishop.

"But Monsignor, try to do something," said the colonel. "We would like to have an understanding."

"I will do my best," replied Fortich, "but I tell you, they are very angry with you." The NPA said that while Cory was offering a cease-fire, the military was reinforcing its units on Negros with four extra battalions. Fortich met with the rebel leaders several times. They were still interested in talking about a cease-fire, and so he began to make plans for a meeting with Cory. She was encouraged, but warned, "Monsignor, I know that you told me that they are willing to talk with me. I like that. But be very careful. I do not want anything to happen to any one of them while they are in transit for a dialogue." He said she was referring to the capture of Salas which had just occurred. But the Salas arrest frightened the Negros rebels, and they called off the meeting.

When it fell through, Fortich attempted to arrange a meeting on nearby Panay Island, the second stop on the trip. He contacted Archbishop Alberto Piamonte in Iloilo City on Panay who spread the word that he wanted to see the NPA leaders. Six of them came down from the hills and said they would send two emissaries to meet Cory. None of this was public knowledge when Cory arrived in Bacolod City October 16.

At a luncheon in the gymnasium of St. Johns Institute, Cory repeated a local joke and introduced Bishop Fortich as Commander Tony, a reference to the title used by leaders of the NPA; everybody laughed. During lunch he passed a note to her. Rebel representatives wanted to meet with her in Iloilo City the next day.

At the press conference that afternoon, reporters asked about her rift with Enrile. Would she do anything to placate him?

"I don't think there is any necessity of placating the defense minister," she replied. "I have told him and General Ramos that both Doy Laurel and I and all the Filipinos appreciate and recognize the fact they did help in the February revolution, and that made it that much easier for us to oust the Marcos dictatorship. When I assumed office, they were saying my government would not last a few days or a few weeks, then it became six months. Let them keep talking. I am convinced this government will continue, because it has the support of the Filipino people," she declared.

She arrived at the Delgado Army base in Iloilo the next morning by helicopter, stepping onto the grass quadrangle to the brisk salutes of an honor guard and smartly saluting back. Breakfast was with the officers of the regional command; she told them they were appreciated, but that she wanted to end the guerrilla war through reconciliation to avoid spilling more blood. They listened politely, reserving their cheers for the announcement of promotions for several of their colleagues, including ten new generals.

Cory was informed about the strength of the NPA—some 2,000 rebel troops in the region, up over 50 percent since the year before, with a slight reduction of the mass base of some 97,000. There were enemy activities in 15 percent of barangays. The meeting seemed innocuous, nothing sensitive or private was discussed, but officials had suddenly barred the press. The miffed reporters were bundled away on buses through streets lined with townspeople and school children waving yellow flags. They headed to a local college, where there would be a rally and meetings with community representatives. Cory was supposed to arrive just after 9, but the crowd would wait for more than an hour, sweltering in the humid heat, protecting their heads from the sun with handkerchiefs and umbrellas. Archbishop Piamonte was also late.

The first meeting of the president—any president—with the Communist rebels was taking place in the Assumption Convent a few miles away.

Cory, the archbishop, and her speechwriter Teddy Locsin sat down at a table with Father Jose Torre representing the NDF, Panay, and Concha Araneta Bojala, a relative of Judy Araneta Roxas, widow of the former president of the Liberal party. The meeting started with a misunderstanding.

"Well . . . ," Cory said.

"Well, what?" they asked.

"I thought you were surrendering?"

"No," they said, "We wanted to talk." They started to repeat the NDF list of demands, in florid rhetoric.

Cory stood up. "I have a mass to attend. I don't have time for this foolishness."

"Wait, wait," they said. "Listen to us." Then they started to talk about some of the specific problems of Panay island, and she listened. They also told her they could act independently of the national leadership.

Cory told them she wanted to start negotiations for a cease-fire. "Until you can learn to trust me and my government, I feel that you don't want to lay down your arms, but at least we should stop killing," she said.

Concha Araneta Bojala wanted to be able to come down from the hills to give birth to her child, and Cory assured her that she could.

They talked for forty minutes. Cory had to leave for the mass, but Locsin stayed behind to listen to their complaints of abuses by local officials. Cory had requested that they draw up a joint statement and it was given to the press later that day. It read, "Father Jose Torre representing the NDF, Panay, and Mrs. Concha Araneta Bojala, representing the CPP Panay, responding to President Aquino's call for a cease-fire, met this morning with President Aquino to discuss the possibility of an island-wide cease-fire. The talks were held in the presence of Monsignor Piamonte; both sides said they were open to the idea of a cease-fire while talks on issues regarding the island of Panay are being discussed."

"Father Torre is one of my priests," the archbishop explained later, "my one and only priest up there. He lost his ministry when he went AWOL. We pray that he will come back if he sees the new government is trying to look after the poor. The priests who are the leftists—it is usually because they love the poor, and they see the government is just giving them the run-around."

Cory said the next step would be for both sides to designate representatives so they could meet on the issues.

Later, at a meeting of community leaders on an auditorium stage flanked by masks of comedy and tragedy, Cory said, "I shall pursue the path of negotiation to the utmost. My chief concern is to stop the killing. With every death of a Filipino, our country dies a little. While that is my chief concern, it is not my only duty. My primary duty is to protect the integrity of the republic and its democratic institutions, insure the safety of my people and guarantee their enjoyment of the basic rights and liberties for which they fought."

She added, "The insurgency is not the only or basic cause of the peace and order problems on this island. A lot of it has to do with the continued presence of gangsters in the hire of the warlords of the past regime. She blamed local officials for the continued activities of these armed bands associated with Marcos loyalists and said, "This particular problem will get my special attention."

She also addressed their gripe about faulty OICs: "I shall say to them now, shape up before you are shipped out." There was laughter, then applause.

In other parts of the country, meetings between local NPA leaders and officials led to several regional cease-fires. Sometimes the military cooperated; other times, it did not. In Negros, a cease-fire was approved by Ramos. In a northern province of Mindanao, Governor Felicidad Pimentel said provincial government and religious leaders, including the bishop, had met with the local NDF team, headed by a rebel priest, had agreed to a de facto cease-fire and were about to sign a formal agreement. She urged Cory to ignore calls for strong military action against the insurgents.

Meanwhile, the full panels of government and NDF negotiators met for the first time to hammer out the differences that remained on immunity and safety guarantees for the rebels' spokespersons.

The conflict with Enrile was becoming as serious a "peace and order" problem to Cory as the insurgents. On the plane back from Iloilo, General Ramos offered to mediate between her and the defense minister. Pimentel said Enrile's critics in the cabinet had decided to tone down their differences.

As Cory's trip south ended, Enrile began a visit to the islands of Cebu and Mindanao. He criticized her for talking only about a cease-fire while the rebels' demand for a "comprehensive political settlement" meant they were out to share power. He said if she gave in to Communist demands, "they can march with music to Malacañang," and that the Communist party and the NPA were already the second government. In Mindanao, he said her talk with Misuari had revived the Muslim secessionist problem. Back in Manila, Laurel echoed Enrile that peace talks would fail.

That same day, Ramos issued a directive saying that some in the armed forces "misconstrued the newly acquired freedom of action as a signal to actively participate in partisan politics," which would divide the military and end its role as the impartial guardian and protector of the people, the nation, the constitution and the flag. Those who wanted to be in politics should leave the military, he said. His statement appeared to be a warning to the RAM officers, who had been making political statements.

One of Enrile's Cebu rallies, sponsored by the pro-Marcos National Movement for Freedom and Democracy, drew about 10,000 people. Cory reportedly asked the local government deputy minister to discourage people from attending, calling it "a new gimmick" of Marcos loyalists to attract support.

In Manila, Laurel spoke out against forcing Enrile to resign. "I want the coalition retained," he said—using a word, "coalition," that would shortly take on significance.

Enrile and his aides also met with military officers on their tour. He lobbed what he hoped would be a new bombshell at her, declaring that on the Sunday of the February revolution, Cory, through her advisors, had agreed to set up a civilian-military coalition government. Enrile would decide matters affecting national security. He admitted he had no written proof, but said she had referred to the accord days before when she told Bishop Fortich at the Bacolod luncheon that she had been "forced into an unholy alliance." He said if he were to resign or be removed, the coalition and the government would collapse.

By abolishing the 1973 constitution under which she had been elected, Cory had forfeited her mandate, Enrile continued. If the new charter were rejected, she should resign. She would have "no moral right to continue as president." He said the Batasan could be convened at any time. And he repeated, with no apparent sense of irony, that Cory's statement to Bishop Fortich meant "she considered our unholy alliance as an agreement and a coalition to topple the Marcos regime."

"Some people are rewriting history," Cory said to some of her aides, but she did not deny the coalition story publicly. "It's not her style," explained an aide. She kept silent on this as she had and would on other Enrile attacks. "Maybe it's part of her fatalism," he mused. "She feels everything will ride itself out; there is divine providence watching over us. 'If I were you, I wouldn't be too worried,' she says. All members of the cabinet are in an uproar, and she is very cool, telling them it's not as black as you think." A palace official denied Cory had ever accepted a formula for powersharing.

Enrile's strategy was to use his verbal assaults on the insurgency policy, the local government officials, alleged corruption in the government, the "left-leaning" cabinet members and the constitution to challenge the legitimacy of Cory's government to build up to a climax at which point he would break away from the government. "There will be a change in the next few months," the RAM boys began telling journalists.

Enrile arrived back from Cebu late for the closing ceremony of a meeting of Mindanao leaders in Malacañang and was going to sit in the audience, when Cory's aides motioned him to take a chair next to her. He remained grim-faced for more than an hour. When Cory spoke to him, he did not turn to face her, but simply nodded his head and looked at her through the corner of his eye.

Cory told the gathering that her "willingness to go to any length for peace" had been construed by some as a sign of weakness. She said "A higher dignity is found in the good use of the presidency to bring peace to our land than by standing on protocol. It does not bother me to be spoken of as weak by some, but let them not make the mistake of putting me to the test, to the test of my commitment to democracy and to the safety and well-being of my people."

However, Cory backtracked on her promise to disband the CHDF. Ramos had argued that in spite of its excesses, the CHDF was needed by the military to fight the Communists. The government needed to reform the paramilitary forces, not get rid of them. She told the group, "We must yield to the public clamor for more responsible guardians of public order than the Civilian Home Defense Forces." But, she said the CHDF would be allowed to continue until "adequate provision is made for the safety of communities by other means, even if it takes a larger military establishment to do it." And there was still no action against the warlords.

Cory increased the military budget and development aid for NPA strongholds. She repeated that a new presidential vote was unnecessary and would be divisive.

In Manila again there were rumors of a coup. Either Enrile would be arrested by pro-Cory troops or he would "separate," in the word of the RAM officers, withdraw his support from the government and confront government forces. Malacañang security forces were beefed up with troops, armored personnel carriers and fire trucks; palace approaches were sealed off. It was explained publicly as security measures against a peasant demonstration for land reform, but it was a contingency plan for armed attack on the palace.

Military commanders in the Visayas islands and Mindanao issued a statement pledging to support Enrile if he were fired. Ramos visited Cory in the palace to assure her that he was with her.

Hoping to calm the situation, Trade and Industry Minister, Joe Concepcion, arranged to call on Enrile. When Cory learned of his intention, she asked, "Why don't you explain to Johnny I am not going to ask for his resignation, that I want him to be part of the cabinet." He passed on Cory's message that she "wished to keep together the team that had sacrificed so much in the revolution." Enrile told Concepcion his grievances against Cory and some of her officials—the lack of a program to fight the insurgents, the government's failure to consult the military on the policy against the NPA, graft and corruption in the administration and the incompetence of some members of the cabinet. Concepcion suggested a meeting with Cory. Enrile was not enthusiastic; he said he would talk with his people.

Enrile launched another attack the next day in a speech before the University of Santo Tomas reserve army officers at Camp Aguinaldo, saying, "The NDF deceived our people by speaking of peace and national reconciliation, while the NPA continues to roam and strike terror in the countryside. If we don't act now, we will pay a very high price in terms of lives lost and blood spilled to preserve freedom and a democratic way of life. Time is running out." After the speech, General Ramos told reporters, "We are all trying very hard to bring everybody together," hinting that he and others were trying to mediate the conflict. A military spokesman said the general wanted to preserve the triumvirate that had led to the success of the February revolution. "Triumvirate" referred to the commander in chief, the defense minister and the chief of staff—"the chain of command." Ramos deliberately eschewed the word "coalition."

After talking with his former law partner, UP president Edgardo Angara, Enrile agreed to a meeting with Cory, and it was arranged for that night on "neutral ground" at Angara's house in Dasmariñas Village, where Enrile also lived. Cory arrived at 10 p.m. after a dinner for journalists who had covered her American trip. Laurel, Concepcion, Ramos, and Locsin were also present. Cory started by apologizing to Enrile "for whatever I may have said that had hurt you." She expected him to make a reciprocal gesture and say he was sorry too.

"No, no, ma'am, not at all," Enrile replied.

"I know we have differences. If we talk about the things that divide us, this meeting will be really short. Why don't we talk about the things we have in common and take up the differences later," Cory suggested. She said she knew he had been impatient with the slow pace of cease-fire talks. "Well, I have been impatient, too," she said. "I think it's time we took a hard line with them."

He replied that if she didn't mind, he would be "very frank."

"Yes, that's very important," said Cory.

Most of the two-hour meeting was spent discussing the insurgency. Enrile told her the government needed a program to fight the rebels and that if there were a cease-fire, it would be followed by a political strategy by the Communists to seize power, banking on the financially-strapped government's inability to carry out economic reforms. The defense minister pressed her to move against the insurgents with a comprehensive approach.

She told him, "You want a hardline counterinsurgency effort. So do

I. I just have to make the effort, if we can, to avoid bloodshed. I have to try."

"Why don't we set a deadline?" Ramos asked.

She said she realized the insurgency had worsened and that she would accept a December deadline.

They talked about the need for a program for rebel returnees. She agreed it was important.

Ramos raised the question of reactivating the provincial peace and order councils which included local government and military officials. Cory promised to do so. Enrile said that it was necessary to replace incompetent, unpopular OICs with better officials.

Cory replied, "You don't have to raise that. I just came from the provinces, and everybody's complaining about the OIC problem."

Enrile was not being specific about his demands, but Laurel was pressing them. Laurel sought to bring up other changes he said the military wanted. "Ma'am," he said, "the army has many demands." "Since when do you speak for the army?" Ramos inquired. Laurel also took the occasion to try to get jobs for some of his Unido members. Cory told him, "Doy, I think you're more of a problem tonight than Johnny." Enrile laughed along with the others.

Enrile said all his speeches had aimed at strengthening the fight against communism, but promised to stop his marathon of verbal attacks against her.

The meeting broke up after midnight. "Let's talk again," Cory said, and Enrile agreed.

The next morning at 8 a.m., Cory, keeping a commitment to address a national conference of Carmelites, met with a hundred nuns at the Carmelite convent, where she had gone to pray while making up her mind about running for president. She told them there was a burden on her shoulders and that sometimes it felt so heavy she asked God to lighten it. She also talked about her meeting with Enrile, which she called a "breakthrough" and "almost a miracle." The tension of the recent days caused her suddenly to shed tears. The nuns quickly surrounded her and told her that God would take care of her. When she had composed herself, she asked them to pray at 10 a.m. when the cabinet meeting would begin. It would be critical. "It's very peaceful and relaxing here," she said. "I wish the cabinet meeting this morning will be like this."

Also at 8 a.m. General Ramos presided over a command conference in the intelligence service conference room in the two-story, white concrete General Headquarters building at Camp Aguinaldo. He won agreement from the generals and colonels to prevent armed conflict between Enrile's forces and the government. Later the officers issued a statement that it was their role to protect the people, assure the stability and security of the nation, and maintain the civilian government supreme over the military. Any splits in the government would benefit only the insurgents. They urged Cory to set a deadline for peace talks with the NPA. In another statement, General Ramos again cautioned military officers against getting involved in partisan political activity.

The cabinet meeting was uneventful. Cory told the ministers there should be a "cease-talk." One participant thought she "exuded confidence" that things could be worked out between her and Enrile. But she was not taking any chances. Concepcion recalled, "I'm normally seated on the other side, but they made me sit down beside Johnny in place of Nene Pimentel."

Amidst continuing rumors of a coup, Cory arrived at the luncheon of the Sigma Delta Phi alumnae association. It was the one-year anniversary of the day she had announced before the same group that she would consider running for president if Marcos called a snap election and a million people signed petitions urging her candidacy.

She revealed that she had met with Enrile the night before. "You have heard many rumors in the past few weeks, rumors of a coup to be staged by Minister Enrile, rumors of counter-action taken by the government. The height was yesterday, when on the one hand I was told I had ordered the arrest of Enrile and on the other Enrile had started his coup by calling on the service chiefs to declare their loyalties one way or the other."

"Those of us who actually made a revolution, as opposed to those who merely talk a good coup or revolution, have nothing to gain by falling out with each other. We have on the contrary a lot to lose by doing so—mainly the meaning of the sacrifices we respectively made to return democracy to our country and the trust reposed on us by the millions of Fillipinos who made the same sacrifices with us."

The conciliatory tone toward the rebels that marked past speeches seemed to fade. "If we fall out with each other, the only gainers are the enemies of freedom: the Marcos loyalists and the die-hard Communists, who by thus far ignoring our offer of peace and our people's burning desire to see an end to killing and fear, increasingly reveal their real intentions for our people, the real character of their regard for our people's well-being. This is why there is no falling out between Minister Enrile and myself. We are not stupid. We did not sacrifice, and more important than that, we did not ask our people to offer the supreme sacrifice of their lives, just to create an opening for their enemies to take control over their lives and their future in the differences that have arisen between us. From the start of our talk last night, that was clear. We are one in seeking the common good, in realizing the potential of our country to recover and to achieve progress and keep its precious freedoms."

She said, "You may say this comes late in the day, but better late than never. It is understandable that we, who had not known each other before, who had made our own plans to restore democracy, should take some time to understand each other. But now we do. Many differences remain, but the common ground of patriotism is clearly shared by all. Our styles will continue to differ; we are different people struck from different models that were created out of radically different experiences. But we are first Filipinos and committed to democracy."

She acknowledged the common impatience at the slow progress of some of the government's initiatives, at the rebels' refusal to accept the government's peace offers, and at the performance of some OICs who were below expectations. She said she would fire OICs found guilty of gross negligence and graft.

Cory was beginning to feel that the Communist leadership was exploiting the cease-fire negotiations for propaganda victories. She was aware that Washington believed that she was naive about the communist threat and unable to deal with the insurgents. She would give both of them stronger rhetoric. She said she would soon set a deadline for the rebels to accept the offer of peace talks or face "a declaration of war." And the peace and order councils would work "to contain the spread of insurgency and put a stop to the abuses of the rebels and their efforts to exploit the democratic space we have created in order to destroy the democracy our people have restored."

But, in fact, she had talked about a deadline for months. The tone of her speech was tough, but there was no real change in policy. After the speech, she responded to a questioner that, "The three government negotiators have just talked with the Communist panel, and we are still hopeful that soon we will hear some favorable answers to our appeal for peace." One of her aides later explained that Cory favored a "situation deadline," not a "calendar deadline" in peace talks with the rebels. She would break off talks if she was convinced the rebels were not "sincere" about peace because they had stepped up their armed attacks.

Bracing against expected criticism for failing to get tough with Enrile, Arroyo said the meeting with the defense minister should not be considered "weakness or indecisiveness" on Cory's part. "If the president is willing to go out of her way to meet Nur Misuari in Jolo and Father Balweg in the Cordilleras, there is no reason why she should not talk to one who is a member of her official family. That is consistent with her policy of reconciliation, consistent with her policy that everything can be settled by talking."

Ramos stressed his loyalty to the president. In a speech on October 23, he said, "I support the chain of command of constitutional authority. I am chief of staff only of the commander in chief. I am in the middle. We [the military] are for the center."

But the "psy war" continued. At a party at the apartment of *Time* correspondent Nelly Sindayen, Captain Robles sat on a hallway floor chatting with several journalists and told them that something would happen by the end of the year. Cory would not last. "What should she do?" a reporter asked. "She ought to fire Enrile," he said, with an enigmatic grin.

A day later, Cory said she would not give in to Enrile's demand to fire left-wing cabinet members or restore the Marcos constitution. She also said she had nothing to do with demands from some of her cabinet members that Enrile resign. "I fight my own battles. If I want to say something, I will say it myself. I may be a woman," she told an interviewer, "but if I was not afraid of someone like Marcos, who had all the forces of the government behind him, I am not about to retreat if there is any necessity to fight."

Her emissaries to the rebels reported that the accord on immunity and safety guarantees for the NDF negotiators could be signed soon. An NDF lawyer confirmed that both sides had reached "almost total agreement" on the matter.

Four days after his reconciliation meeting with Cory, Enrile spoke to about 6,000 people at an anti-communist rally organized by Marcos loyalists in Rizal Park and criticized the government for its failures to revive the economy, create jobs and stop corruption. He said he was speaking for the armed forces as well as himself.

Indeed, there was increasing talk and newspaper accounts of corruption by some cabinet ministers, particularly the heads of the natural resources and public works ministries, accused of taking bribes for awarding concessions and contracts. One columnist wrote, "The President isn't a cloistered nun to remain ignorant of all these shenanigans."

Meanwhile, people had a frightening sense of déjà vu about the pre-martial law days after a series of bombings hit two Manila fast food shops and the Mondragon building owned by one of Cory's supporters. The widespread assumption was that the blasts were set by the loyalists or elements of the military.

At an anti-communist rally in Manila, Enrile's daughter Katrina wore an "ABC" sticker; it meant "Anyone but Cory." Her father told the largely loyalist crowd of 20,000 that there would be more bombings in Manila—and that the culprits were the NPA. The audience waved placards of pro-Marcos organizations and flashed the Marcos "V" sign. One banner said, "Go, Rambo, go" and another, "Minister Rambo Enrile—no retreat, no surrender." A few had "Johnny Rambo" T-shirts.

Washington announced its strong support for the Aquino government. Press Secretary Teodoro "Teddy" Benigno declared that a coup would not be possible because, he said, Cory had "one big advantage . . . which has to be considered very, very significantly, the complete and unqualified support of the United States." He noted that most senior officers had gone to U.S. military schools. "The military is traditionally very sensitive to signals from Washington," he said. "The military has always been linked intimately with its counterpart in the United States." Both nationalists and military officers chafed at the remark.

Washington, although it had encouraged Enrile's criticism of Cory's handling of the insurgency, did not like his destabilizing challenge to her government and expressed that concern to him and his allies. Cayetano noticed the change in their line. When he had coffee with his Embassy friends, they continued to praise Enrile's anti-communist stand, but objected to his questioning the legitimacy of Cory's government.

Cory was not "deliriously happy" about Enrile's attacks, but she still wanted reconciliation. Her policy was to calm Enrile as much as she could, stay at the center and wait for the plebiscite on the constitution. She told officials of the Manila and Makati stock exchanges she hoped people would no longer talk about instability once the charter was ratified.

Before the public, Cory maintained the same line on the insurgency she had held out since March. She told a nurses' convention that she was bound by her Christian conviction, as they were by professional ethics, to save rather than destroy life. But should the insurgency "prove as incurable as cancer, then it must be removed by the drastic surgery of warfare." She said nothing about the deadline she had mentioned a week earlier.

Enrile repeated his line, too, telling the nurses the next day that the military was a partner in a coalition government with Cory, that the government could not have survived without it. "We preceded almost everybody who is now in government. We were the wielders of power before anybody took her or his oath to become a part of the government, and so no one can tell us they handed us an appointment or a position. . . . "Suppose we did not attach ourselves to that government in that crucial hour, do you think that government could survive?" Enrile asked.

And Laurel continued to raise suspicions about where he stood. He classed as "premature" a report he and Enrile had made a deal to run a Laurel-Enrile ticket in the next presidential election. A few days later, he told a press conference that the Aquino government would remain unstable unless it got a "decisive majority" in the constitutional plebiscite. And he proposed that the approval of his and Cory's terms of office be separated from the vote on the charter. He said that would resolve the "moral issue" including the appointive nature of the constitutional commission, the revolutionary status of the government, and the question of who really won the February elections. He also said, "If my conviction tells me to reject the draft constitution, I will campaign against its ratification."

Cory sought to play down the crisis. "I do not feel threatened by Minister Enrile, because I do not consider him an adversary," Cory told an interviewer. "All of us contributed in the ouster of Mr. Marcos." She ignored Enrile's repeated claims of a coalition government.

Ramos continued to separate himself from Enrile. After a morning jog with soldiers, he told reporters that NPA hit teams were not a serious threat to Manila, though Enrile had said they had infiltrated the city. The NPA had announced that as many as a thousand "armed city partisans" had entered the city to provide protection to NDF representatives during the peace talks. Ramos believed the units would not carry out assaults in the capital while the rebels were trying to achieve a cease-fire. At a forum, he said that Cory's policy for dealing with the insurgents was "very similar, if not identical, to what was worked out during the late forties and early fifties," when the Huk rebellion was crushed by "all-out force and all-out friendship." And he suggested that government discussions of the matter were better held in private.

Cory was pessimistic about the outcome of events. "It's hopeless," she thought. "Enrile and I will never get together."

God Save the Queen

THE RAM OFFICERS' "PSY WAR" was escalating. They were contacting their classmates and friends in command positions, telling them of plans for a "surgical operation" that would remove "left-leaning" officials, but keep Cory in power. They were spreading the word in the military that Cory would welcome a coup to purge her leftist ministers. They hinted that General Ramos was on their side—that "the chief of staff has been informed about this, and we have to make the preparations." However, Ramos was aware of their activities. He would jog with them and talk with them, emphasizing the need to obey the chain of command. The RAM boys had told reporters to expect a "psy war" campaign. Now they were saying that they were importing weapons and training special strike forces and would move before the end of the year. Reporters and others also began to hear about the Corpus Plaza Miranda letter. Enrile's boys were trying to get Corpus to support their coup plan by publicly revealing the letter, but he was unwilling to comply.

"They were rumors that came out of intense disappointments," said a high-ranking military officer involved in the plot. "It was a way of transmitting our thoughts, our feelings. We were hoping the people in the coffee shops [the politicians who met there] could feel how the military feels, being shut out from decision-making processes, from participating in the government." They thought their "psy war" tactics would persuade Cory to give in to Enrile's demands.

Enrile pressed the claim that he and Cory had agreed to a coalition government in February. He also admitted that he had planned to set up a military junta, that the people had supported his military revolt. "The leaders of the opposition were not there; they only appeared on the last day. At that point we had complete control of the republic's military organization, except for a few units. President Marcos was already dealing with us. He was not dealing with the opposition. We could have effectively run the country at that point. In fact, we were exercising governmental powers. Only then did they [the opposition] appear at our camp. We readily and willingly transferred power to them." His statement, of course, was untrue.

He continued, "If I am asked to resign, I'll have to consult the people who asked me to represent them in the government. First, the records must show that Mrs. Aquino did not in fact give me a job. I was holding the position before she took her oath of office. Second, I was holding a position even higher than that of minister of defense. We were in control of the government."

Laurel repeated Enrile's demand for a change in the cabinet.

Cory said Enrile's statements were honest differences of opinion allowed in their new democracy.

November, three months before the vote on the constitution, was a dangerous time. If there were to be a coup, it had to be before the government was legitimized by the plebiscite. At the start of the month, the NDF proposed the government accept a one-hundred-day cease-fire beginning December 10, International Human Rights Day. It eliminated its demand that armed forces troops withdraw from NPA areas and the CHDF be abolished. It asked only that "notorious units" of the CHDF be dissolved and "notorious" regular military units be deactivated, with local police confined to anti-crime functions. It also called for disarming and disbanding of private armies, goons, fanatical sects, and "Marcos die-hards." It said the new proposal had nothing to do with Cory's deadline.

A palace spokesman said the offer showed "the willingness of both sides to achieve peace." At a National Security Council briefing on the peace proposal, Cory said it represented a step forward, but she asked for discussion on the length of the cease-fire. The military representative said he thought one hundred days was too long, but the consensus was to find a period somewhere between the NDF proposal and the thirty days the armed forces leadership supported. Enrile emptied all his cartridges against the cease-fire. He said it was dangerous for the country, that no cease-fire had ever succeeded anywhere in the world, and that the Communists were simply trying to stall. Cory responded there was no way she would backtrack from her moral commitment to halt the violence. In the end, Enrile said he would abide by whatever was agreed upon, and the NSC authorized government negotiators to discuss the cease-fire mechanics with the NDF the next day.

The Commission on Elections set February 2 as the date for the vote on the constitution. After a meeting of Unido party leaders, who indicated support of the charter, Laurel softened his criticism and suggested he might reconsider his "noncommittal" stand.

The Presidential Commission on Human Rights asked Ramos to freeze promotions of members of the military who had committed violations of human rights. He replied that the commission should give him a list of people it knew had committed abuses and it would take action, but that promotion was a matter between the selection board and the commander in chief—the president.

That evening Victor Corpus was called to a meeting with Captain Robles and Navy Lieutenant Alex Pama. Corpus's old classmates had petitioned for his return, and he had been reinstated in the army October 8 and promoted three grades to lieutenant colonel. Military officals said the new rank was in recognition of his experience in working with the insurgents; he would serve as an instructor and researcher on the Communist party and the NPA. Corpus set to work writing an alternative strategy to deal with the guerrilla war for the MND Study Group, headed by Robles.

At their November 3 meeting, Robles and Pama talked about the chaos in the country, the corruption, the communist threat. They asked Corpus to join them in a coup. He would announce publicly what he had already written in his letter, that the Communists, not Marcos, were responsible for the Plaza Miranda bombing.

Corpus refused. They told him in strong terms they would release the letter, anyway. It would back up Enrile's attacks on the government as soft on communism, make people believe that the recent bombings in Manila were also the work of the Communists, and torpedo the peace talks. It would trigger a crisis that would set the stage for the coup. Corpus objected to its release, but the officers told him they had to move and repeated in a veiled threat an invitation to join them. Again, he refused.

The Enrile-RAM coup plan was called "God Save the Queen." It called for seizure by commando strike forces of communications systems, radio and television stations, newspapers, and power and water facilities while Cory was on an announced visit to Japan, November 10–13. Taking control of the media would prevent a repeat of the people power outpouring of the February revolution. Left-leaning cabinet members and activists would be killed.

The 1984 KBL-dominated parliament would reconvene, and Enrile would take charge as the head of a civilian-military junta. Cory would be part of the junta, because the plotters did not want to contest her popularity with the people, but she would have to accede to Enrile's demands. The plan showed an astonishing ignorance of her character and sense of mission; she would no more give in to Enrile than Ninoy had to Marcos.

Tuesday, November 4, at a birthday party attended by generals and other top officers at the Fort Bonifacio home of Marine commander Brigadier General Brigido Paredes, Enrile called on those present to support his plan.

That night there was a movement of troops in the capital to strengthen security at Malacañang and Air Force headquarters at Villamor Air Base. Neighbors sighted helicopters hovering over the palace. There were speculations that the RAM boys would carry out a coup before Cory left for Japan.

Meanwhile, government representatives spoke positively of the NDF peace proposal; they were optimistic they would reach an agreement the next day. But, talks stalled over the terms and mechanics of the cease-fire. They had agreed on the proposal for security and immunity guarantees but not on the definition of hositilities nor the period for the truce. The military was still pushing for a short cease-fire to prevent the NPA from using the time to build up its forces.

The security situation began to heat up. The NPA announced it had deployed some of its units in Manila "to counter any attempt to stage a coup against the Aquino government." Ramos was keeping tabs on the RAM boys' plans through informants inside their group; he knew their decisions almost as soon as they were made. However, he preferred not to move against them directly, but to use the media in his turn. One of his officers called a reporter for *Business Day,* a respected daily newspaper, which duly on Wednesday, November 5, detailed the plan for a "surgical operation" called "God Save the Queen." The report said military leaders were worried about a bloody backlash and foresaw scenarios of Enrile being "forced to step down by certain foreign powers" or of instituting a repressive regime which, in either case, would cause bloodshed and create advantages for the Communists. Cory saw the story, but as far as her aides could tell she had no reaction.

Manila was awash with rumors—broadcast over some radio stations—that Cory had fired Enrile after discovering a coup plot.

Some thought the rumors were part of RAM's "psy war" to pressure the government for change. But officials in Malacañang were getting daily threats that they considered credible, letters and phone calls about who would jail them, who would kill them, where they would be taken. "It's good we had more than a decade of practice at this," said Saguisag, who had been a human rights lawyer during the Marcos years. "We were threatened all the time during the seventies. If you were not used to this, you could easily call it quits."

Cory did not flinch. "She's tough as nails. You don't threaten her; she stiffens," Saguisag said. "It was astonishing, sometimes befuddling about her," remarked another of her aides "Her calm, her serenity, her poise. She can talk as if this thing were not a crisis beginning to overwhelm her." Cory's reaction was that the threats had to be taken into account, but she would not let the rumors dictate the tempo of her life.

However, she began to show concern when Locsin reported to her that many military officers believed she would welcome a coup to rescue her from incompetent or leftist advisors. That was serious. It could neutralize the army and allow Enrile's boys to move against her.

Ramos, in a speech to a religious club called Martha's Vineyard, said Enrile's assessment of the insurgency situation was correct and the government had to take action to implement the strategy recommended by the military. The government's efforts to deal with the guerrillas had been made more difficult by its administrative paralysis; Cory for example, had ordered her ministers to submit plans for dealing with rebel returnees, but there still was no program in operation.

Ramos also emphasized that the armed forces placed the highest premium on unity. "We are working hard so that the chain of command led by President Aquino, Minister Enrile and I remains undisrupted at all levels in the military." He noted that the military commanders had stated they would steer clear of politics.

However, Cory learned what had taken place at the Paredes gathering. Her confidence in Ramos was shaken because he had not told her; she thought it was impossible that he did not know of the discussion.

She called him, and he explained that he had been checking out the facts before he informed her. His practice was first to verify reports, which involved conferring with his commanders, before he notified the president. "We do not like to be panicky," explained a high-ranking military official.

Ramos would play an even more important role in the following days. He was an enigma to many people. He had gone along with Marcos when his colleague, Rafael Ileto, now deputy defense minister, had refused to endorse martial law and had been put out to pasture in the diplomatic service. Some said it was because Ramos was a professional and did not see his role as mixing in politics. Others said he would serve any master. He had not joined or encouraged the original RAM coup plot against Marcos or even the young officers' criticism of the dictator, and he joined the revolution only after it appeared he would be arrested by the Marcos regime.

On November 6, several newspapers headlined the report of the Corpus letter which had been leaked the day before to local and foreign journalists. That same day, Ramos issued a statement citing the *Business Day* story and warning "military adventurists against embarking on such a rash course of action because it could be bloody and destabilizing." He ordered the army, constabulary, air force, and navy commanders to "take immediate actions to neutralize any such plots, if any, and to reorient any personnel involved" towards loyalty to the military chain of command headed by the president. He also activated a contingency plan against armed operations in Manila.

Early in the morning, Ramos visited his service commanders to find out where their loyalties lay and to try to forestall the coup. They promised to abide by his orders and the chain of command.

Ramos confronted Enrile and argued against his plan. He told him that it could lead to fighting within the military. Finally, Enrile yielded; Ramos got assurances that nothing would happen.

He also met with the RAM plotters, afraid they would act independently, and told them that if they went ahead, he feared for the country. He argued that it was crucial to keep the armed forces united. If it were divided, the country would be polarized, and the Communists could take advantage of the crisis. He told them that the military had to operate with the support of the people, and it had therefore to preserve the Aquino government, which was popular at home and recognized abroad.

"All right, it's called off," they told him. "It's really nothing; we're just preparing to protect the life of the minister." But the RAM boys continued contacting field officers to solicit support.

"There are just too many cleavages, and there's just too much factionalism even at the lower levels," Ramos commented.

In the midst of all the tension, Ramos saw Ray Cline, former deputy chief of the CIA and now executive director of the Georgetown Center for Strategic and International Studies, and retired General Robert Sweitzer; both were connected with the conservative American Security Council. They also met with Enrile.

The Cline-Sweitzer visit may have been connected to the appearance of another American whose presence raised suspicions in the local press, retired General John Singlaub, president of the World Anti-Communist League, who helped the Reagan administration supply "private" aid to the anti-Sandinista rebels, the "contras," and was the member of the board of an American arms firm that had smuggled weapons to Iran. Singlaub also talked with Enrile, and there are two accounts of what occurred.

The first, Enrile's version, is that Singlaub visited to ask for military protection for an expedition to search for the Yamashita treasure—a fortune of gold, platinum, and silver sequestered by World War II Japanese General Tomoyuki Yamashita from Burma, Thailand, Singapore, and Malaysia and hidden in scattered sites in the Philippines, one of them a receptacle at the bottom of a bay. The general could not return for the booty after the war: he had been hanged by U.S. military commander, General Douglas MacArthur. Singlaub said the treasure was worth $8 billion. Sweitzer had also talked to Enrile about it. Enrile was not sure if they were working together. He said he thought the plan absurd.

But Singlaub's mission may have involved less fantasy. He reportedly told Enrile, "You're our man to fight the Communists." Singlaub got the required government permits for his treasure-hunting company, Nippon Star, and cabinet members laughed about his foolishness. But could it have been an elaborate cover?

Cory stepped up her defenses. The National Capital Region Defense Command (NCRDC) was deployed to secure television stations and other strategic public utilities, and she ordered the head of the Presidential Security Guard to "repel all predatory forces approaching Malacañang under any pretext."

But she resisted confronting the coup plotters. "Enrile wants my job; there's nothing I can do to satisfy him. Why should I see him?" Her aides argued that she was the commander in chief and pressed her to fire him lest he become too much of a danger. She felt it was not the time to move, but they persuaded her to talk with the plotters, and the meeting was set for Friday morning. Cory seemed lighthearted to her aides and members of the cabinet.

Military intelligence told the palace they had found a hit list with names of people in government, business, media, the president's family, labor and cause-oriented groups. At the top was the name of KMU and Partido ng Bayan leader, Rolando Olalia.

Cory called Cardinal Sin and Joe Concepcion to join her in a meeting with top military officials at Malacañang later that day.

The military officals advised her not to go to Japan.

"No, I am committed to go," she replied. "If something happens, that is the will of God."

Cardinal Sin thought how tranquil she was. To Concepcion she seemed worried, but not frightened.

The military discussed the precautions they were taking against the "God Save the Queen" plot. Cory asked Cardinal Sin to postpone his trip to Rome scheduled for the next day, and she asked Sin and Concepcion to see what they could do to help the situation. Cory had reservations about using people power; she was concerned that people might be slaughtered.

Adding to her uncertainty about Ramos was intelligence from a group of retired generals saying that Ramos would stay with Enrile to preserve military supremacy. Cory talked with Ramos the evening of November 6. They discussed the coup plot. He told her he had been talking to the commanders.

That same night, Corpus met with General Luis Villareal, head of the National Intelligence Coordinating Agency, and told him what he knew of the RAM boys' plans. Villareal ordered him to prepare a statement to deliver at a press conference the next morning appealing to his fellow officers not to support the coup.

The RAM boys issued a press release calling the talk of a plot "foolish communist propaganda aimed at destabilizing the triumvirate of Aquino, Ramos, and Defense Minister Juan Ponce Enrile."

That day, a grenade exploded inside a movie theater and injured some twenty people.

With his general penchant for finding the wrong moment to make the wrong comments, Laurel gave a speech urging a military solution to the insurgency problem. "I have strongly recommended a clearcut, swift and decisive policy on the insurgency movement," he said. And he gave Cory a list of OICs he wanted removed, including six provincial governors and ninety-four mayors, whom he charged with graft and corruption, incompetence, and having previous criminal records.

The next day, Cory spent the morning meeting individually with the chiefs of the different military commands. She put to them what had happened Tuesday night. They did not deny the facts. She told them a coup was not the answer, that a clash would only benefit the Communists. She asked them to come to her with their problems. She asked for their pledges of support against any attempted coup, but she told her aides later that she did not find the meetings productive. Cory also held meetings with all key provincial commanders and told them she was counting on them. She would not cancel her trip to Japan.

The same morning, Corpus met with General Renato de Villa, commander of the Philippine Constabulary at Camp Crane. De Villa told him the plot had been defused and to hold his statement. Corpus left the document, in the form of an open letter to Robles, with De Villa and proceeded to his press conference in a nearby conference room. He told the press that he had been present when the plot to bomb the Liberal party meeting at Plaza Miranda was being planned by Joma Sison, Commander Dante, and other Communist Central Committee members. (Sison and Dante later denied the charges.) He said he had planned to reveal the details of the bombing after the resolution of the Ninoy Aquino-Rolando Galman murder case. He said he though that if the truth about the bombing were known earlier, people might believe Marcos was also telling the truth when he said the Communists killed Ninoy. He said he had given copies of the Plaza Miranda letter to friends in the military but that Enrile had not leaked it. Armed Forces Vice Chief of Staff Mison later said the military would not arrest Sison and Dante, but the case would be reopened for investigation. Many people thought the letter was a RAM disinformation plot aimed at destabilizing the government. When Cory was asked at a press conference why Corpus had been recommissioned and promoted, she denied the reinstatement papers had come across her desk.

Corpus's open letter to Robles, pulled back from publication at the last minute, would nevertheless be circulated among the military especially to young officers and members of RAM who might be vulnerable to recruitment by the plotters.

The letter, reproduced exactly, said:

Nov 7
To Capt. Rex Robles
Dear Rex,

That Monday night of Nov 3 when we met in your office was perhaps the most frightful night of my life. You may not have noticed, but it was the very first time in my life that I really trembled with fear. This was when you started relating to me the scenario of a coup: of PMAers killing PMAers, of classmates killing classmates, of any attempt at peoples' power being bombarded or sprayed with bullets, of death squads which you will personally supervise doing "surgical operations", etc. etc.

When you asked me to join your coup attempt (my part being to expose the Plaza Miranda Bombing incident much earlier than previously planned to trigger a crisis and start the ball rolling for the coup), I was shocked to say the least. Aside from assuring me of a made future if I join, you dangled the idea that Min. Enrile follows up his people man-to-man and that he has quite a long memory. I realized at the moment how dangerous your group has become.

Since that horrifying night to this very moment, I haven't had the luxury of sleep, believe me.

I know you may not be able to forgive me for what I am going to say now, and that I may rank no. 1 in your death list if your coup succeeds; nevertheless I now take this opportunity to tell you: NO! NO! NO!

You may succeed in seizing power, but the question you should ponder is: can you hold on to it? Even if you use all the repressive measures in the book, without popular support and with only your handful of Marcos loyalists to depend on, you will fail. By such a putsch, you will only drive the idle force in our society to the waiting arms of the left. Surely you will not receive the blessings of Cardinal

Sin and all his bishops. What you will get instead is the ire of the multitude of faithfuls.

What will you do if the people, except for your handful of Marcos diehards, suddenly stop all work leaving shops, factories and streets empty? Or if three million people march in the street daily, or picket the palace where your boss hopes to sit one day? Are you going to bombard and spray them with gunfire as you said you would? You will surely have another rebellion or revolution in your hands and this time it will most probably be the left who will be at the forefront. It will be the communists who will ultimately benefit from all these (sic) foolishness of yours.

So I appeal to you, sir: Stop that Goddamn plan of yours. It will only lead to death of our new-found democracy. It will lead to national suicide. It will lead the NAFP to self-destruction.

Though you were my former upper class in the academy, I take this liberty to tell you: Wake up, Goddammit!!

Respectfully yours, Victor Corpus

P.S. If in the next days or so, you finally achieve your aim of toppling the Cory gov't, I hope you will only give me 30 push-ups for writing you this letter. But if I may add, I am no longer trembling in fear with the thought and I may be facing your future "death squad" or firing squad—or whatever.

By the way, Sir. Do you know that I was called to active duty only the other day? And now—this! What a way to celebrate my return to the NAFP! A BIG BANG WELCOME—indeed!!!

Corpus added the following to his typed note in script:

One ominous and disturbing statement of your keeps ringing in my mind to the effect that you have reserved a special pistol for Minister Enrile alone in the event that he does not go along with you.

Robles refused to discuss the letter.

After his press conference, Corpus went into hiding, spending some time living in the quarters of the Presidential Security Guard in Malacañang Park.

Cardinal Sin called Enrile that day to persuade him not to go through with his attempts to seize power. He told him, "If you are a member of the cabinet, you are not supposed to be talking outside. All the ministers are supposed to be coordinating and you are talking in different wavelengths."

Enrile answered, " . . . communism."

Sin told him, "It has been there for seventeen years, you have not solved the problem; the Communists are increasing." He added, "Johnny, you may be right, but history will condemn you if there is bloodshed."

In the afternoon, Cory held a press conference. Journalists had protested a note on the press office bulletin board that only questions about Japan would be permitted; she calmed them by saying that, of course, she would entertain other topics. She sat behind a carved wooden table on a platform at the front of the press conference room in Kalayaan ("Freedom") Hall on the palace grounds.

Would she comment on Butz's remark that the army was on red alert and feared a coup?

"Every time I plan a trip abroad, there is so much talk about a coup," she declared. "Each time I say if I believed there would be a coup, I would not be leaving the country. The best proof of this is I am ready to go. Also, I think in staging a coup, one does not announce it. There's just so much talk about it. I am confident there will not be a coup."

Did she know whether the coup talk was related to the cease-fire negotiations?

She repeated, "My knowledge of coups is that one does not advertise this, especially the way it has been talked about so openly in the newspapers and even in the magazines from abroad. I am just not familiar with an announced coup."

Pressed, Cory acknowledged that she had met with Ramos the day before to talk about the "God Save the Queen" plot rumors. "I made it very clear to him, and he agreed with me, that definitely we should not allow anything like this to happen, because we will all be the losers if we fight each other. He assured me he had been talking to the commanders and other people to make sure the military observes the professionalism required in their career."

Did she forsee any scenario in which she would ask for Enrile's resignation?

Her brief answer suggested another question: "Right now, no."

She also promised to look into the Corpus letter on the Plaza Miranda bombing, though she noted that Salonga, one of the worst injured of the victims—he had been blinded in an eye, made deaf in one ear and had dozens of shrapnel fragments inside his body— believed Marcos was responsible for the crime. Later, she expressed skepticism about the letter to her aides, and many of them continued to believe that Marcos was behind the attack.

Mitra, who was also injured in the bombing, said that Corpus had told him his story. "I immediately reported it to General Ramos. I didn't think it was necessary for me to inform the president."

Cory said there was no longer a need to specify a deadline for peace talks with the NDF. "The fact that they are responding negates the very idea of a deadline," she said.

Ramos arranged a meeting between Cory and Enrile Friday evening.

"I've heard about these rumors of a coup," she told Enrile.

"So have I," he responded.

"Just assure me that nothing happens while I'm in Japan," she said.

"I'll see what I can do, because I may not be able to control the boys," he replied. "Ma'am, I don't think they have anything against you, but there are some hotheads in the military, and I'm trying to contain them."

She said, "Johnny, you have a lot of moral persuasion on these people. I think you can do it."

"I'll do my best, ma'am."

They also discussed the removal of some OICs sought by Enrile and Laurel.

"When I come back we can take that up in more detail," she told him.

This talk, like others with Enrile, was cordial, but she was convinced it had been futile.

Malacañang palace, now a museum, was closed until Cory's return from Japan. "For repairs," the government said.

If that day needed an anti-climax, it was again Laurel, who announced in a speech that he would support the constitution after all. However, he said voters should be asked separately whether they wanted new presidential elections. And as a fallback, they should be asked whether they wanted the 1935 or 1973 constitutions in the event the new one failed to be approved.

On Saturday, the various actors in the drama held meetings and decided their next moves.

Ramos, pressing his efforts to assure loyalty to the president, met for four hours with some forty senior commanders and members of RAM at Camp Aguinaldo. The military was divided, with many discontent over Cory's response to the Communists. But they agreed to respect the chain of command. Ramos promised to present a list of their recommendations to the president upon her return from Japan.

223

Enrile conferred with the RAM members.

Sin and Concepcion met and discussed the use of people power and other options. Members of the pro-Aquino parties and political groups were also on "red alert." Bandila leader Noel Soriano set in motion a telephone chain to mobilize his people to be ready, unarmed, to surround the television and radio stations if that were necessary. Others were prepared to fight in the streets.

On Sunday, the Manila International Airport customs collector expressed alarm about the importation of arms by defense ministry officials. "How can we demonstrate the government's sincerity in wanting peace when the MND officials are gearing up for battle?" he asked. "Unless these arms are for other purposes, I fear they may not bide well for those of us who aspire for political stability in this country." He added that the MND's custom liaison authorized to pick up the arms shipment was being investigated for trying to smuggle electronic components and wristwatches into the country.

Ramos and General Mison went to see Cory to assure her that nothing would happen in her absence. Ramos also met again with the RAM boys, sure of his own support, but afraid of a precipitate action by this small group that, though it would be defeated, could divide the armed forces.

When Cory learned that the cardinal, thinking things had cooled down, had decided to proceed to Rome, she phoned him and asked him to stay. He agreed.

Finally, she went public with her knowledge of the coup rumors and her determination to oppose any effort to dislodge her government. It was an unlikely occasion, a nationally televised speech to an international dental conference at the Philippine Convention Center.

"I will not allow the New Armed Forces of the Philippines to be destroyed by a handful of misguided elements," she said. "On the eve of my departure, the country is awash with rumors of an impending coup or an emergency contrived to justify an uncalled-for action by some military units on the pretext of effecting changes in my government."

"These rumors, fueled by a few self-appointed messiahs who would want to dictate how this government should be run, is an insult to the integrity of the majority of the New Armed Forces of the Philippines that have tried to adhere to the highest standards of professionalism," she said.

"They betray, on the part of the perpetrators, a shameless disregard for the welfare of our people in the pursuit of personal ambition or misguided ideas of the common good." She said a coup would benefit the insurgents. "The soldier should bear this in mind always."

"I shall oppose any attempt from any quarter to interfere with or dictate to my government, whether blatantly or, as the rumored plan "God Save the Queen" would have it, to protect the presidency—but from whom? Well, this queen doesn't want to be saved."

"Much as I am said to dislike unsolicited advice, I reject unsolicited coups or for that matter, any actions that violate the law or intefere with the regular process of government. This includes any actions taken by the forces of the other extreme, the Left."

"To our people, I say be calm, but also be vigilant. What we have won, no one can take away from us unless we let them. If it should be necessary, however, I shall once more ask you to take to the streets."

Cory met Sunday night with eight cabinet ministers. They reviewed the situation in the light of rumors of yet another coup plot. She reported on her meetings with the generals and with Enrile and told them that Enrile was not likely to stop destabilizing her government until he took over. They were concerned that if she left the country, Enrile would move in. She said preparations had been made to secure Malacañang. She would go ahead with her trip, but would do what needed to be done to stabilize her government on her return.

Coup Redux

DESPITE THE REASSURANCES, the coup plan had not been abandoned. Late Sunday, the Marcos loyalist forces and the military rebels were given the signal to move beginning Tuesday morning at 2 a.m. Arms would be distributed to 700 soldiers, and the colonels would enter Malacañang from surrounding safehouses. At the same time there would be raids on Communist underground sites. Left-leaning cabinet members would be detained. A civilian-military junta would be formed with Cory as its head.

Ramos responded by reactivating the National Capital Region Defense Command, which was put directly under the Armed Forces Headquarters command, and took full control of all military and police forces in Manila. It was set up ostensibly to deal with Enrile's charge that the insurgents had infiltrated Manila, but was really a counter-coup force. RAM leader Colonel Red Kapunan's MND anti-terrorist battalion was put under the NCRDC instead of the defense ministry, so that Enrile's boys were integrated into the force.

In the face of these new developments, Cory remained determined to go to Japan, rejecting again her advisors' urgings that she stay home. "If I don't go," she said, "we will have lost the 'psy war'.

They would have made a laughing stock of the presidency." Cory said publicly that the coup rumors had hurt the country's attempt to attract new investment, and she would try to dispel that effect in Japan. The Japanese government was also apprehensive that during her presence in Tokyo there might be a coup. "They didn't want to go all out on the visit for fear that she would be toppled," said a palace official.

Shortly before she was to leave for Japan, the palace received a report that she would be assassinated at the Manila airport. A sharpshooter in a helicopter would fire at her during the departure ceremonies. She laughed off the story.

Enrile and his allies pressed ahead on their insistance that Cory's was a coalition government. At the Monday morning press round-table at the Manila Hotel, Mindanao political leader Homobono Adaza declared that at a meeting with Enrile he had attended as an opposition leader during the second day of the revolution, an agreement had been reached for a provisional coalition government, with the military, led by Enrile and Ramos, having exclusive control over the armed forces, and Cory and Laurel taking civilian authority. Adaza had moved close to the Enrile camp out of anger at having been frozen out of top government posts; he'd been rewarded for his campaign efforts only by membership on several corporate boards that were lucrative but powerless.

Luis Villafuerte, the other Cory representative at the meeting, denied utterly Adaza's claim.

But Adaza seemed to have the last word: "Evidence of the coalition government is that President Aquino cannot remove Minister Enrile. The revolutionary government depends on the support of the military."

Enrile and Ramos saw Cory off at the airport at 10 a.m. Before she boarded the plane, she said that "any coup or other military action by misguided elements must contend with my opposition, which means the power of the people, in order to succeed."

When he returned to his headquarters at Camp Aguinaldo, Ramos received reports that Enrile's officers were moving to take unauthorized actions against leftists that night. He would spend the rest of the day and part of the night moving from camp to camp, talking with the men, trying to keep things under control.

When Ramos attempted to contact Enrile by phone, he got no response, and he rushed to the Ministry of National Defense across the parade ground with his service commanders and vice chief of staff. They found Enrile and tried to talk things over with him. Ramos gave him the Corpus "Dear Rex" letter. There are two versions of what ensued. One is that Ramos pointed to the section that said that one of the plotters had been assigned to kill Enrile if he did not follow the script. "These are the people you think are your boys," he said. Enrile was dazed when he saw it. His head slumped to the table. Ramos reportedly said he had never seen him so stunned. Enrile himself later said only that the section had been misinterpreted, that early on, in a solemn pact, each had promised to shoot any of the others who failed to keep his commitment to the shared cause.

Ramos and Enrile talked from 11 a.m. to 3:30 p.m. Ramos emphasized again that he would present Cory with a list of the military's grievances and recommendations, including the dismissal of some ministers, a more central role for the military in planning the anti-insurgency campaign, a shorter cease-fire period, a concrete demonstration of strength against the insurgents, and a human rights committee to investigate NPA abuses. But Ramos was not taking any chances. He banned all movements of troops, armor, and aircraft in Manila without his prior clearance. Commanders in the city's military camps were ordered to keep watch over suspicious troop movements. Even so, KMU chief Olalia accused Ramos of "coddling" the military and said subversion charges should be filed against the plotters.

Her first day in Tokyo put Cory in high spirits. Prime Minister Yasuhiro Nakasone told her that his government would give her $447 million in new loans on top of a previous commitment of $471 million in development assistance and grants. Japan had confirmed its role as the Philippines' largest donor, greater than the United States, providing 40 percent of the country's foreign aid.

An embarrassing diplomatic incident occurred later when Emperor Hirohito asked Cory in a private meeting whether her family had suffered during the war. Naturally candid, she said, yes, her uncle, his wife, and their two children had been killed by the Japanese.

The emperor was shaken. He apologized and bowed and apologized and bowed.

"Don't think about it; it's all right," she told him.

"Oh, no, I must make amends," he insisted, continuing to express contrition.

Afterwards, she told her press spokesman, Teddy Benigno, about the scene, and he told the press. The Japanese were in an uproar: the emperor was never supposed to apologize, nor a visiting dignitary reveal what they talked about. Cory herself was highly embarrassed.

In the Philippines, government and NDF negotiators met again that day, pledging not to adjourn until an agreement was approved. A government negotiator said they had agreed the cease-fire would be from thirty to one hundred days. The main issue was safeguards. They also had not agreed on what would be considered hostile acts. The government wanted to include rebel patrols, "tax" collections, and propagandizing, and told the NDF panel it was finding it difficult to convince the military to go along even with what Cory was willing to accept.

Following a series of NPA attacks, Ramos ordered troops in two regions to "track down, apprehend, and neutralize the communist . . . New People's Army terrorists without let-up."

Meanwhile, Laurel kept busy with public statements. A coalition government existed by "implied, informal, unwritten" agreement, he said and noted there was no documentary evidence the Aquino-Laurel ticket had won the February elections. In the midst of the uncertainty, he sought to beef up his own security and seemed embarrassed when his efforts were discovered. He said he had "no knowledge" of a shipment of guns and ammunition which had arrived at the airport consigned to him, but later his office said that Laurel had bought the arms after the defense ministry refused to provide them.

Several violent incidents occurred in the next few days. Police shot a man holding identification from the military's Offic : of Joint Staff Intelligence who attempted to blow up a downtown building. They said they shot him when he was about to pull the pin of a grenade; a Marcos calendar was in his bag. That evening, Olalia disappeared. His mutilated body, with signs of torture, was found the next day in a grassy lot where it had been dumped. His hands had been tied with a handkerchief and a belt, and newspaper had been stuffed in his mouth. His eyes were shot out. His driver was also found dead. Olalia had told an Australian diplomat at lunch earlier that day that he feared he was being followed and would be killed. Palace officials believed the murder was a part of the strategy of a coup.

In Tokyo, at a press conference before her departure, Cory commented about Enrile, "He is not an enemy of mine although he issued the arrest orders for my husband. At the moment, I have no intention of replacing him."

When she arrived in Manila Thursday, a welcoming party came

aboard the plane. Cory looked at Joker Arroyo, smiled, and said, "Joker, am I still . . . ?" Everybody roared. Less amusing was a report Cory heard of a plot to shoot her as she got off the plane.

Cory was horrified and enraged by the murder of Olalia. She ordered a multi-agency investigation and offered a $10,000 reward for information leading to the arrest and conviction of his killers. She visited the body at the University of the Philippines chapel the morning after her arrival home. At a televised press conference, she had a demeanor of great solemnity and sadness. "Every resource and power of my government will be brought to bear," she said slowly in a heavy voice that cracked with emotion. "I want to see justice done."

The NDF negotiators called off a scheduled meeting with the government panel. They said the murder of Olalia had put them in danger. They would not resume talks until his killers had been caught and justice had been done.

On Saturday, Cory received the memo by Ramos and his generals that set down their recommendations on how to counter the insurgency. It called for firing some cabinet ministers, reactivating the national security council, weeding out corruption in government, and replacing some OICs. Enrile endorsed the proposals in a separate letter.

That same day, the federal prosecutor filed murder charges against twenty-five soldiers and one civilian for the killings of Ninoy Aquino and Rolando Galman. Former General Fabian Ver and former Major General Prospero Olivas were charged as accessories.

The KMU announced it would hold a general strike the following Monday. It said the assassination of Olalia was a "logical result of the president's indecisiveness and compromising attitude in dealing with the Marcos holdovers, a fact that had emboldened Enrile and his cohorts to plot and freely engage in bloody intrigues." It called for his ouster.

Cory called on the union and other leftist organizations for "sobriety." She would not move against Enrile yet; she was trying to be doubly sure that when she did, she was in full command. Cory still was uncertain how the factions within the military stood in relation to her government. "Why don't you fire Enrile," a friend asked. "What if I fire him and he doesn't want to vacate his office? Who's going to enforce it?" she replied.

On Saturday, Noboyuki Wakaoji, the Manila general manager of Mitsui & Co., Japan's largest trading company, was kidnapped on his way home from a round of golf. He had accompanied Cory on her visit and returned to Manila the day before his abduction. The kidnapping prompted banner headlines in Japan.

On Sunday, Cory spoke on the peace process at a United Nations "First Earth Run" peace rally at the Luneta. She said, "There is a possibility that our initiative may fail, but first we have to remove all doubts." If the talks did not succeed, she was ready "to lead the war against the enemies of peace." At an emergency cabinet meeting, Cory said the Olalia murder and Wakaoji kidnapping were "directed at me, destabilizing or negating what I've done."

On her TV program, Cory promised she would take forceful action against "people who just want to destabilize government," but she also rejected reports that a military faction was about to stage a coup against her. She parried charges that she was indecisive with the comment: "One must fight when one can win. I am convinced there is a time to fight. I want to be sure I have the necessary forces and support all the way." She said, "I am a kindhearted person, but I am not afraid; I am, like Ninoy, a fatalist." She would wait for evidence before firing any cabinet members accused of wrongdoing.

Wasn't there enough evidence already? Hadn't there been coup attempts in October and early this month? "We don't know if there were," said Saguisag. "They were trying to raise the 'psy war' to a high level. Enrile was doing everything to be martyrized." If he was fired only because he was critical of the insurgency, there would be a high political cost. Without any evidence against Enrile, "people would say he was fired because he was an anti-communist," Saguisag said. There could be, he said, "an uprising." Her cabinet members were biting their fingernails, thinking Enrile was getting the better of her, and she was telling them the situation was not really so bad.

Cory thought the achievement of a cease-fire would add to stability, and pressed her representatives to reach an agreement before the end of the month.

Then, two more terrorist explosions went off. A fragmentation grenade hurled into the balcony of a movie theater caused twenty people to be hospitalized, and a time bomb in a department store two blocks away injured thirty-five people twenty-five minutes later. They brought to eight the bombing incidents in the last few weeks. Military intelligence reports pointed to the loyalists, but investigators lacked hard evidence to make arrests.

On November 19, half a million people marched fifteen miles

through the streets for Olalia's funeral. There were many red flags as well as some NDF banners and placards that said, "Enrile resign." Cory's advisor, Father Bernas, celebrated the funeral mass. Several Western embassies sent representatives, excluding the United States, which earlier in the year had refused Olalia a visitor's visa. He had been granted a three-month traveling fellowship by the Eisenhower Foundation, but then had been uninvited. The U.S. Embassy in Manila said the Foundation could not find people willing to talk with him.

Military intelligence discovered a new coup plan through men planted among Enrile's RAM boys. Their ranks were heavily infiltrated, and their secret radio frequencies were being monitored. Most of the RAM leaders had come from the PMA class of 1971, but some had decided that loyalty to their classmates was less compelling than their commitment to an armed forces respectful of constitutional rule. Acknowledging the source of Malacañang's information, Benigno said RAM "has sort of become very loose and many parts of it have cracked up already." The coup plotters would fall through the cracks.

According to military intelligence, the plan was for the loyalist group, protected by certain military elements, to convene the Batasan on Sunday, November 23, declare a failure of the presidential election, and name former speaker Nicanor Yñiguez acting president. Then new elections would be called. RAM officers and their supporters would move 2 a.m. Sunday to seize radio and TV stations, newspaper offices, public utilities, and the palace. They would escort the former MPs to the Batasan, then wait for other forces to arrive and declare their support.

Colonel Gringo Honasan, chief of the MDN Security Group, who had used his alliance with the defense minister to place his classmates in sensitive positions around the capital and in nearby provinces, controlled troops within striking distance of Malacañang. The plotters assumed that, as in the February revolution, Ramos, faced with the revolt, would be forced to join them.

The next day, Friday, Ramos and Cory talked on the phone and then met for an hour and a half at her office. Ramos told Cory of the plot. They also discussed the insurgency, and he pressed the senior generals' demands. Afterwards, some of Cory's ministers and advisors were telephoned, informed that there were reports of unauthorized troop movements, and warned to stand by.

Benigno told reporters, "A small fragment of the military is not just talking, but threatening as a matter of fact to take power by launching a coup." He said, "There is a suspicion that some right-wing elements in the military, a combination of the right-wing in the military and Marcos loyalists are involved." He said Cory could check these groups only "as far as the police and military will help her. If she says I am in control of the armed forces and the police, she would be telling a lie." He said Cory was preparing "to strike and strike effectively" against forces out to destabilize her government, but "she does not have the kind of political and military footing she needs" to strike now.

Cory's supporters, most of them unarmed, were waiting for the word to go out into the streets to defend the government TV and radio stations and the palace. She did not give the signal.

Her strategy was still to press forward with the campaign for ratification of the constitution. This would give the government stability—if it could last that long. The RAM boys would have to move off the political stage. But she was concerned that they would move to disrupt preparations for the plebiscite.

The confluence of events was pushing Enrile and the RAM boys to act. The signing of the cease-fire seemed imminent. So was the probable sacking of Enrile. The show of force of the Left at Olalia's funeral—the red banners and NDF flags—was the first attempt by the Communists to claim legal public space. It could presage increased above-ground organizing efforts.

Friday evening, commanders loyal to Ramos tried to convince the men in the coup not to go through with it.

Saturday, November 22, was the day toward which everything of the past few months had been building.

In the morning, some 500 RAM supporters and 1,000 civilians began a demonstration at Camp Sergio Osmeña in Cebu City, the main military installation in the Central Visayas region and headquarters of the regional command; it lasted all day. The rally was led by Lieutenant Colonel Tiburcio Fusillero, provincial commander of Negros Oriental province until he was placed under technical arrest for punching a human rights official. The regional commander told reporters the rally was "not an attack against the government. It is just an attack against communism."

The troops called for the ouster of incompetent and left-leaning cabinet ministers, replacement of corrupt OICs, reconvening the parliament, holding new presidential elections, military participation in peace talks with the insurgents, and tougher action against the rebels—the same demands Enrile had been making for months.

Some 2,500 soldiers and 1,000 civilians at Camp Rafael Rodriguez in Butuan City in Mindanao also began a demonstration. The rallies in the southern islands were planned to incite rebellions in key cities and be the signal for the coup.

Later, Ramos phoned Enrile, told him he knew of a coup plan underway and asked him to stop it. Enrile denied anything was afoot, but when Ramos insisted, he promised to act.

Troops were put on red alert at noon, and Ramos began to contact his commanders. Forces sent to guard the Batasan took up positions inside the building and at strategic junctions of access roads. Soldiers also guarded public utilities and radio and television stations. TV stations, which normally closed at midnight, were asked to keep broadcasting into Sunday morning in case the government wanted to make an announcement.

Forces inside the three military camps in Manila were in full battle gear, waiting for further instructions. Heavily armed troops stood guard at the entrance of Camp Aguinaldo. Off-duty soldiers were ordered to remain inside the gates.

Military intelligence monitored the arrival of about 100 troops from camps in southern Luzon. They also knew of preparations in a scout ranger camp, but there was no movement. Other rebel troops would be frozen in place. Service commanders were ordered to secure and monitor their units. Provincial commanders were directed to be alert for groups of armed men heading for Manila. In the capital, checkpoints were put up to bar entry of pro-Enrile troops. Tank and commando units guarded the approaches to the palace.

In the city that day, rumors of an impending coup spread. Seeking without much success to promote a feeling of normalcy, Ramos kept a date to lecture on the NPA at the Central United Methodist Church. He spoke to Cory in the afternoon, then tried to contact Enrile, but he would be unable to reach him all evening and into the night. Ramos met for several hours with the major commanders and the joint chiefs at Camp Aguinaldo.

At about seven, Cory called key staff and ministers to tell those who had not been alerted about the coup threat and to ask them to be ready for a Sunday morning cabinet meeting. Tensions rose further when Ulbert Ulama Tugung, a Muslim supporter of Cory's who had been named chairman of the West Mindanao autonomous region, was gunned down as he stepped out of his hotel in Manila.

Enrile that evening relaxed at a dinner party hosted by economic development chief Winnie Monsod, his neighbor in Dasmariñas Village. Another guest at the dinner was Cory's sister-in-law, Lupita.

In Wack Wack, further north in the city, some seventy ex-Nacionalista and KBL MPs arrived at the home of Antonio Carag, former member of parliament from Enrile's home province, Cagayan. RAM members of the class of 1971 were also there, along with some former soldiers loyal to Marcos who had gone AWOL or been dismissed from the service after the February revolution. Cayetano would say later that it was the Nacionalista party's regular monthly social. Enrile left the Monsod dinner party and arrived at Carag's at about eleven.

The Nacionalista and Marcos loyalists had for months been talking openly about their plan to reconvene the Batasan, name former Speaker Nicanor Yñiguez acting president and call for new elections. Cayetano later denied reports they planned to take over the Batasan that night. "That's stupid," he declared. "There is only one entrance and exit to the subdivision of Carag's place. That's the worst place to start. They could put a squad of soldiers in front of that gate, and we are holed up."

Six truckloads of armed men from Honasan's MND Security Group, some in civilian clothing, entered Camp Aguinaldo that night. They were not stopped, because Ramos did not want to precipitate a clash. Two trucks of armed men went to where the Marcos loyalists were meeting. Other armed men in private cars were also monitored by military officers. Two members of the MND Security Group in civilian clothes and riding motorcycles were stopped by police while doing surveillance of the Batasan.

There were only about one hundred RAM officers leading the plot, the Security Group itself had about seven hundred men, but they expected to get massive support from the field. They thought they had the backing of most of the services, or that they would at least be neutral. They had become victims of their own propaganda.

Ramos sent for Honasan and Robles so he could try again to dissuade them, but they would not come: word came back they were "unavailable." Instead, Captain Felix Turingan and Major Noe Wong, Honasan's deputy, arrived to see Ramos at 10 p.m., and he and other senior officers tried to cool them off.

"Why are you in such a hurry to do something? Do you not care about the blood that will be spilled because of your plans?" They in turn invited Ramos to join them. He refused.

Turingan responded, "We will go it alone then. I am sorry this thing has to happen, sir. There are certain things that we have to do."

"What will you do if we stop you," Ramos asked.

"We will move in, sir, and use reasonable force."

Ramos had been called the man in the middle, the question mark, the Hamlet. But now he no longer hesitated.

He told them, "I want to make it clear that I am not with you. If you do anything foolish, we will meet you with maximum force."

Ramos talked with his service commanders and key staff officers. Then he issued a radio message at 1 a.m. to commanders throughout the country detailing the plot and instructing troops that their mission was "to preserve the unity of military institutions to enable us to perform our constitutional and inherent mission of protecting the people, maintaining law and order, and preserving the stability, security and integrity of the republic." He said the armed forces stood behind the government of President Aquino. The message had been prepared beforehand in typescript. Ramos penned an addition in his own hand: "Disregard any orders from MND or Colonel Honasan and MND staff." Later, some officers said they had been told that Ramos was with the coup and had not been disabused of that until this statement.

"My chief of staff is and has been a team player, even with President Marcos," explained Brigadier General Alexander Aguirre, NAFP chief of operations. "He didn't decide for Cory or Enrile, because he did not want to break up the triumvirate. He thought he could make Enrile stop his attacks on the government when the recommendations had been attended to. That is why, up to the last moment, he did not insert the term, "disregard MND." He tried to arouse public opinion by leaking some of these actions they did without connecting it to Enrile. He sought to give him more flexibility to take appropriate actions, not to go with it, and to discourage his people below."

Honasan, Robles, and Turingan had to decide their course of action by 4:30 a.m., but they had little alternative. They had gotten commitments, but the troops they expected did not support them or did not arrive. Some troops reported to be on their way disappeared. Ramos had turned the tide. The wire he sent was the signal many had been waiting for. Even the RAM boys' troops inside Camp Aguinaldo could not be mobilized.

At 4:30 a.m., Ramos received a message that the coup had been aborted. An hour later, he went out jogging—at the same time, checking conditions in the camp.

Weeks later, he would say on television, "If we did not act the way we acted during a series of weekends, we would not be here talking on this talk show. We were reacting to certain movements of forces and certain movements of supplies. If we did not act the way we did, then maybe the situation would be much worse now and not as stable as it is today." He added, "I am not completely satisfied with the stability yet."

Cory kept vigil at home until dawn. Armored personnel carriers stood guard during the night outside her white villa and at the palace a few blocks away. Ramos called her several times, the last in the early morning. She told Arroyo to summon the cabinet. Enrile was not invited.

The meeting began at 8 a.m. Cory looked tired. It pained her that Enrile had to go. She felt that she might not be president were it not for his actions in sparking the revolution, though she knew also that he had been forced by events to take refuge in Camp Aguinaldo. She was tense when she called the meeting to order. It would last for three-and-a-half hours.

Ramos briefed the ministers on the plot. He also reported the rumor that at one point Enrile had lost complete control of the RAM boys.

"We cannot continue this way," Cory said.

When Cory asked Ramos if she should fire Enrile, he said, "Yes, Mrs. President, but please don't humiliate him." He would later say that he went along with the firing of Enrile to avert a polarization that could lead to civil war.

Cory announced that she would accept everyone's resignation and asked them to write them out on the spot. She declared that changes in the cabinet would be necessary, because it was important for people to see her as a president who was decisive and in full control of her government. Her actions were essential to preserve her credibility. It was, indeed, an understatement. The criticisms of her failure to move against Enrile had become a crescendo in the press and conversations among the political class. When she finally summarized the decisions she had made, the ministers spontaneously stood and applauded.

NPA units in Manila. "There are New People's Army rebels in Manila, but there's nothing new about it. They have been here even during the time of [President] Magsaysay," he said, referring to the Huks. "Maybe there are left-leaning cabinet members, but they are free to think their own way."

That afternoon at Rizal Park, where Cory attended the proclamation of the National Eucharistic Year, the light rain did not dampen the enthusiasm of the crowd of 15,000 which cheered her report of Enrile's firing. She said she would make other changes in the cabinet in the following days.

Benigno said disciplinary action would be up to Ileto but expected that the plotters would not be severely punished. He said the government was not in a position to implicate Enrile.

Ileto said later that Enrile's RAM boys had "tendered their courtesy resignations," and an "informal investigation" into the coup plot would be launched. He said that he would not take action against Enrile "even if he were involved in the coup plot," since he was not a soldier, and that it was too early to decide if charges would be filed against the RAM plotters. But they would be reassigned to "areas where their specialties can be properly utilized." A high-ranking officer explained, "We could have pounced on them and held them for conspiracy to rebellion. But they had a following, and we didn't want to create a division."

The National Intelligence Coordinating Agency was assigned to investigate the coup plot, but it was unlikely to come up with the full story. It would reach too high, to a not inconsequential number of generals who had been amenable to the coup plans or whose actions might at least raise questions about their loyalty to the government. Cory agreed with the military not to press the issue.

A few days later, Cory fired several other cabinet ministers, Ernesto Maceda, charged with taking bribes for logging concessions, and Rogaciano Mercado, accused of corruption in distributing public works contracts. The resignation of Pimentel was accepted a few days after that. Labor Minister Sanchez held on a few weeks longer, but Cory announced his imminent removal after a week of threats by the KMU that it would strike if he were fired. She does not like threats, Saguisag explained. Cory did not cite evidence against the men accused of corruption, but said people in government service had to be concerned about public perceptions.

All the firings were difficult. Mercado was the main political leader of her brother's party in Bulacan province and had joined him in fighting central Luzon battles against Marcos. Maceda was a family friend who had been Ninoy's political aide during the years in Boston. Pimentel had been jailed for fighting the Marcos dictatorship and had been a leader in the 1978 ticket for parliament Ninoy had headed. Sanchez was a member of the lawyers' human rights group of Arroyo and Saguisag. The first three had been guilty of corruption or severe mismanagement, but sacking Sanchez was a concession to business interests who simply thought that the labor minister was too pro-labor. He was replaced by Franklin Drilon, a corporate lawyer who had been vice-president of a business federation. At a time when Cory had focused little personal attention on improving the situation of labor, the appointment raised new questions about her priorities and judgment. Reporter James Clad of the *Far Eastern Economic Review*, the major regional business magazine, called Sanchez's firing a big mistake. "He carried progressive credentials that would allow him to make the KMU bite their tongue and accept strike settlements," he said. "He had given a progressive tone to the government. Now it was contracting into a technocratic center of business people with strong U.S. links."

Pimentel was named special advisor on national affairs, with cabinet rank. Cory, with a finely honed sense of poetic justice, also withdrew Homobono Adaza's appointment to board seats on two government corporations and gave them to Pimentel, his arch-rival. Maceda, fired because of credible rumors, although there was no solid proof, was given the title ambassador-at-large. Mercado, apparently nailed by conclusive evidence, did not receive a consolation prize.

In Manila, it was business as usual. Laurel, in the hospital with flu, had a nephew read a speech prepared for a business group. This one attacked the Freedom Constitution for causing "unease and alarm" and paralyzing the government service by making every worker a casual employee. He said perceptions of the government's instability emboldened its challengers.

Cory turned her attention to the negotiations with the NPA. She was in a good position; she appeared in control of the military, which was more united than it had been in years. She felt the Communist leadership was waffling, taking advantage of the government.

Cory wanted a cease-fire during the Christmas holidays. She

realized that if she did not succeed then, when Filipinos were psychologically more malleable and people had a tendency to compromise, it would be much harder to do so later on.

On November 25, government and NDF negotiators met for a marathon eight-hour session in Manila. Then the government representatives met with the military. "We are nearing an agreement," they told reporters.

The military had provided a position paper on the agreement and, at the end, got additional "refinements." It secured a ban on rebels carrying fire arms in population centers and the expansion of "hostile acts" to include armed extortion, coercion and molestation in addition to actual shooting. The cease-fire would go into effect on December 10, International Human Rights Day, and last for sixty days.

Club Filipino the afternoon of November 27 was jammed with reporters and photographers squeezed into rows of folding chairs. Government and rebel negotiators sat at a yellow-covered table on a raised platform. Behind them, white curtains with delicate green flowers and cross-hatched window panels made of mother-of-pearl provided an incongruous backdrop. It was the room where Cory had held her inauguration just nine months before.

The negotiators grinned as the cease-fire agreement passed from one to the other for their signatures; this ended seventeen years of war between government forces and NPA guerrillas. The negotiations had taken less than four months. Two of the adversaries hugged, and flashbulbs popped. An irreverent journalist yelled, "Kiss, kiss!"

In the end, both sides made concessions. Negotiations on "taxation" by the insurgents and procurement of arms during the cease-fire period were postponed. The government did not concede to the NDF the status of belligerency or recognize the rebels' territorial claims.

That day, Cory made two visits to fortify her spirit and share feelings with the souls that gave her strength and guidance. She went to Ninoy's grave and to the Carmelite convent.

On the last day of the eventful month, Cory took stock. Addressing a meeting of the Asian Development Bank Women's Club—wives of ADB executives—she relished her victory over the men who had sought to defeat her.

"It has often been said that Marcos was the first male chauvinist to underestimate me. He was not the last to pay for that mistake."

"One distinct quality I have observed in the men who would

discount my abilities, diminish my role, or who cannot bring themselves to imagine that I shall rule this country for the entire term of a presidency, is their ability to out-talk me at every opportunity."

Lately, she said, "there have arisen a crop of garrulous men with better and brighter ideas on how to run my government or what I should do with myself. And again, their addresses have been longer, wordier, and delivered with more dramatic inflections, better-placed pauses, more body English than I would ever manage on a rostrum. For, those who love to hear themselves talk do work hard at it."

But she said, "After all is said and done—or should I say, said and undone—I would like to think that I have managed to have the last word and the last task of having to set things back in order after these men were finished."

She added, unnecessarily, "It is not I who have been consigned to the bedroom of history."

Victory

THE WEEKS LEADING UP TO the constitutional plebiscite on February 2, 1987, were the most dangerous that Cory had faced as president. On January 4, the government had signed a pact with MNLF leader Nur Misuari under which he agreed to give up demands for a separate state in return for a referendum in five southern islands on the question of Muslim autonomy. MILF rebels led by Hashim Salamat, angered at being cut out of the negotiations, had attacked fourteen targets, including a provincial capital building, two hotels, four bridges, power lines, a university, and other public places in Mindanao. Then, the palace received intelligence that they might strike in Manila.

There were also reports that Marcos loyalists would attempt to seize some radio stations in the capital the weekend of January 17-18. Further intelligence said armed groups would move to destabilize the government. On January 17, Ramos called his commanders to a meeting and placed the armed forces on alert. Road blocks with armored personnel carriers, water cannon, and riot troops were set up on streets leading to the palace. Orders were given to arrest any uniformed troops traveling at night, and Ramos did not leave his headquarters to sleep. Rumors of a coup spread.

Nevertheless, Cory went to Mindanao on Saturday to campaign for ratification of the constitution. The next day, she spoke to MILF leader Haji Murad and invited his organization to a dialogue in Malacañang. He agreed to pass the invitation on to Salamat and offered her flowers, symbolizing the quest for peace and unity, together with a paper outlining his group's positions. On Tuesday, January 20, TV stations showed her taped appeal calling on Filipinos to be patient in their demands for reforms and to approve the constitution. "Believe me when I say that my government is out eventually to redress your grievances," she said. "Without [the constitution], our fledgling democracy will crumble, and I dread to think of what may happen to our country."

Meanwhile, the Farmers' Movement of the Philippines (KMP) was planning a demonstration demanding that Cory carry out her promises of land reform. Its members were angry and they had already protested by camping in tents for a week outside the ministry of agrarian reform. The government had granted plots to only 6,000 peasants, although it had promised to help four million. The KMP believed that Cory was stalling or that she had no commitment to land reform.

On Thursday, January 22, 10,000 people, most of them peasant farmers, massed to move to Malacañang. KMP demonstrators had in two previous marches been refused permission to approach the palace. This time, they said, there would be a confrontation; some carried clubs and weapons. When they got to Mendiola Bridge on the approach to the palace, they met a phalanx of 500 police and a contingent of marines. The police carried shields with the words "Maximum Tolerance" stenciled in yellow. They were backed by two water cannons and eight fire trucks. KMP chairman Jaime Tadeo reportedly shouted, "Charge Malacañang; break down the barricades!" The protestors began to push against the line of troops.

Suddenly, there was pandemonium. Police said the demonstrators attacked with iron pipes, wooden clubs, and rocks and also fired shots at them. Without a warning, the troops discharged handguns and automatic rifles into the crowd. Demonstrators dropped to the ground and screamed. Some of them fired back or threw rocks and sticks at the police. After a minute, the volley was over, though a few troops chased and fired at fleeing demonstrators. The toll was twenty protestors dead and over a hundred wounded. Three soldiers were injured by bullets and one was hurt by a stone. An hour later, police fired shots and tear gas to disperse 3,000 demonstrators who had moved to Bonifacio Square.

That same day, government and Communist negotiators, citing threats to their lives, suspended peace talks indefinitely. The NDF closed the office it had opened in the National Press Club building and returned to the underground. After the killings, it issued a statement attacking the government for the violence against the demonstrators, saying, "The Aquino government has ripped off its mask of democratic liberalism and bared itself to be no more than the deceitful successor to the fascist Marcos dictatorship."

In a late evening TV address, Cory expressed her "deep regrets" and urged calm after the "tragedy that struck our nation." She ordered the release of any demonstrators that had been arrested and said an independent commission would investigate the killings. "In the period before the plebiscite, attempts to destabilize the government and defeat our democratic aims will intensify. I urge our people to maintain sobriety."

Ramos said his troops had overreacted and that they would behave differently in the future. "We want to let everyone know that the policy of the military is maximum tolerance, especially now that we have a democracy," he said.

The next day, Cory set up a Citizens Mendiola Commission to investigate the shootings, but some of her supporters on the left were disillusioned. Maria Serena "Maris" Diokno resigned from the government negotiating panel, saying, "In the past few weeks I have found it increasingly difficult to defend the position of the government on a wide range of issues. Regardless of whatever provocation might have eminated from the ranks of the demonstrators, the killings were unjustified." Five members of the Presidential Commission on Human Rights, including Maris's father, Pepe Diokno, and some of its staff members also quit. However, Bayan leader Leandro Alejandro said his organization did not hold Cory responsible for the killings. With supreme irony, Enrile criticized Cory for the attack on the demonstrators. He said, "There is blood on the hands of the government" and asked, "Why was the president not at Malacañang to take charge of her troops?"

That same day, Cory was politically embarrassed when Homobono Adaza released a tape of a phone conversation in which she and

Teddy Locsin, in New York during her September trip to the United States, talked to Joker Arroyo in Manila. They were concerned about the language the Constitutional Commission had just approved which said, "The Philippines, consistent with the national interest, adopts and pursues a policy of freedom from nuclear weapons in its territory." This could conflict with Washington's free use of its bases. Cory had pledged not to interfere with the drafting of the constitution, but she was worried that the measure might hurt her attempts to secure American aid. Arroyo said he would see the style committee chairman, Soc Rodrigo; shortly afterwards, the commission "clarified" the provision, saying that "consistent with the national interest" meant "subject to the national interest." When the tape was revealed, Cory ordered Justice Minister Netpali Gonzales to prosecute Adaza under a Marcos-era law which set a six-month penalty for illegal wiretapping or possessing a tape of wiretapped communications. It was believed that he had secured the tape from military sources who had been monitoring palace communications.

Sunday was also Cory's fifty-fourth birthday, and she spent it with her family. About five hundred demonstrators paraded near Malacañang with a black banner that read "Happy birthday, Cory." They carried cardboard coffins commemorating the victims of what had come to be known as the "Mendiola Massacre."

The KMP called an "indignation rally" for Monday. Cory ordered that the demonstrators be allowed to file past the shooting site; government representatives reached an agreement that the marchers would go close to the palace, but then detour into side streets. A delegation would meet with Cory later in the week. On Monday afternoon, 15,000 protestors strode past the place where the killings had occurred. A line of government officials and the president's staff and secretaries met the demonstrators in front of the palace. Among them were Rene Saguisag, Joe Concepcion, Noel Soriano (now National Security Council chairman), Nene Pimentel, and other cabinet ministers; they linked arms with nuns and priests and walked among the marchers as they, with clenched fists, passed the palace gates.

During these days, elements of another machination were being put into place. In Waikiki, Hawaii, Imelda Marcos visited The Military Shop and bought $2,000 worth of camouflage pants and T-shirts, combat boots, and jackets. A chartered Boeing 707 waited on the runway of Honolulu International Airport.

In the early morning of Tuesday, January 27, at least 500 mutinous troops commenced the operation of a plan to attack nine military and civilian targets, including broadcast facilities, in an attempt that would extend further than any of the previous military plots. Armed forces were put on alert after midnight when several truckloads of troops were seen moving into Manila from camps to the north. The first attack occurred an hour later, when about 200 soldiers with red-and-blue "Guardian" headbands seized the Channel 7 television and radio complex and took up positions throughout the building and on the roof. They were led by Air Force Colonel Oscar Canlas, an intelligence specialist under former armed forces chief Ver, who had become close to Danding Cojuangco while in charge of intelligence in central Luzon. Rebellious soldiers later said Danding had helped to finance the action. The loyalists at the media complex said they were attempting to save the country from a drift toward communism. Civilian supporters brought them food and shouted, "Marcos forever." Some mutineers said Marcos would return and go on the air to rally his forces.

The military command reacted swiftly, deploying hundreds of government troops, some armed with machine guns, around the station. Police tried to disperse the crowd with fire hoses, tear gas, and warning shots. Ramos arrived to talk with the rebels in a police van outside the station. He called on them to surrender, saying "There is no hope for your cause, whatever it is," but they refused.

Elsewhere in Manila, more than fifty mutinous officers entered Villamor Air Base. After a four-hour gun battle, in which one rebel soldier was killed and eighteen wounded, they surrendered. At Sangley Point Air Base, south of the city, some forty loyalists held two high-ranking officers hostage until daybreak, then surrendered. Another sixty soldiers tried unsuccessfully to take over the government's Channel 4 TV station, and still others targeted the main power company. Ramos ordered troops confined to their camps and set up eighteen roadblocks to stop reinforcements from moving toward the capital. More than a hundred troops were arrested on their way from the north to take over the ministry of defense and armed forces general headquarters. Government forces secured the other media centers.

In a live television address in the morning, Cory said, "The situation is well in hand. People should keep calm. Our troops, responding with exemplary speed, thwarted attempts of certain groups of misguided military personnel to seize key installations. This attempt reflects the inability of some elements, both in the military and in the civilian sector, to face the fact that the civilian government is here to stay and that nothing will derail our efforts to establish full constitutional democracy in the coming plebiscite."

She urged the loyalist troops to surrender. "Their situation is hopeless. Every moment of delay merely compounds the gravity of their crime." She warned, "There may have to be intensive military operations around Channel 7. Do not stay there or you will be hurt." There would be no more leniency. "Let me be perfectly clear: we will not treat this like the Manila Hotel incident." She promised courts-martial for the leaders. "There is a time for reconciliation and a time for justice and retribution," she said. "That time has come."

Ramos announced at noon that the coup attempt had been crushed and appealed to those holding out to surrender, but they refused. Up to five thousand people gathered in the streets surrounding the station. Marcos loyalists and government supporters threw stones at each other until troops dispersed the crowd.

Cory had ordered Ramos to arrest and detain the rebels, but Ramos would not or could not comply. The military turned to "psy war," bringing the rebels' wives and children to the street outside the station and playing rock music, particularly Paul Anka's "I'm just a lonely boy." By Wednesday night, at least a thousand troops of the National Capital Regional Command, led by Brigadier General Alexander Aguirre and backed by armored personnel carriers and heavy weapons surrounded Channel 7. Ramos set a 10:30 p.m. Wednesday deadline for the surrender of the mutinous troops; when it passed, government forces began to lob tear-gas canisters into the building. Meanwhile, Ramos was confronted by about a hundred RAM officers led by Gringo Honasan, who met with him at Camp Aguinaldo for five hours during the night. They demanded leniency for the loyalists and the airing of their grievances on radio and TV; they threatened rebellion if any military blood was shed. The MND had issued a press release after the last November coup that the RAM boys would be reassigned, but this had never been implemented.

Ramos responded by suspending the attack, and early Thursday morning, Canlas went to Camp Aguinaldo for negotiations. At 3:30 a.m. Thursday, after several hours of talks, the rebels agreed to leave the station. The accord was announced later in the morning at a news conference at armed forces headquarters, with Canlas and other armed loyalists present. Ramos said the mutineers were not under arrest, but would be taken to Fort Bonifacio for processing. "Everybody is entitled to due process." But Canlas was allowed to return to Channel 7. When the loyalists returned, some said they would not accept the agreement because it left open the possibility they would be arrested. Cory expressed her irritation at this soft treatment through a statement by a spokesman who said she was reiterating her order for punishment of those involved.

Later that day—Wednesday night Washington time—the U.S. government received a request from Malacañang to look into reports of the Boeing 707, which had been spotted by a Filipino consular official at the airport in Honolulu. The State Department sent a representative who, Marcos said, gave him a written warning that he would be "physically prevented" from boarding any plane going to the Philippines. "Now I am being treated like a prisoner," he complained. "What am I to do, poor little me, who was your ally for so many years? I can only do whatever you tell me to do." He denied any connection with the aborted coup. The rebels finally left the station Thursday afternoon, only after it was reported that the Americans had thwarted Marcos's plans to return. The morning agreement with Ramos had been just a delaying tactic.

Ramos seemed to balk at Cory's demand the loyalist troops be court-martialed, saying it would be "premature" to speak of prosecution before investigation. Ileto made a similar statement. Nevertheless, Cory said the occupation of the TV station had been part of an attempt to overthrow the government and those involved would be dealt with. She said she had ordered the preparation of rebellion charges against any civilians involved and courts-martial against the rebel military officers. "Every one implicated in this crime, civilian and military, will be held to the fullest account."

The next day, Ramos ordered the arrest of Brigadier General Jose Maria Zumel, Colonel Rolando Abadilla, and several other officers for their involvement in the plot. They, like the Guardians, had been involved in the Manila Hotel incident. Ramos said 13 officers, 359 enlisted men and 137 civilians were being held. There were reports that some loyalists troops had been paid as much as $7,500 for their participation; a palace official said the money came from Marcos. The armed forces were put on alert to guard against further threats.

That same day, NDF announced that it would formally withdraw from the peace talks. The negotiations had not gotten beyond the agenda. The government would discuss only matters that would fit within the draft constitution, which ruled out most of the insurgents' demands, including a coalition government that would share power with them, a ban on investment by multinational companies, and immediate distribution of farmland.

It was the weekend before the plebiscite, and Cory went to Mindanao for the final campaign push. She told 75,000 people in Davao, "I let them go after the Manila Hotel incident, but this time it is too much. I forgave everybody then, because it was the first attempt, but this time it is different. Everybody has to respect law and order."

Cory had spent all of January campaigning in a fashion that resembled a traditional political race. At provincial rallies, she made promises for new roads, irrigation systems, flood control, and classrooms. She pledged to pay back money owed by the government to sugar planters, and she awarded land patents to farmers. The country was flooded with yellow stickers that showed only Cory's face and the word "yes." The campaign slogan on banners and placards around the nation was "Yes to Cory, yes to country, yes to democracy, and yes to the constitution." Sometimes the variation was "yes to stability and yes to growth." But the constitution wasn't the issue—Cory was. Fifty thousand people, including government workers with banners emblazoned with their agency names, attended the final campaign rally, Saturday, at the Luneta. She told them, "I have been accused of favoring the leftists, while others accuse me of siding with the rightists, but I am only for you, my beloved countrymen."

The "yes" vote was supported by PDP-Laban, the Salonga Liberals, Bandila, and moderate groups such as the Christian Democrats. Unido remained divided. Partido ng Bayan changed its "critical yes" to a "no" after the killings of the KMP demonstrators. The KMU said "no," though some of its affiliates voted "yes." A right-wing coalition, whose leaders included Enrile and Tolentino, was formed to fight the charter, with the slogan "No to Cory, no to communism, and no to the constitution."

On election day, there was little violence and few incidents of attempted fraud or ballot box stealing. In Mindanao, nine people were killed in NPA attacks on polling places.

Cory's advisors had said she needed a big turn-out and a 65-percent win to establish her credibility. She got that and more. The victory was overwhelming, over 76 percent, including wide margins in many areas of Communist strength. Even Marcos's home province, Ilocos Norte, approved the charter, although Enrile's Cagayan province turned it down by a small margin. The overall military vote was 50-50. The 250,000-member armed forces was still polarized internally, much of it alienated from the government. In the short term, it would continue to be a threat.

But the long-term challenge would be the leftist insurgents, who, though politically weakened by the vote, had resumed encounters with the military. Many of the guerillas had come down from the hills during the cease-fire and had spent Christmas with their families. Cory knew that the large majority were not ideological Communists, but peasants who fought out of desperation because of repression by the military and warlords and in the belief there was no other way to end their economic misery. She hoped that the weeks with their families had stoked their desire to return home and that many would have faith in her promise to improve their conditions. She would pursue a policy of encouraging regional cease-fires and establish a program for rebel returnees. There appeared to be a struggle inside the Communist party over whether to resume the war or attempt a political and electoral opposition. Commander Dante said the Left had made a mistake by opposing the constitution. Defections from the NPA would strengthen the moderates. However, if she could not control military abuses, disarm the warlords, or deal with the peasants' economic plight, she would not end the rebellion. Less than two days after the cease-fire ended, the military chased NPA fighters out of a peasant village and then turned their guns on the residents, massacring 17 and injuring many other, including young children.

National elections would take place May 11; local and regional elections were set for August 24. Afterwards, Cory would share power with the newly elected legislators and officials while she sought to hold her fractious country together.

But, whatever the future brought, she had already achieved a monumental success. She had proved to her countrymen and to an astonished world that a political neophyte with little besides courage, tenacity and innate good sense could embark on a moral crusade and defeat a dictator who had controlled the country through brutality and bribes for twenty years.

Reference Notes

The information for this book was gathered from a wide variety of sources, including newspapers, books, and interviews. Controversial or questionable facts were cross-checked, and items that were initially drawn from newspaper articles were confirmed though personal interviews. Individuals who were close observers or participants in the events reviewed all sections of the manuscript. For cases in which information about an event was pieced together in equal parts from several sources, those sources are listed together. In most cases, to avoid long citations, I give only a single source. Given multiple sources, I preferred to cite press reports because they are more readily available than personal sources to researchers who wish to investigate these topics.

BOOKS CITED

Agoncillo, Teodoro, *A Short History of the Philippines*, The New American Library, New York, 1975
Arillo, Cecilio T., *Breakaway*, CTA & Associates, Manila, 1986
Crisostomo, Isabelo T., *Cory: Profile of a President*, J. Kriz Publishing Enterprises, Manila, 1986
Joaquin, Nick, *The Aquinos of Tarlac*, Solar Publishing Corp, Manila, 1986
Kerkvliet, Benedict, *The Huk Rebellion*, University of California Press, Berkeley, 1977
Larkin, John A., *The Pampangans*, University of California Press, Berkeley, 1972
Maramba, Asuncion David, ed., *Ninoy Aquino: The Man, The Legend*, Cacho Hermanos, Manila, 1984
Mercado, Monila Allarey, ed., *People Power*, The James R. Reuter, S.J. Foundation, Manila, 1986
Porzio, Giovanni, *Cory*, Arnoldo Mondadori Editore, Milan, 1986

The following periodicals are cited frequently in the notes by these abbreviations:

Asian Wall Street Journal—AWSJ
Bulletin Today—BT*
Business Day—BD
Far Eastern Economic Review—FEER
Manila Bulletin—MB*

Manila Chronicle—MC
Manila Times—MT
Philippine Daily Express—PDE
Philippine Daily Inquirer—PDI
Philippine Tribune—PT

Periodicals not cited frequently, and those with shorter names, are spelled out.

Citations from *Time* and *Newsweek* are in most cases from the Asian editions; page numbers may vary from those of the American editions.

*After the revolution, *Bulletin Today* changed its name to *Manila Bulletin*.

Preface

"the official who handles . . . her own book": phone conversation with Carmen Stelton, Nov. 18, 1986

Chapter 1, Return

3 The story of Ninoy's return and assassination combines material from Ken Kashiwahara, "Aquino's final journey," p. 106, p. 108; and Cory Aquino, "Ninoy loved you," p. 142, both in *Ninoy Aquino: The Man, The Legend;* "Taiwan military official sent Aquino says US Journalist," BD June 7, 1984, p. 15; "The Aquino Plot," *Time,* Oct. 22, 1984, p. 10; *Asiaweek,* Nov. 2, 1984, p. 24

4 Ninoy's speech is available in Benigno Aquino, "Letters—Prison & Exile," Aquino Family & La Ignaciana Apostolic Center, Manila, October 1983, pp. 64–67

5 "Don't forget to go . . . to me in prison": Crisostomo, p. 97

5 "I'm coming with him . . . exit door: "Taiwan military official sent Aquino off, says US Journalist," p. 15

6 His face showed . . . before him: interview, Ernesto Lichauco, husband of Ninoy's sister Maur, Nov. 16, 1986

6 Marcos had asked . . . should be present: interview, Juan Ponce Enrile, Dec. 23, 1986

6 At 2:30 a.m. . . . telephone: Cory's children and their birthdates are: Maria Elena (Ballsy), August 1955; Aurora (Pinky), December 1957; Benigno III (Nonoy), February 1960; Victoria Elena (Viel), October 1961; and Kristine (Kris), February 1971.

6 Ballsy recalled that evening's event in "Ballsy," *Fookien Times Yearbook,* Manila, 1985–86, p. 37a; also in Crisostomo, pp. 99–100; Aquino, "Ninoy loved you," p. 142; "Cory is blunt, says close pal," *MT,* Feb. 28, 1986, p. 4

7 "We'd better pray . . . we can do": Arnold Zeitlin, "Cory remembers," from *Boston Magazine,* Sept. 1986, in *The Philippine Star,* Sept. 17, 1986, p. 7

7 "Do the people . . . few friends: Monila Allarey Mercado, ed, *People Power,* The James R. Reuter, S.J. Foundation, Manila, 1986, p. 12

8 Cory was overwhelmed . . . love for Ninoy: Aquino, "Ninoy loved you," p. 143

8 It eased her sadness: Cory Aquino in *People Power,* p. 15

8 Cory leaned down . . . and democracy: interview, Aurora Aquino, Nov. 16, 1986

8 She had no . . . would involve: Cory Aquino, "Speech to Makati Rotary Club," Dec. 6, 1983, in *Mr. & Ms.,* Dec. 27, 1983

8 When she kissed . . . smiling: "Aquino funeral plans bared," *BT,* Aug. 25, 1983, p. 1

8 "If only one . . . come out": interview, Max Soliven, Oct. 29, 1986

9 Cory was astonished . . . Ninoy's hearse: Aquino, "Ninoy loved you," p. 143

9 She turned down . . . him rest: interview, Agapito "Butz" Aquino, Oct. 14, 1986

9 The family . . . difficult: interview, Paul Aquino, Oct. 20, 1986

9 "Ninoy, who . . . in turn": Aquino, "Ninoy loved you," p. 143

10 She was exhausted . . . faint now": Cory Aquino in *People Power,* p. 17

10 She felt tears . . . people uncomfortable: Neni Sta. Romana Cruz, "Life with Ninoy," in *Ninoy Aquino,* p. 60

10 And, she . . . get done: Riassa Lamson Espinosa, "The new president: an enigma even to followers," *BD,* Feb. 26, 1986, p. 5

Chapter 2, Growing Up

11 Maria Corazon . . . Jose Cojuangco: One of the children was stillborn; the other died at one-and-a-half from meningitis. Cory's living brothers and sisters are Pedro (Pepe), Josephine, Teresita (Terry), Jose Jr. (Peping), Maria Paz (Passy)

11 The Cojuangco's . . . intermarry. Crisostomo, pp. 6-7

11 Cory's great grandfather . . . Jose married Mantera Estrella from Bulacan.

Reference Notes

11 Cojuangco's only son, Melecio . . . : Melecio married Tecla Chichioco

12 In Paniqui, they . . . armed forces: The story of Ysidra and General Luna is from a political party official and a member of the Cojuangco family, both of whom asked to remain anonymous.

12 He served as . . . ran the government: Don Juan Sumulong favored a gradual approach to independence, rather than the immediate break advocated by the nationalists. He was later elected a senator and was an unsuccessful candidate for vice president in 1935.

12 Cory's parents . . . : Material about Cory's childhood is taken from an interview with an anonymous relative; Betty Go Belmonte, "President Cory's early years," *Fookien Times Yearbook*, 1985–86, Manila pp. 31, 32; William Stewart and Nelly Sindayen, "A Christmas Conversation," *Time*, Jan. 5, 1987, p. 16; Crisostomo, p. 15

13 Her father managed . . . : Paniqui Sugar Mill was founded in 1929.

13 Philippine Bank . . . four brothers: interview, Jose "Peping" Cojuangco, Dec. 11, 1986. Peping said Ysidra "probably put up most of the funds."

13 Cory's best . . . sisters: Aurora Aquino, Nov. 16, 1986

13 Cory remembers meeting . . . Lupita: Joaquin, p. 250

14 "It is up to you . . . charm": Betty Go Belmonte, p. 33

14 She saw Ninoy . . . older man: Joaquin, p. 250

15 Cory was impressed . . . industry: Joaquin, 250; "My life with Ninoy," *Diplomacy*, Seoul, Oct. 25, 1986, p. 14

15 "As a lover . . . person": Joaquin, p. 250

15 "Ninoy was . . . queens": Agapito "Butz" Aquino, Oct. 14, 1986

15 She did not . . . Filipino men: Aurora Aquino, Nov. 16, 1986

15 Pacing . . . friends: interview, Tessie Aquino Oreta, Oct. 20, 1986

15 Imelda would marry . . . crush on her: Aurora Aquino, Nov. 16, 1986

15 Cory returned . . . a discipline: Belmonte, p. 34

15 Cory did not have . . . existence": interview, Florence "Flory" Aguas, Dec 29, 1986

16 On one date . . . marry you": Joaquin, p. 251

16 "Ninoy was . . . hand"; "wouldn't let . . . tomorrow": Aurora Aquino, Nov. 16, 1986

Chapter 3, Roots of Unrest

17 This chapter relies especially on material from John. A. Larkin, *The Pampangans*, University of California Press, Berkeley, 1972; Teodoro A. Agoncillo, *A Short History of the Philippines*, The New American Library, New York, 1975; Benedict J. Kerkvliet, *The Huk Rebellion*, University of California Press, Berkeley, 1977; and discussions with Luis Taruc, former Huk leader, and Professor George Henry Weightman, Department of Sociology, Herbert Lehman College of the City University of New York.

18 After the United States . . . in the Philippines. It was the occasion for his famous remark to the captain of his flagship, "You may fire when you are ready, Gridley." Agoncillo, p. 106

19 Men like Theodore . . . did not prevail: interview, Weightman, Feb. 1, 1987

19 Filipinos had the right . . . posts as well: Larkin, p. 134

20 The Americans promised . . . be established: from the Jones Law passed by the U.S. Congress in 1916, Agoncillo, p. 183

20 "There was a crash . . . in the south: Weightman, Feb. 1, 1987

20 Public works . . . and businessmen: Larkin, p. 135

20 The U.S. did nothing . . . Philippine society: Larkin, p. 135

21 The Democratic presidents . . . farms in California: Weightman, Feb. 1, 1987

21 One politician . . . were holding": interview, Antonio "Tony" Cuenco, Oct. 30, 1986. Cuenco, a former assemblyman and congressman, would be appointed Cory Aquino's political affairs minister. His father was a governor and his grandfather was a senator.

21 Cory's grandfather . . . in these parties": Agoncillo, p. 196

22 Neither tenant . . . virtual serfs: Kerkvliet, p. 22

22 Traditionally, the division . . . molasses: interview, Luis Taruc, Nov. 13, 1986

22 Tenants had to pay . . . chapel: Kerkvliet, p. 16

23 For Luis Taruc . . . Cojuangco hacienda workers: Taruc, Nov. 13, 1986

23 Taruc, turned . . . mayor was a Huk: ibid. Taruc's Socialist Party had entered an alliance with the Communists and other leftist groups in 1938.

24 Most of the landlords . . . as local officials: Kerkvliet, p. 116

24 The U.S. also gave . . . troops to return: ibid., p. 115

24 or were . . . bandits: Weightman, Feb. 1, 1986

24 In one case . . . as town mayor: Kerkvliet, p. 113

24 Many of the Huks . . . for the attacks: Taruc, Nov. 13, 1986

25 The Concepcion municipal . . . official approval: Kerkvliet, p. 145

26 MacArthur, the son . . . business connections: Weightman, Feb. 1, 1987

26 MacArthur and U.S. High . . . collaborators: Agoncillo, 251. President Osmeña was vice-president of the Commonwealth when he was evacuated by the Americans in December 1941 along with President Manuel Quezon. Roxas stayed and collaborated with the Japanese. Osmeña became president of the exile government when Quezon died in 1944. Agoncillo adds, "The first thing congress did was to pass a law giving its members three years' back pay corresponding to the three years of Japanese occupation."

26 Repression increased . . . or disappeared: Kerkvliet, p. 151

26 They founded . . . called Huks: The full name was Hukbong Mapagpalaya ng Bayan (The Peoples Army of Liberation of the Country).

26 The army's demands . . . abolition of tenancy: Kerkvliet, p. 171

27 Lansdale, then a . . . station chief: He initially carried out sabotage missions in Communist North Vietnam in violation of a truce negotiated with the American-backed South at an international conference in Geneva.

Chapter 4, Ninoy

30 Ninoy and the Laurel . . . only friend: Joaquin, pp. 193, 195

30 Nearly a decade . . . rebellion: ibid., p. 242

30 Taruc spent . . . school: Luis Taruc, Nov. 13, 1986. Taruc accepted, and his son became a doctor. The son paid back the assistance by working for several years on the Cojuangco family plantation. Taruc was released in 1968 and was later jailed again briefly by Marcos under martial law. He was released, became a member of Marcos's land reform agency, and defended government policies. He kept a similar post in the Aquino administration.

30 Back from . . . father: Joaquin, p. 255

30 "Ninoy forced . . . image: William Stewart and Nelly Sindayen, "A Christmas Conversation," *Time*, Jan. 5, 1987, p. 16

30 Cory promised . . . children: notes from interview by *Village Voice* reporter Joe Conason, March 1986

31 She soon . . . other people: "On Ninoy's birthday, Cory talks about her husband and best friend," *Panorama*, Nov. 25, 1985, p. 5

31 However . . . wakes: Neni Sta. Romana Cruz, "Life with Ninoy," in *Ninoy Aquino*, p. 56

31 sometimes . . . sleep afterward: Stewart and Sindayen, p. 17

31 She relieved . . . addict. Crisostomo, p. 23

31 When she went from the fleas: "On Ninoy's birthday, Cory . . . ," p. 68

31 She picked . . . once a month: Stewart and Sindayen, p. 17

31 a Spanish company: Compañía de Tabacos de Filipinas (Tabacalera)

31 Perhaps to put . . . small farmers: He said, "It will pave the way for the sale to bona fide planters on a long-term basis of portions of the hacienda."

31 The agency . . . Tenure Act": The sugar mill was bought in 1957 with a $2.1 million loan from Manufacturers Hanover Trust Company of New York. At a time when the country was under exchange controls because of low dollar reserves, the Central Bank covered the loan by depositing U.S. dollars with the bank. Cojuangco proposed a clause in the agreement that, "There shall be a simultaneous purchase of Hacienda Luisita with the purchase of the [mill] shares, with a view to distributing this hacienda to small farmers in line with the Administration's social justice program."

31 Ninoy told . . . agreement: Joaquin, p. 274

32 "If I become . . . in-laws away": interview with a close political associate of the Cojuangcos, not for attribution.

32 During this . . . to Sukarno: Joaquin, pp. 268–71

32 "Marcos hated . . . himself": Soliven, Oct. 29, 1986

32 Cory did not meddle . . . eating out: Agapito "Butz" Aquino, Oct. 14, 1986

33 "She was the . . . food": Tessie Oreta, Oct. 20, 1986

33 Years later . . . quiet: Belinda Olivares-Cunanan, "To lead by example; to inspire," *Mr.&Ms.*, Dec. 5–12, 1985, p. 18

33 As governor, his tasks . . . Party: Joaquin, p. 288

33 He also . . . abroad: Taruc, Nov. 17, 1986

33 Years later . . . his son: Francisco Cruz, a leader of the radical coalition Bayan, in Bacolod City, Negros, Oct. 16, 1986

34 Dante had . . . getting in: Even today, though members of the public can't pass the guard posts without permission, when Dante arrives, he is allowed to pass and is saluted by ex-rebels who now work as security men.

34 "You cannot . . . dialogue": interview, Jose "Apeng" Yap, Dec. 29, 1986

34 "The Huks . . . social change": Joaquin, p. 321

34 They would meet . . . situation: Aurora Aquino, Nov. 16, 1986

34 "I am the wife . . . gives speeches: Joaquin, pp. 314–15

34 Ninoy was the . . . elected: Patterned on the American system, a third of the 24 were chosen every two years.

35 "it was doubtful . . . system: "Facts about Hacienda Luisita," published by Federation of Land Reform Farmers, 1986

35 Ninoy supported . . . Vietnamese: Joaquin, p. 337

35 Nevertheless . . . U.S. bases: Luis Mauricio, "The man behind the myth and why the myth was born," *Veritas*, Aug. 19, 1984, p. 4

35 Through a Senate . . . land reform: Aurora Aquino, Nov. 16, 1986

35 Ninoy allowed . . . and regulations: Taruc, Nov. 13, 1986. He was in prison during the period, but his son worked at the hacienda.

36 "Political hypocrisy . . . survival?": Luis Beltran, "Remembering Ninoy," in *Ninoy Aquino*, 121. When Marcos was elected president in 1965—on a platform of stopping inflation and ending graft and corruption—Cory's cousin Danding gave money to a renegade Huk commander to insure that villagers voted for Marcos. Taruc, Nov. 17, 1986

36 As the crisis . . . defense: Enrile became justice minister in 1968 and defense minister in 1970.

37 When the military . . . laughed: Yap, Dec. 29, 1986

37 The American owned . . . gathered dust: interview, Jovito Salonga, Feb. 27, 1986

38 "No president . . . support": Yap, Dec. 29, 1986

38 In the morning . . . as offices: interview, Francisco "Soc" Rodrigo, Nov. 22, 1986; and Soliven, Oct. 29, 1986

38 She turned off . . . for Ninoy: "Cory Aquino on Ninoy's assassination," *Veritas*, Jan. 1, 1984, p. 8

39 Her husband . . . weakness: Florence "Flory" Aguas, Dec. 29, 1986

39 Cory went to mass . . . normally: Crisostomo, p. 75

39 Ninoy and Diokno . . . water: Benigno Aquino, "Letters—Prison & Exile," pp. 2–6

39 "Cory was . . . anything": Salonga, Dec. 24, 1986

39 He was behind . . . next day: Betty Go Belmonte, "What the Lord told Cory Aquino during Ninoy's trip home," *Philippine Star*, Vol. III, No. 3

39 A few months . . . gratitude!": Benigno Aquino, "Letters—Prison & Exile," pp. 6–15

40 Cory was . . . him: interviews with two sources, including a close friend of Cory who confirmed the report; neither would be quoted.

40 It was . . . Ninoy: Cory Aquino, "Ninoy turned to God," in *Ninoy Aquino*, p. 98

40 Cory and Ninoy . . . his opponents: ibid.

40 It was a . . . seen with her: Rosario Liquicia, "Tough year for Mrs. Aquino," *MB*, Aug. 22, 1984

40 People snubbed . . . unkind: Aquino, "Ninoy turned to God," p. 99

40 She did not tell . . . anxieties: Cory Aquino, speech at forum, "Women for Justice and Freedom," sponsored by Concerned Women of the Philippines, Oct. 15, 1983

41 "That's enough . . . finished," Cory said: Aurora Aquino, Nov. 16, 1986

41 His years . . . new Cory Aquino": Cory Aquino's speech at College of Mount St. Vincent, Riverdale, NY, Sept. 21, 1986

41 For the first time . . . repressed: "I support any movement that will unite all of us," *Veritas*, May 29, 1986, p. 14

42 Making love . . . masking tape: Cory Aquino, from a Dec. 6 speech to Makati Rotary Club, in *Mr. & Ms.*, Dec. 27, 1983

42 "Even if we're . . . private: Diane Sawyer interview, "60 Minutes," CBS-TV, Sept. 14, 1986.

42 Ninoy conducted . . . newspapers: Paul Aquino, Oct. 20, 1986

42 Once . . . Lupita: ibid.

43 often smuggling . . . clothes: Max Soliven, "Cory must act decisively on cabinet revamp," *Philippine Star*, Nov. 29, 1986, p. 4

43 Ninoy was . . . role: Butz Aquino, Oct. 14, 1986

43 She said . . . "brainwashing": "Aquino is quiet on politics in interview," *AWSJ*, Mar. 13, 1986, p. 8

43 One day . . . has to do it" Aurora Aquino, Nov. 16, 1986

43 When Cory asked . . . would emerge: "Aquino is quiet on politics in interview," p. 8

43 Then, he raised . . . transport firms: The bank's name had been changed to First United Bank. The transport firm was the Patranco Bus company.

43 Cory cried . . . time: Porzio, p. 39

44 He was afraid . . . gone crazy: Yap, Dec. 29, 1986

44 Cory was against . . . were huge: Cory Aquino, "To vote or boycott is only a question of strategy," *Mr. & Ms.*, Feb. 24, 1984, p. 22

44 Allowed to go . . . transacted this": Ernesto Lichauco, Nov. 16, 1986

45 "This is the end . . . an election": "Cory Aquino tells how she scolded cabinet," *BD*, Mar. 7, 1986, p. 5

45 Marcos began . . . potential threat: The opposition denounced the electoral frauds, and to cool down the dissent, Marcos dangled the possibility of exile before Ninoy. Marcos let out word to Ninoy's friends to be quiet or they would disrupt the negotiations. It turned out to be a ploy to silence the critics.

45 In December . . . for his exile: Vic Barranco, "Go to America," in *Ninoy Aquino*, p. 101

45 Just before he . . . decades earlier: The response to the court action was that the agreements were unenforceable because there were no tenants on Hacienda Luisita, the Central Bank accord did not indicate which "small farmers" would benefit, the hacienda was outside the scope of land reform, and there was no agrarian unrest there. (From decision of the Regional Trial Court of Manila, Civil Case No. 131654, Dec. 2, 1985, Judge Bernardo P. Pardo)

45 The years in . . . Camelot: Aurora Magdalena, "Boston: A Camelot for Ninoy and Cory," *Veritas*, Aug. 19, 1984, p. 12

46 At a dinner . . . she is." Arnold Zeitlin, "Cory remembers Boston," from *Boston Magazine*, in *The Philippine Star*, Sept. 17, 1986, p. 7

46 She liked to read . . . but secretly," he replied: Letty Jimenez-Magsanoc, "Everything that's happening to me should have happened to Ninoy," *Mr. & Ms.*, Aug 16, 1985, p. 19

46 "He even knew . . . another command": Antonio "Tony" Cuenco, Oct. 30, 1986

46 Somebody once told . . . give in," answered Ninoy: Aurora Aquino, Nov. 16, 1986

46 Cory told a visitor . . . common sense: interview, Heherson "Sonny" Alvarez, Oct. 27, 1986. He would be named Cory's agrarian reform minister.

46 Jovito Salonga . . . a comment": Salonga, Dec. 24, 1986

47 In Boston . . . substantive changes: Belinda Olivares-Cunanan, "To lead by example; to inspire," *Mr. & Ms.*, Dec. 6, 1985, p. 18

47 She and Ninoy . . . reconciliation: "Boston memories," *PDE*, May 1, 1986, p. 5

47 Ninoy visited . . . parliamentary struggle: Yap, Dec. 29, 1986

47 She was sometimes . . . of guests: Oreta, Oct. 20, 1986

47 Once, a big rain . . . stay in exile": Alvarez, Oct. 27, 1986

47 "Doy, I'll . . . changed his mind: Lorna Kalaw-Tirol, "Ninoy's widow comes into her own," *Panorama*, Dec. 2, 1984, p. 16

48 "Why don't you . . . my chances": Porzio, p. 50; and interview, Lupita Aquino Kashiwahara, Nov. 25, 1986

48 Secretary of State . . . in the United States: Kashiwahara, Nov. 25, 1986

48 Ninoy had difficulties . . . from traveling: Yap, Dec. 29, 1986

48 FBI agents . . . "Nightline": Kashiwahara, Nov. 27, 1986. (Her husband is ABC correspondent Ken Kashiwahara.)

48 Finally, in 1983 . . . offers of help: Max Soliven, Oct. 29, 1986

48 He was sure . . . to move: Luis Beltran, "Remembering Ninoy," in *Ninoy Aquino*, p. 122

49 He wrote a . . . were experts: interview, Angelito Banayo, Dec. 5, 1986. Banayo would be appointed Cory Aquino's Postmaster General.

49 His mother warned . . . out of me." Aurora Aquino, Nov. 16, 1986

49 Cory did not want . . . so soon: ibid.

49 She told him . . . calloused: "My life with Ninoy," *Diplomacy*, Seoul, Oct. 25, 1986, p. 16

49 "Do you think . . . excuse": Zeitlin, p. 7

49 In June, she wrote . . . have to do": Belmonte, "President Cory's early years," *Diplomacy*, Seoul, Oct. 25, 1986, p. 12

49 Cory was frightened . . . prescribe drugs: Zeitlin, p. 7

50 At dinner, Cory . . . felt," Cory said: ibid.

50 In the morning . . . sadness: "My life with Ninoy," p. 16

50 On the way . . . Fort Bonifacio: Zeitlin, p. 7

50 "See you . . . good-bye: "My life with Ninoy," p. 16

50 "Just call . . . stop," she said: Crisostomo, p. 95

Chapter 5, The Opposition

51 hundreds . . . went up: "Aquino assassination: a year later," *BD*, Aug. 7, 1984, p. 20

52 "Even though . . . any land.": interview by author, Feb. 23, 1986.

52 Bishop Antonio . . . owners: interview, Bishop Antonio Mabutas of Davao, Feb. 18, 1986

52 "Nobody can . . . system," he said: interview, Jose Romero, Feb. 10, 1986

53 The other members . . . labor federation: They were, in the same order, Dante Santos, Luciano Salazar, Amado Dizon, and Ernesto Herrera.

53 "Even in the . . . ordered it": Jesselynn de la Cruz, "August thoughts from the Aquinos," *Veritas*, Aug. 19, 1984, p. 6

53 One theory . . . successor: "The Aquino Legacy," *FEER*, Aug. 30, 1984, p. 24

53 Cory said . . . place: "Aquino remains to QC Church," *BT*, Aug. 24, 1983, p. 1

54 She was very . . . to say: Porzio, p. 73

55 Cory thanked . . . resigns": "Demonstrations mark Aquino's birthday," *BD*, Nov. 28, 1983, p. 16

55 She called on . . . be afraid: Cory Aquino, Makati Rotary Club Speech, Dec. 6, 1983, in *Mr. & Ms.*, Dec. 27, 1983

56 "through the years . . . consideration: Cory Aquino, "To vote or boycott is only a question of strategy, *Mr. & Ms.*, Feb. 24, 1984, p. 22

56 "This is the . . . accept": interview, Noel Tolentino, was appointed by Cory as president of TV Channel 13, which was sequestered by the government. Dec. 16, 1986

56 At no time . . . political leader": "Cory is for participation," *Malaya*, Mar. 1, 1984, p. 1

57 She told them . . . April 6, 1978": "Mrs. Aquino urges people to give support to Namfrel," *Metro Manila Times*, Mar. 29, 1984

57 "It is unfortunate . . . situation": "Mrs. Aquino explains poll stand," *BT*, Mar. 2, 1984, p. 1

57 "When I crack . . . stories": Nini Sta. Romana-Cruz, "Please do not overestimate me," *Mr. & Ms.*, May 25, 1984, p. 29

57 "No, I don't . . . replied": "We are sending a message to Marcos," *Newsweek*, Aug. 20, 1984, p. 52

57 "When Ninoy . . . Cory Aquino": "Interview—Cory Aquino," *Asiaweek*, Mar. 16, 1984, p. 25

57 "Where do we . . . leading to?": "Prophet in his own country," *Veritas*, Aug. 26, 1984, p. 8

57 "The option . . . ambitions": "Millions turn out to remember Ninoy," *BD*, Aug. 22, 1984, p. 24

57 "It has been . . . might": "Aquino extolled on anniversary," *BT*, Aug. 22, 1984, p. 1

58 "saturnalia . . . forces": "The case against the military," *Newsweek*, Oct. 29, 1984, p. 10

58 "Wasn't Ninoy . . . approval: Crisostomo, p. 115

59 "Justice is not . . . power": "Cory still blames FM for Ninoy slay," *BD*, Oct. 25, 1984, p. 21

59 "I know there are . . . Pacific": U.S. Information Service, U.S. Embassy, Manila, Oct. 23, 1984

59 "People will be . . . reduced numbers: Aurora Aquino, Nov. 16, 1986

59 "A lot of people . . . changed": "RP tradition burdens Aquino's poll campaign," *Malaya*, Jan. 29, 1986, p. 6

59 "Cory Aquino . . . gone": Tessie Oreta, Oct. 20, 1986

Chapter 6, The Candidate

61 The people who had organized . . . group: The story of the convenor group and its meetings comes largely from interviews with Emanuel "Noel" Soriano, business consultant and former University of the Philippines president, who served as its secretary. Information about the National Unification Conference (NUC) comes from Francisco "Soc" Rodrigo, its secretary, and from Cecilia Muñoz Palma, its president.

61 Eleven potential . . . signed: Those who signed were Agapito "Butz" Aquino, Jose Diokno, Teofisto Guingona, Raul Manglapus, Ramon Mitra, Ambrosio Padilla, Aquilino Pimentel, Rafael Salas, and Jovito Salonga. Manglapus and Salas, who lived in the U.S., had representatives sign for them.

61 "Please stop . . . Gonzales: Belinda Olivares-Cunanan, "To lead by example; to inspire," *Mr.&Ms.*, Dec. 6, 1985, p. 9

62 "Are we . . . my head": Aurora Aquino, Nov. 16, 1986

62 leading political prisoners: Father Edicio de la Torre, Horacio "Boy" Morales, and Nemesio Prudente, of the Philippine College of Commerce.

62 "We badly . . . unity: "Cory urges unity," *Malaya*, Feb. 28, 1985, p. 8

62 account of a passenger: she was Rebecca Quijono.

62 The NUC conference . . . handkerchief: Soriano, Oct. 30, 1986.

62 The day before . . . with men: Belinda Olivares-Cunanan, "Cory comes into her own," *Mr.&Ms.*, March 22, 1985, p. 28

62 "If there's . . . candidate": "Muñoz Palma talks about woman power," *BT*, Mar. 12, 1985, p. 1

63 "I feel like . . . like it": Rodrigo, Nov. 22, 1986

63 They were . . . altogether: Olivares-Cunanan, "Cory comes into her own," p. 28

63 A few days . . . assertive: ibid.

63 "When I joined . . . inflexible: ibid.

63 "Look . . . to do?: William Stewart and Nelly Sindayen, "A Christmas Conversation," *Time*, Jan. 5, 1986, p. 17

63 "I cannot be . . . another": Olivares-Cunanan, "Cory comes into her own," p. 28

63 She felt . . . for her: Stewart and Sindayen, p. 17

64 "Have pity . . . mine": Olivares-Cunanan, "Cory Aquino: to lead by example; to inspire," p. 9

65 "We know that . . . transition": "Cory Aquino warns of Red takeover," *BT*, Aug. 17, 1985, p. 1

65 "Perhaps it . . . hardships": Cory reiterates decision not to run," *BD*, Sept. 18, 1985, p. 22

65 "What do . . . Aguas: Florence "Flory" Aguas, Dec. 29, 1986

66 "Cory please . . . yourself": Vicente Paterno in *People Power*, p. 44

66 "Please Lord . . . elections": Olivares-Cunanan, "Cory Aquino: to lead," p. 9

66 "without her knowledge": interview, Emigdio "Ding" Tanjuatco, Nov. 10, 1986

66 "If you are . . . to run?": interview, Joaquin "Chino" Roces, Nov. 11, 1986

67 When Laurel . . . encouragement: interview, Laurel spokesman Manuel Malvar, Dec. 17, 1986

67 "My family . . . signing": Aguas, Dec. 29, 1986

67 "I do not seek . . . candidacy: "Cory will run if . . . ," *Mr. &Ms.*, Oct. 25, 1985, p. 4

67 "She did not . . . snap vote: Olivares-Cunanan, "Cory Aquino: to lead," p. 10

67 She also . . . to raise: Aurora Aquino, Nov. 16, 1986

67 "When a certificate . . . way": Tanjuatco, Nov. 10, 1986

68 "That whole . . . inevitable": Olivares-Cunanan," Cory Aquino: to lead," p. 10

68 "My God . . . our people?": Sandra Burton, "Starting the campaign with hope and a prayer," *Time*, Jan. 5, 1987, p. 18

68 On Sunday . . . to the people: Olivares-Cunanan, "Cory Aquino: to lead," p. 10

68 a candidate . . . from Marcos: Burton, p. 18

68 Cory began to . . . older daughters: "Gosh, I've just got to do this," *FEER*, Dec. 19, 1985

68 She prayed . . . assassination: Olivares-Cunanan, "Cory Aquino: to lead," p. 10

69 "I do not think . . . anymore": Aurora Aquino, Nov. 16, 1986

69 They talked . . . Marcos regime: Soriano, Oct. 30, 1986

69 "Doy, I hope . . . each other": Olivares-Cunanan, "Cory Aquino: to lead," p. 10

69 Cory would say . . . to give in: Angelito Banayo, Dec. 5, 1986

69 Cory did not . . . leadership: Palma, Nov. 17, 1986

69 She thought . . . groups: Tanjuatco, Nov. 10, 1986

69 He was suspicious . . . to Cory: Rodrigo, Nov. 22, 1986; and Belinda Olivares-Cunanan, "Doy, how could you," *Mr. &Ms.*, Nov. 22, 1985, p. 12

70 "That's the . . . cannot": Olivares-Cunanan, "Cory Aquino: to lead," p. 10

70 "The tremendous . . . guidance": Rodrigo, Nov. 22, 1986

70 As she was . . . reborn in her: "The remarkable rise of a widow in yellow," *Newsweek*, Mar. 10, 1986, p. 167

70 "We must . . . best known": "Cory enters the fray," *Time*, Dec. 16, 1985, p. 8

70 What is . . . would win: Rodrigo, Nov. 22, 1986

70 Roces called . . . signatures": Roces, Nov. 11, 1985

70 "I've been . . . to stop": Soriano, Oct. 30, 1986

71 "I will never . . . election bill: "Unido insists on Laurel," *Times Journal*, Nov. 28, 1985, p. 1

71 But, after the . . . was to run: Soriano, Oct. 30, 1986

71 "Doy, I know . . . than you": Olivares-Cunanan, "Cory Aquino: to lead," p. 11

71 "If you're . . . help me soon": ibid.

71 "If I were . . . want to hear": "Cory drops hint on running," *Malaya*, Dec. 2, 1985, p. 1

71 "My number one . . . investigation: "Cory is not surprised," *Malaya*, Dec. 3, 1985, p. 1

72 Mondragon: it was owned by Jose Antonio Gonzalez who would be named Cory's tourism minister.

72 She said the major . . . soil: "Cory to run vs. FM! *Malaya*, Dec. 4, 1985, p. 1

72 "Who knows . . . my stand": "Aquino still wavers on bases," *Times Journal*, Dec. 19, 1985, p. 1

72 Her economic . . . achieve change: "Cory to run vs. FM": *Malaya*, Dec. 4, 1986, p. 1; and "Cory declares she will run in snap elections," *BD*, Dec. 4, 1986, p. 12

72 "All they have . . . violence": "Trial for FM—Cory," *PDI*, Dec. 13, 1985, p.1

72 Cory noticed . . . faith in her: Olivares-Cunanan, "Cory Aquino: to lead," p. 18

73 There was also . . . support for Cory: "U.S. pushing Laurel to join Aquino," *Honolulu Advertiser*, Dec. 5, 1985. This is widely believed, but Laurel spokesman Manuel Malvar denied it.

73 "Let us go . . . he told him: "Laurel blames Cory's advisors for collapse," *Malaya*, Dec. 10, 1985 p. 1; and Rodrigo, Nov. 22, 1986

73 When Rodrigo . . . like this?: Rodrigo, Nov. 22, 1986

73 "May I invite . . . waiting for": Soriano, Oct. 30, 1986

73 Laurel responded . . . slot: "Laurel denies withdraw yarn; Kalaw for VP," *PDE*, Dec. 8, 1985, p. 1

74 "May I ask . . . morning": Soriano, Oct. 30, 1986

74 "Why did you not . . . opposition party": Rodrigo, Nov. 22, 1986

74 Cory replied . . . broke up: Rodrigo.

74 "if I had . . . us": ibid.

75 She told . . . Laban ng Bayan coalition: "Finishing what Ninoy started," *FEER*, Dec. 19, 1985, p. 40

75 Laurel rejected . . . mate: "Aquino-Laurel break-up," *PDE*, Dec. 9, 1985, p. 1

75 Doy's . . . abused: said by Rene Espina, in "Aquino-Laurel break-up," p. 1

75 "Your Eminence . . . I will do it": interview, Jaime Cardinal Sin, Mar. 3, 1986

75 "If she . . . he said: "Laurel blames Cory's advisors for collapse," *Malaya*, Dec. 10, 1985, p. 1

76 Cory visited Cardinal . . . of Arc": Cardinal Sin in *People Power*, p. 48

76 "You are wise . . . decide": Cardinal Sin, Mar. 3, 1986

76 "The Laurels . . . your brothers": Aurora Aquino, Nov. 16, 1986

76 "We've agreed . . . later": Jose "Peping" Cojuangco, Dec. 11, 1986

Chapter 7, The Campaign

77 "As you can . . . eye bags": "Marcos faces biggest challenge in years," *AWSJ*, Dec. 14, 1986, p. 1

77 Back in Manila . . . simple situations: interview, Captain Rex Robles, Nov. 20, 1986

78 Elden Cruz . . . : the husband of Ballsy (Maria Elena)

78 She said she . . . regime": "Big Cory-Doy rally," *BT*, Dec. 16, 1985, p. 1

78 "join me . . . different from Marcos": "Contrasting styles clash in campaign," *BD*, Dec. 17, 1985, p. 20

78 "The Philippines . . . splendor": "Big Cory-Doy rally," p. 1

78 "I might sound . . . from fear": Aurora Aquino in *People Power*, pp. 47–8

79 "She was oozing . . . sad experiences": Antonio "Tony" Cuenco, Oct. 30, 1986

80 helped . . . pills: Lupita Kashiwahara, Nov. 27, 1986

80 "That is . . . theme": interview with journalist, not for attribution.

80 "I will retire . . . about it.": Porzio, p. 99

81 "Sometimes . . . know": "Cory needs P250 M for polls," *BD*, Dec. 6, 1985, p. 15

81 "Sometimes I can't . . . it is Cory.": "Aquino is quiet on politics interview," *AWSJ*, Mar. 13, 1986, p. 8

81 "I learned . . . my best": FM wasted RP wealth, says Cory," *Malaya*, Dec. 28, 1985, p. 1

81 "I do not . . . the government: "Cruel fate leads simple politician's wife to top," *BD*, Feb. 26, 1986, p. 8

81 "In a brainstorming . . . sisters: Emanuel "Noel" Soriano, Dec. 22, 1986

81 Cory declared that . . . in 1958: "Mrs. A talks on hacienda issue," *BT*, Dec. 31, 1985, p. 1

81 "We pay . . . she said: "Expropriation of Luisita politically motivated: Cory,"

BD, Dec. 30, 1985, p. 18. The family repeated its arguments and said it would appeal. See second footnote for p. 59. From "Hitting the family spread," *Asiaweek*, Jan. 26, 1986, p. 18

81 They got up to . . . needed: interview, Eulelio Lerum, Nov. 19, 1986. Lerum is president of the National Labor Union, which represents many Hacienda Luisita workers.

81 "It is not . . . co-owners," she said: "Hitting the family spread," p. 18

82 "I am . . . flexible": "Aquino still wavers on basis," *Times Journal*, Dec. 19, 1985, p. 1, from *Asiaweek*, Dec. 20, 1985

82 "What else . . . she replied: Jose "Peping" Cojuangco, Dec. 11, 1986

82 She also complained . . . a year: "Hidden wealth recall urged," *BT*, Jan. 1, 1986, p. 1

83 He said some . . . Party: "Opposition will give RP to communists—FM," *PDE*, Dec. 31, 1985, p. 1

83 "Are we going . . . he asked": 'What's Aquino's govt program?' Perez asks," *PDE*, Dec. 17, 1985, p. 1

83 "kind of embarrassing . . . woman": "Contrasting styles clash in campaign," *BD*, Dec. 17, 1985, p. 20

83 "If that is . . . his reforms: "FM links Aquino camp to communists," *PDE*, Dec. 24, 1985, p. 1

83 And he warned . . . a while": "How FM, Aquino see issues," *BD*, Dec. 26, 1985, p. 20

83 The Reform . . . if she won: "Halfway through campaign FM faces foe's groundswell," *Malaya*, Jan. 9, 1986, p. 1

84 By Christmas . . . percent of that. "Cory blitzes through provinces as Marcos marks time in palace," *BD*, Dec. 23, 1985, p. 28

84 At first . . . would win: "Cory says all support welcome," *BT*, Jan. 4, 1986, p. 1; and "Leytenos agog over Cory, give 'thumbs down' to FM," *Malaya*, Jan. 5, 1986, p. 8

84 In Cebu . . . elected in 1984: "Cory's people power," *Malaya*, Feb. 6, 1986, p. 16

84 In one town . . . to end it: "Tabuk warriors welcome Cory-Doy in Kalinga," *PDI*, Jan. 8, 1986, p. 1; and "Aquino disavows red link, says boycott won't hurt her," *BD*, Jan. 8, 1986, p. 1

85 Marcos countered . . . property: "Marcos warns nation," BT, Jan. 1, 1986, p. 1

85 He said one . . . government: "Opposition dared to present plan on anti-insurgency," *PDE*, Jan. 1, 1986, p. 1

85 Cory had said . . . everybody's help": "The Aquino Challenge," *Asiaweek*, Jan. 26, 1986, p. 13

85 "I will not appoint . . . in communism": "Aquino reaffirms anti-communist stand," *BT*, Jan. 12, 1986, p. 1

85 "All along . . . been dead": "I don't believe that he will never give up," *FEER*, Feb. 20, 1986, p. 11

85 He said . . . "anti-fascism": "Sison bares support for Cory," *BD*, Jan. 2, 1986, p. 12

86 On New Year's . . . technical support: "Laurel signs merger pact; Jovy hedges," *Malaya*, Jan. 4, 1986, p. 1

86 He argued . . . rebellion: "Cory knew of Ninoy's setting up of NPA—FM," *PDE*, Jan. 5, 1986, p. 1

86 "I'm a woman . . . government": "Cory refutes landgrab rap," *Malaya*, Dec. 29, 1985, p. 1

86 "Ninoy fought . . . fight": "Unido, Laban join forces," *BT*, Jan. 3, 1986, p. 1

87 "I continue . . . the press. ".5-M greet Cory, Doy in Cebu City," *Malaya*, Jan. 12, 1986, p. 1

87 A brouhaha . . . the country: "No such deal—Aquino," *BT*, Jan. 14, 1986, p. 1; and "Secessionist deal bared," *BT*, Jan. 15, 1986, p. 1

87 "Our opponent . . . manicured": "Cory doesn't wear makeup or manicure her nails, says Imelda," *PDI*, Jan. 14, 1986, p. 3

87 "Like you . . . justice: "Negros crowds mob A-L team," *BD*, Dec. 23, 1985, p. 28

87 "Cory, you are . . . another widow: "Cory-Doy tandem rallies Antiqueños," *Malaya*, Jan. 14, 1986, p. 1; and "Cory reaches Iloilo," *BD*, Jan. 15, 1986, p. 12

87 As the campaign . . . confrontation": "Marcos to be tried for human rights violations, Cory says," *BD*, Jan. 2, 1986, p. 22

88 "If the votes . . . retirable": "Cory pledges to lead demos if FM defies people's will," *BD*, Jan. 16, 1986, p. 19

88 She suggested . . . insurgency: "Marcos to be tried for human rights violations, Cory says," p. 22

88 Cory outlined her program . . . monopolies: Published by Aquino for President campaign and reprinted by *PDI*, Jan. 18, 19, 20, 1986.

89 The original draft . . . the parents": Soriano, Dec. 22, 1986

89 Once, on the way . . . the teeth: Lupita Kashiwahara, Nov. 27, 1986

90 "I was too . . . to go": interview with journalist, not for attribution.

90 On the island of Negros . . . passed through: Kashiwahara, Nov. 27, 1986

90 She called on him . . . if he dares": "Cory: FM is Miranda bomber," *PDI*, Jan. 21, 1986, p. 2

90 Marcos, apparently . . . bedroom": "FM: women's place is bedroom," *PDI*, Jan. 21, 1986, p. 1

90 "How do you . . . opponents": "Tearing down the dictatorship, rebuilding democracy," *PDI*, Jan. 26, 28, 29, 1986

91 Cory made a return . . . processing zone: "Aquino says no to Bataan nuclear plant," *Malaya*, Feb. 1, 1986, p. 1

91 "I dare you . . . but bullets": "Cory dares Marcos to take up the gun," *PDI*, Feb. 3, 1986, p. 1

91 "The yellow revolution . . . new beginning": author's notes

Chapter 8, The Election

93 "The fields . . . heads": "Cory's people power," *Malaya*, Feb. 6, 1986, p. 16

93 She would ask . . . her desperation: "Aquino warns of 'angry people'; she's just desperate, says Marcos," *BD*, Feb. 7, 1986, p. 19

93 Cardinal Sin . . . fraud: "FM, Cory: 'Keep Cool'," *PDI*, Feb. 7, 1986, p. 1

94 Cory would think . . . his party: "The people's power," *Newsweek*, Feb. 24, 1986, p. 10

94 Members of the Reformist . . . polling booths: Paul Aquino, Oct. 20, 1986

94 "Today is . . . to win": "Cory Aquino claims victory," *BT*, Feb. 8, 1986, p. 1

95 The Regional . . . for Marcos: "Cory enjoys lead," *PDI*, Feb. 10, 1986, p. 1

95 Marines landed . . . canvass: "Opposition fight turns to Batasan," *PDE* Feb. 20, 1986, p. 1

95 In Tarlac . . . Marcos votes: "Marcos fights to stem the 'Cory' Tide," *FEER*, Feb. 20, 1986, p. 11

95 In one . . . existed: "Opposition fight turns to Batasan," *PDE*, Feb. 20, 1986, p. 1

95 The opposition . . . intimidation: "Aquino hits U.S. proposal," *BT*, Feb. 13, 1986, p. 1

96 "The Marcos spell . . . we know it": "We have prevailed," *MT*, Feb. 8, 1986, p. 1

96 Her "secret . . . counted: Paul Aquino, Oct. 20, 1986

96 Cory, acting . . . demonstrations: Author's notes, and "Aquino seeks FM meet-

ing," *BT*, Feb. 9, 1986, p. 1; "Concede, Cory tells Marcos," *Times Journal*, Feb. 9, p. 1; "Cory asks Marcos to concede defeat," *BD*, Feb. 9, p. 7

96 "These are . . . percent: "Cory to FM: Concede to preserve peace," *PDI*, Feb. 9, 1986, p. 2

97 The Reform . . . to be heard: "Moderate opposition, Church, reformist military in alliance," *BD*, Feb. 17, 1986, p. 5

97 Back in Washington . . . stable democracy": press release, U.S. Embassy, Manila, Feb. 11, 1986

98 "There you are . . . president: "Cory urges RP's allies to stop supporting FM," *BD*, Feb. 12, 1986, p. 2

98 She was angered . . . he had sent: "Aquino seeks European, Japanese boycott of FM," *BD*, Feb. 20, 1986, p. 20

98 "No Filipino . . . of Marcos: "Aquino airs appeal to U.S.," *BT*, Feb. 12, 1986, p. 1

98 Ongpin . . . the Left: "The people's power," *Newsweek*, Feb. 24, 1986, p. 10

98 She said she "knew . . . and honor": "Cory's statement," *Malaya*, Feb. 12, 1986, p. 3

99 She rejected the idea . . . leadership: "Moderate opposition, Church, reformist military in alliance," p. 5

99 "I have not talked . . . to him": Armando Doronila, "Shared power is ruled out," *MT*, Feb. 22, 1986, p. 1

99 And she did not . . . carry them out: Fulgencio Factoran, "Non-cooperation, not civil disobedience," *BD*, Feb. 21, 1986, p. 6

99 "Oh my gosh . . . laughter: Noel Tolentino, Dec. 16, 1986.

100 The president of . . . strike: "Big businessmen back Cory," *MT*, Feb. 22, 1986, p. 1

100 She had been to . . . of that!: Cardinal Sin, Mar. 3, 1986

100 A week after . . . credible result: "Aquino to ignore official canvass," *Times Journal*, Feb. 15, 1986, p. 1

101 "Mr. Marcos controls . . . to go?": "When is he going to go?," *Sunday Times*, Feb. 16, 1986, p. 1

101 The report cited . . . some areas: "Cory could have won by a landslide," *MC*, Aug. 24, 1986, p. 1

101 Reagan issued . . . U.S. bases: "Everybody lost," *Newsweek*, Feb. 24, 1986, p. 8

102 No politicians . . . invited: Florence "Flory" Aguas, Dec. 29, 1986

102 "Look . . . to know: interview, Solita "Winnie" Monsod, Dec. 17, 1986

102 I have to . . . I won": "Aquino is quiet on politics in interview," *AWSJ*, Mar. 13, 1986, p. 8

102 The big turnout . . . to the people: ibid.

102 There was, however . . . demonstrations: "Aquino's weak stance bewailed," *Sunday Times*, Feb. 21, 1986, p. 16

102 "The majority . . . her": Tolentino, Dec. 16, 1986

103 "Many of my . . . harder": Doronila, p. 1

103 The next . . . economic aid: Crisostomo, p. 197

103 "What can I . . . polls": Crisostomo, p. 196

103 "Don't see . . . told them: "FM the next Duvalier—Cory," *PDI*, Feb. 20, 1986, p. 1

103 "Although this . . . two-party system: "Cory meets Habib, presses for transition of power," *Malaya*, Feb. 18, 1986, p. 1

104 On Friday . . . with Marcos: Doronila, p. 1

104 She told him . . . government: "Cory is safe in Cebu," *Sunday Times*, Feb. 23, 1986, p. 1

104 "Wait and . . . told him: "Habib off today for US," *BT*, Feb. 22, 1986, p. 1

104 Cory did . . . trust Reagan: Doronila, p. 1
104 Habib would . . . economic aid: Doronila, p. 1

Chapter 9, Revolution

105 Juan Ponce Enrile . . . born Feb. 14, 1924: "Enrile: from peasant boy to defense minister," *The Philippine Star*, Nov. 24, 1986, p. 6
105 Then in the 1980s . . . of Cagayan: Arillo, p. 127
106 Enrile responded . . . and arms: Arillo, p. 137
106 Some people . . . coup: Enrile allegedly had gotten a report that Ver was plotting, in the event of Marcos's death, to install Imelda as president for six months, then seize power himself.
106 Ver's son . . . Marcos refused: Alfred McCoy, Marian Wilkinson, Gwen Robinson, "Coup! The real story behind the February revolt," *Veritas*, October 1986, part I, p. 5
107 They met during . . . machine guns: McCoy, Wilkinson, Robinson, part I, p. 6
107 The strategy . . . figurehead: interview with Ministry of National Defense (MND) officer, not for attribution.
107 "Stop pushing . . . he told them: "Marcos plays rough," *Newsweek*, Jan. 27, 1986, p. 6
107 "Don't exacerbate . . . tolerating you": interview with MND officer, not for attribution.
107 "It gave us . . . involved: ibid.
108 Leading Aquino . . . money: McCoy, Wilkinson, Robinson, part I, p.7
108 In January . . . defend yourselves": Captain Rex Robles, Nov. 20, 1986
108 "We have to . . . being my own?": "I don't believe that he will never give up," *FEER*, Feb. 20, 1986, p. 11
108 However, her brother . . . the better": Jose "Peping" Cojuangco, Dec. 11, 1986
108 Some representatives . . . the president: Robles, Nov. 20, 1986
108 A week before . . . their plans: McCoy, Wilkinson, Robinson, part I, p. 7
108 "We knew something . . . preempted": interview with MND officer, not for attribution.
109 The CIA station . . . self-defense: McCoy, Wilkinson, Robinson, part I, p. 8
109 Ver, kept . . . approached: ibid.
109 On Wednesday . . . his future: ibid.
110 Enrile's troops . . . of arms: Arillo, p. 150
110 "Don't let her . . . Robles warned: Robles, Nov. 20, 1986
110 "There's no way . . . organized them: Cojuangco, Dec. 11, 1986
110 At midnight . . . join the junta: McCoy, Wilkinson, Robinson, part I, p. 2
110 The rebellious . . . attack plans: ibid.
110 That morning . . . Fort Bonifacio: Arillo, pp. 9–10
111 Enrile telephoned Ramos . . . went to Camp Aguinaldo: *People Power*, p. 104; and McCoy, Wilkinson, Robinson, part I, p. 2
111 the Japanese ambassador: Kiyoshi Somiya
111 "Go to the . . . end of your life": Cardinal Sin, Mar. 3, 1986
111 "Go to Camp . . . in danger": McCoy, Wilkinson, Robinson, part II, p. 3
112 She said there . . . turn over power: "Cebu rejects FM rule," *Malaya*, Feb. 23, 1986, p. 1
112 Journalist Belinda . . . camp Aguinaldo: interview, Belinda Olivares, Dec. 18, 1986. (Ms. Olivares generally is known by her maiden name, but signs her articles Olivares-Cunanan.)

113 "I was informed . . . to the camp": McCoy, Wilkinson, Robinson, part II, p. 3
113 "As of now . . . the movement: Arillo, pp. 21–22
113 Ramos declared . . . military reformists: Arillo, pp. 24–25
113 "I am not making . . . my mind": Arillo, p. 27
114 After the broadcast . . . the next morning: Olivares, Dec. 18, 1986
114 The opposition . . . friends: ibid.
114 Cory called . . . minutes later: Miguel Perez-Rubio, Dec. 15, 1986
114 It was their . . . assassination: Porzio, p. 112
114 She asked Enrile . . . presidency: Arillo, p. 68
114 "Madam . . . to pray": Crisostomo, p. 208
115 Ver begged . . . the palace": McCoy, Wilkinson, Robinson, part II, p. 3
115 At 9 p.m. . . . . motorcycle: Cojuangco, Dec. 11, 1986
115 The gate . . . building: Antonio "Tony" Cuenco, Oct. 30, 1986
115 Cory went . . . radio reports: Cojuangco, Dec. 11, 1986
115 She slept . . . defend her: Porzio, p. 112
115 "I am deeply . . . to eat": Cardinal Sin in *People Power*, p. 105; Cardinal Sin, Dec. 27, 1986.
116 Cory would later . . . laymen: quote from Cory Aquino, "I support any movement that will unite all of us," *Veritas*, May 29, 1986, p. 14
116 "Justice, is it true . . . be careful": Cecilia Muñoz Palma in *People Power*, p. 106
117 she said a lot . . . on the plane: "Aquino is quiet on politics in interview," *AWSJ*, Mar. 13, 1986, p. 8
117 She called Cardinal . . . our prayers": Cardinal Sin in *People Power*, p. 119
117 "An overwhelming . . . against us": Arillo, p. 72
118 Enrile called . . . hold the tanks: Crisostomo, p. 222
118 "On Sunday . . . Corazon C. Aquino": "New govt under Cory set up," *BD*, Feb. 25, 1986, p. 1
118 Enrile told opposition leaders: Ernesto Maceda, former Ambassador Jose Laurel III, and Batangas Governor Jose Laurel IV
118 He declared . . . preconditions: "Opposition may form own govt," *PDE*, Feb. 24, 1986, p. 1
118 Across the . . . embraced the rebels: Military officer, not for attribution.
118 In Washington . . . in the U.S.: U.S. State Dept.
119 "I am responsible . . . to them": Jose "Apeng" Yap, Dec. 29, 1986
120 "If you do . . . by myself": Cory Aquino in *People Power*, p. 209
120 For the . . . vigilance: "Aquino greets followers," *BD*, Feb. 25, 1986, p. 3
120 Enrile told him . . . military operation": Luis Villafuerte, Dec. 19 and 28, 1986. Villafuerte became Cory's minister of reorganization.
120 "It should be . . . the country": Cardinal Sin, Mar. 3, 1986
120 The U.S. also . . . the suggestion: Cardinal Sin, Dec. 27, 1986
120 Washington knew . . . assault: interview, Allan Croghan, U.S. press officer, Manila, Dec. 12, 1986
120 "We felt . . . side": interview, military officers, not for attribution.
121 Ver was already . . . other side: McCoy, Wilkinson, Robinson, part II, p. 6
121 "No way am I . . . in the past": Cory Aquino, p. 209, and Rafael Ongpin, pp.233–4, in *People Power*.
121 "I have decided . . . civilian president": Belinda Olivares-Cunanan, "Cory insisted on being a civilian president," *PDI*, Oct. 17, 1986, p. 5
121 General Ramos recommended . . . refused": Ongpin in *People Power*, p. 234
122 "I wouldn't want . . . bring me": Olivares-Cunanan, "Cory insisted," p. 5
122 "I just want . . . Mrs. Aquino": Crisostomo, p. 230
123 Bosworth phoned Cory . . . leave the country": Porzio, p. 116

Reference Notes

Chapter 10, The Presidency

124 She did not . . . speeches: Tessie Oreta, Oct. 20, 1986

124 She believed . . . moved her: interview, Jose Concepcion, Dec. 24, 1986

124 During . . . steel": Agapito "Butz" Aquino, Oct. 14, 1986

125 "The whole . . . her face": Solita "Winnie" Monsod, Dec. 17, 1986

125 "It takes . . . forgive them": "Cory Aquino on Ninoy's assassination," *Veritas*, Jan. 1, 1984, p. 8

125 "Women are . . . of peace": William Stewart and Nelly Sindayen, "A Christmas Conversation," *Time*, Jan. 5, 1987, p. 17

125 Singapore's . . . her people": "U.S. no stranger to Mrs. Aquino," *Philippine Star*, Sept. 15, 1986

125 "I always have . . . my own boss": The presidency must be something; even my mother-in-law apologizes to me," *Sunday Inquirer Magazine*, June 8, 1986, p. 8

126 "Oh, Miguel . . . President more": Miguel Perez-Rubio, Dec. 15, 1986

126 Marcos, presiding . . . everyone else: ibid.

126 "Now I know . . . lionized": Paul Aquino, Oct. 20, 1986

126 "I guess . . . red lights": "U.S. no stranger to Mrs. Aquino," *Philippine Star*, Sept. 15, 1986

126 "Before, I used . . . it's different": "The presidency must be something . . . ", pp. 28–29

126 "One day . . . Cory government": Rene Saguisag, Dec. 13, 1986

127 Some opposition . . . appointees: Jose "Apeng" Yap, Dec. 29, 1986

127 Enrile would . . . appointments: Juan Ponce Enrile, Dec. 23, 1986

127 "How many . . . Salonga?": "Holding it all together," *FEER*, Aug. 28, 1986

128 "You said we . . . later that day: Cecilia Muñoz Palma, Nov. 17, 1986

128 other members of the cabinet: Cory also chose Saguisag as her spokesman, and former journalist Teodoro "Teddy" Locsin, Jr., whose family's *Free Press* magazine had been closed under martial law, was made information minister (he was later press spokesman and then speechwriter). Palma proposed Mita Pardo de Tavera for minister of social services. She had worked with her in the Medical Action Group, a human rights organization. Cory appointed her several days later. Cory also later named Letitia Shahani, a former United Nations official who had left her job to campaign for Cory, as deputy foreign minister. Shahani's father had been an ambassador, and her brother was General Ramos.

128 When Cory reported . . . six-figure incomes: Enrile listed his worth as over $1 million, Laurel as nearly $1 million, Concepcion about $1.5 million, Ongpin nearly $1.5 million, Mitra about $863,000. Saguisag, the human rights lawyer, was at the bottom, at just $22,000. "Aquino reports P17.7 M," *MB*, Apr. 18, 1986, p. 1

129 "The need . . . the decisions": Angelito Banayo, Dec. 5, 1986

130 "I've had . . . work together": "Cory Aquino tells how she scolded cabinet," *BD*, Mar. 7, 1986, p. 5

130 "Thank God . . . her aides: interview, Teodoro "Teddy" Locsin, Jan. 2, 1987

130 In a committee . . . respectively: interview, Luis Villafuerte, Dec. 19, 1986

131 "We have to . . . do it": Palma, Nov. 17, 1986

131 Its general secretary . . . Batasan: "Unido describes Aquino gov't dictatorial; alliance near end?" *BD*, Apr. 2, 1986, p. 14

132 "They were . . . much weight": interview, Aquilino Pimentel, Oct. 28, 1986

133 On the island . . . appointments: Seth Mydans, "Aquino is pulling up the establishment by its roots," *New York Times*, Aug. 17, 1986, sec. 4

133 In his home . . . February election: interview, Anthony Spaeth, correspondent, *AWSJ*, Jan. 5, 1987

133 A Unido governor . . . in 1992," he said: interview, Leandro Verceles, Dec. 23, 1986

133 Of the hundreds . . . about appointments: Spaeth, Jan. 5, 1987

134 "I beg you . . . to freedom": speech May 23, 1986

135 "If there are . . . to share": Noel Tolentino, Dec. 16, 1986

135 She and her aides . . . referendum: Locsin, Jan. 2, 1987

136 They wished . . . policy: Saguisag, Dec. 13, 1986

136 In an effort . . . for review: "Aquino shows tough mettle amid problems," *Malaya*, June 4, 1986, p. 1

137 "You lost . . . disgust: heard by author during interview with Salonga, Dec. 24, 1986

137 "You release . . . leading them": Saguisag, Dec. 13, 1986

137 A trip . . . world leaders: "We have to reach out," *Asiaweek*, Sept. 28, 1986, p. 14

Chapter 11, Confronting the Military and the Rebels

140 "I have had . . . world": "Cory bares talks with communists," *BD*, Mar. 10, 1986, p. 1

140 Saguisag . . . conflict: "Cory may take bold steps," *Sunday Times*, Mar. 2, 1986, p. 1

140 The National . . . those gains: "NDF hails Aquino ascension," *BD*, Mar. 5, 1986, p. 12

140 She announced the restoration . . . was to succeed: "Cory showing political skills," *MT*, Mar. 3, 1986, p. 1

140 Cory's mother-in-law . . . were none: Aurora Aquino, Dec. 28, 1986

141 "Marcos is not . . . the country: "Can Cory's yellow blend with the NPA's red?" *PDI*, June 4, 1986, p. 3

142 Cory ordered . . . peace talks: "Ceasefire on in Mindanao," *MB*, Mar. 18, 1986, p. 1

142 "Only by exposing . . . of our country": speech Mar. 22, 1986

143 "The coup rumors . . . Marcos's KBL: interview, Renato Cayetano, Dec. 19, 1986

143 "Of course . . . support me": "Aquino admits own set of cronies," *PT*, Apr. 24, 1986, p. 4

143 They said they . . . impossible: "NPA cadres cautious in reacting to Cory's win," *BD*, Mar. 25, 1986, p. 18

143 In a statement . . . spheres": "Giving peace another chance," *Asiaweek*, May 4, 1986, p. 20

143 Tony Cuenco . . . dismantled: "Aquino eyes solid political mass base," *BD*, Apr. 11, 1986, p. 22

143 In a speech in April . . . renege on any": speech, University of the Philippines graduation, Apr. 20, 1986

144 He announced that the army . . . cease-fire: "Giving peace another chance," p. 20

144 He said also . . . selectively: "Stronger civilian-military links urged," *BD*, Apr. 23, 1986, p. 5

144 A group of KBL . . . president: "Batasan eyes new president," *PDE*, Apr. 1, 1986, p. 1

144 "Let them reconvene . . . they want," she said: "MPs in 'rump' session won't be arrested—Cory," *Manila Evening Post*, Apr. 11, 1986, p.1

145 Laurel, appearing . . . economic stability: "Stronger civilian-military links urged," p. 5

145 In May . . . talks: "Insurgency: Cory's real problem," *Sunday Times*, June 15, 1986, p. 6

145 "Nene . . . to him": interview with journalist, not for attribution, confirmed by Teodoro "Teddy" Locsin, Jan. 4, 1987

145 "In this period . . . New York": Locsin, Jan. 4, 1987

145 "If I were to . . . her surrender: "Aquino, rebels hold dialogue," *MB*, May 24, 1986, p. 1

145 Later in the day . . . for its continued existence": speech May 23, 1986

147 Some of Cory's ministers . . . knew it: Luis Villafuerte, Dec. 28, 1986

147 She told the military . . . till victory: "Aquino warns rebs: ceasefire or war," *PDE*, May 25, 1986, p. 1

147 Cory said in her speech . . . insurgent leadership: "Can Cory's yellow blend," p. 34; interview, Locsin, Jan. 2, 1987

147 "They tell her . . . them off": Locsin, Jan. 2, 1986

147 Enrile would say . . . reconciliation": Juan Ponce Enrile, Dec. 23, 1986

148 Speaking through . . . armed forces: " 'Fragile coalition' worries communists," *Malaya*, June 2, 1986, p. 1

148 "It would have been . . . each other": "The presidency must be something; even my mother-in-law apologizes to me," *Sunday Inquirer Magazine*, June 8, 1986, p. 8

148 She said that . . . Fabian Ver: "Cory vows all effort for peace," *MT*, June 13, 1986, p. 1

148 "The military is not . . . in detention: "Can Cory's yellow blend," p. 34

148 The problem is . . . in jail": "I won't abandon Enrile—Aquino," *MT*, June 20, 1986, p. 1

148 "It is unsettling . . . political detainees: "Aquino sees Ramos, denies coup rumors," *MB*, June 20, 1986, p. 1

149 Cory saw . . . their region: "Mindanao group to brief Cory," *MC*, June 18, 1986, p. 2

149 "I'm not one . . . of Churches: "Aquino sees Ramos," p. 1

149 That same day . . . lose them: "Loyalists don't worry Aquino," *MC*, June 21, 1986, p. 1

149 "If things are . . . here anymore": "Aquino admits she would be helpless in a coup d'etat," *PT*, June 21, 1986, p. 1

149 NDF leader Tony . . . reform program: "NDF leaders praise Aquino but call for more reforms," *MB*, June 24, 1986, p. 1

Chapter 12, The Manila Hotel Incident

151 The 75-year-old . . . to Cory: "Aquino wins first round vs. loyalists," *BD*, July 9, 1986, p. 5

151 "I'm not really afraid . . . bother me": "Despite difficulties, we got results," *PT*, June 4, 1986, p. 1

152 The plan had . . . hold Cory hostage: "Marcos waiting, watching events," *Manila Evening Post*, July 7, 1986, p. 1

152 The palace learned . . . Abadilla men": Teodoro "Teddy" Locsin, Jan. 2, 1987

153 "When they started . . . situation": "Aquino wins first round vs. loyalists," p. 5

154 "I hereby order . . . to the Philippines": "Tolentino takes oath as veep; claims he is 'acting president'," *BD*, July 7, 1986, p. 1

154 Inside the . . . back there": Marcos's conversations are based on "Allegiance? No way—Recto," *PDI*, July 11, 1986, p. 1; "Marcos gave phone orders during coup," *MC*, Aug. 17, 1986, p. 1; and "FM involved in coup," *News Herald*, Aug. 18, 1986, p. 6

155 Enrile ordered . . . for the moment": "Leave them alone," *Peoples Journal*, July 7, 1986, p. 1

155 He said, "How do . . . attack them?: Niñez Cacho-Olivares, "Wake up, Mrs. Aquino," *BD*, July 10, 1986, p. 4

155 She said she would . . . action," she said: "File sedition raps vs. Tolentino—Aquino," *MT*, July 7, 1986. p. 1

155 "We have only one . . . need to panic": "Cory faces armed challenge," *MC*, July 7, 1986, p. 1

156 He said Tolentino . . . actions: "Leave them alone," p. 1

156 In Honolulu . . . developments": "Marcos waiting, watching events," *Manila Evening Post*, July 7, 1986, p. 1

156 "Maybe seventy-two . . . she agreed: interview, Enrile, Dec. 23, 1986

156 "I want to reassure . . . here on": "The president's statement," *Malaya*, July 8, 1986, p. 1; and "Aquino gives ultimatum: leave Manila Hotel or else," *MT*, July 8, 1986, p. 1

156 "This is not . . . cool head": "'Foolish attempt'—Cory," *News Herald*, July 8, 1986, p. 1

156 "I don't know . . . she declared: "Tolentino gov't collapses; troopers yield," *MB*, July 8, 1986, p. 1

157 "Let us not . . . embarrassing them": "Putsch collapses," *News Herald*, July 8, 1986, p. 1

157 "There has been . . . the people": "Tolentino calls for early polls," *PT*, July 8, 1986, p. 1

157 "We did not . . . told another journalist: "Poor parody of February," *MC*, July 8, 1986, p. 1

157 Marcos, keeping . . . the country: "FM disowns coup try; blames Cory," *News Herald*, July 8, 1986, p. 1

157 Enrile told . . . had happened": "Generals quit, vow anti-red campaign," *Manila Evening Post*, July 8, 1986, p. 1

157 "We welcome you . . . our fold": "Manila's armed farce," *Asiaweek*, July 20, 1986, p. 10

157 "We understand the pressure . . . be fulfilled": "No charges to be filed vs. soldiers," *MB*, July 9, 1986, p. 1

158 "The push-ups . . . afterward: "Cory asks for Tolentino's loyalty," *BD*, July 10, 1986, p. 28

158 "My supporters . . . the leaders": "Rebellion charge vs. Tolentino held": *MT*, July 9, 1986, p. 1

158 "It's easy for you . . . inquired Ramos: Locsin, Jan. 2, 1987

158 "They shouldn't . . . Laurel: "Cory not keen on loyalist charges," *PDI*, July 26, 1986, p. 1

158 "Okay, okay . . . of Tolentino": "No charges to be filed vs. soldiers," p. 1

159 Some in the . . . warn the president: Luis Villafuerte, Dec. 28, 1986

159 "I am glad . . . behind us": "Loyalists go free," *PDI*, July 10, 1986, p. 1

159 "Any group . . . open arms": "Wake up, Mrs. Aquino," p. 4

159 She told a meeting . . . single life": "Leniency pays," *MB*, July 11, 1986, p. 1

159 "I was really . . . going on": "Aquino wants to find out truth on Manila Hotel siege," *Sunday Times*, July 20, 1986, p. 6

159 General Ramos sent . . . by the president: memo from Ramos on "Achieving Unity in the New AFP," July 16, 1986

160 President Reagan . . . permit that": "No evidence of FM involvement—Reagan," *MB*, July 11, 1986, p. 1

160 Enrile said . . . and brandy: "No charges yet vs. coup leaders—MOJ," *Malaya*, July 22, 1986, p. 1

160 "I too felt . . . Hotel incident": "Cory not keen on loyalist charges," p. 1

161 "I hoped . . . of this": "Door still open for clemency," *MB*, July 31, 1986, p. 1

161 "I don't see . . . to justice": "No more clemency for Tolentino & Co.," *PDI*, Aug. 1, 1986, p. 1

161 "I still consider . . . dormant": "Tolentino on oath: only to the republic," *PDE*, Aug. 9, 1986, p. 1

161 Tolentino refused to pay . . . attraction: "Rebellion raps vs. Tolentino dropped," *BD*, Sept. 2, 1986, p. 12

161 "A room with a coup": *FEER*, July 17, 1986, p. 14

162 "Based on testimony . . . to have known": Jose Concepcion, Dec. 24, 1986

Chapter 13, Peace Talks

164 Cory called Butz . . . wants," she said: Agapito "Butz" Aquino, Oct. 18, 1986

165 "Yes, immediately . . . government": Butz Aquino, Oct. 18, 1986

165 "What are they . . . Locsin: Teodoro "Teddy" Locsin, Jan. 4, 1987

165 Cory ordered . . . not move: "Cory acts to remove warlords," *MC*, July 16, 1986, p. 1

166 "Johnny we have . . . press reports: "Holding it all together," *FEER*, Aug. 28, 1986

166 "Madame . . . told her: Juan Ponce Enrile, Dec. 23, 1986

166 She repeated . . . the rebels: "Cory, Enrile views don't jibe on TV," *MC*, July 18, 1986, p. 1

166 The Communist . . . reactionary: "Many people disillusioned—CPP," *PDE*, Aug. 27, 1986, p. 1

166 In August . . . families: "Aquino chides lawyers for apathy," *MT*, Aug. 30, 1986, p. 1

166 In 1913 . . . of the land: Alan Robles, "The 'Muslim problem': a worsening conflict," *MC*, Jan. 4, 1987, p. 10

167 NDF negotiators . . . NDF officials: "Aquino asks NPA to stop hostilities," *MT*, Aug. 20, 1986, p. 1

168 Lieutenant Victor Corpus . . . happened to him: interview, Victor Corpus, Dec. 20, 1986

169 Military officials . . . of the region: "Cory overrules PSG, insists on Jolo meet," *PDI*, Sept. 2, 1986, p. 1

169 "Misuari does not . . . protocol": "Aquino, Misuari agree on halt to hostilities," *MT*, Sept. 6, 1986, p. 1

169 "Our struggle . . . Philippines": "Cory flies south; Nur set to listen," *PDI*, Sept. 5, 1986, p. 1

170 "We have been . . . the Philippines": "The wounds of war take time to heal," *MC*, Sept. 8, 1986, p. 8

170 When Misuari came . . . guards: Locsin, Jan. 2, 1987

170 "Everybody forgot . . . listen": Butz Aquino, Oct. 18, 1986

170 "I came here . . . to attain peace": "Peace in Mindanao," *New Day*, Sept. 8, 1986, p. 1

170 Cory felt his eyes . . . her up: "Aquino warns U.S. not to meddle," *BD*, Sept. 11, 1986, p. 21

170 "It must be very . . . is concerned": ibid.
171 Misuri said he appreciated . . . our people": "Peace in Mindanao," p. 1
171 Cory was furious . . . never consult": Locsin, Jan. 2, 1987
171 "Let's just . . . fuming: ibid.
171 Enrile said . . . Butz Aquino": Enrile, Dec. 23, 1986
171 "I knew . . . Front": ibid.
172 "It has been our . . . our forces": "A meeting of several compromises," *PDI*, Sept. 16, 1986, p. 6
172 She had come . . . for justice": "Aquino, Balweg meet; peace accord is signed," *MB*, Sept. 14, 1986, p. 1
172 "The key to . . . nationwide": "Talking peace in the high mountains," *Veritas*, Nov. 27, 1986, p. 14
172 "We have a common . . . loss of lives," he said: "Aquino, Balweg meet," p. 1
173 "We could work . . . explained later: Enrile, Dec. 23, 1986
173 Balweg drove . . . the next week: Filipino guerrilla heroes have become popular film subjects. Commander Dante and Victor Corpus no sooner got out of the military prisons where they had spent most of the past decade than they were hired as consultants for the movie versions of their lives.

Chapter 14, Economy

175 She later would . . . aid the poor: speech before conference of Christian Democratic International, Dec. 13, 1986
175 In Manhattan . . . capacity: speech given Sept. 19, 1986
176 "My heart . . . to pay": Solita "Winnie" Monsod, Dec. 17, 1986
176 In December . . . Spaeth concluded: Anthony Spaeth, Jan. 5, 1987
176 The government is . . . union": Monsod, Dec. 17, 1986
176 There were no well-organized . . . efficiently: "US discounts Aquino Ouster," *AWSJ*, Nov. 16, 1986, p. 5
177 After providing . . . treasury: "P3.9-B employment program suspended," *MT*, Dec. 2, 1986, p. 1
177 Investment from January . . . 38 percent: Jose Galang, "A new strategy for industrial renaissance," *FEER*, Nov. 6, 1986, p. 81
178 In her speech . . . of political power": speech, May 1, 1986
179 "Business wants . . . grievances of labor": speech to Philippine Chamber of Commerce and Industry, at Manila Hotel, July 21, 1986
179 The next month . . . the problem: "Aquino orders crackdown on strikes," *MT*, Aug. 14, 1986, p. 1
179 Sugar workers who . . . good idea": interview by author, Jan. 30. 1986
180 "Do what you . . . rice and corn: Heherson "Sonny" Alvarez, Oct. 27, 1986
180 "Peasant members . . . not in use: "Farmers set to march in Malacañang," *PDI*, Oct. 18, 1986, p. 1
180 Cory explained . . . the money": answer to author's question at press conference, Nov. 17, 1986
180 "Land reform was . . . business community": Angelito Banayo, Dec. 5, 1986
180 "At this stage . . . signals": Alvarez, Jan. 6, 1987
180 In South Cotabato . . . the tenants: "FFF exposes harassment of South Cotabato tenants," *Malaya*, Nov. 4, 1986, p. 15
181 Luis Taruc . . . landowners: Luis Taruc, Nov. 17, 1986
181 The Cojuangcos . . . December, 1986: "Hacienda Luisita residents restive," *MT*, Nov. 10, 1986, p. 1

181 Alvarez was . . . nationwide," he said: author's notes, Manila Hotel r●
table, Dec. 8, 1986

Chapter 15, The Game of Politics

182 Once during . . . moral crusade": Jose "Apeng" Yap, Dec. 29, 1986

183 Partido ng Bayan: It was set up after the revolution by leftist leaders, including Sison and Dante and KMU leader Rolando Olalia.

183 Cory acknowledged . . . shake down: "Holding it all together," *FEER*, Aug. 28, 1986

183 Enrile said he considered . . . the KBL: "A big joke," *PT*, June 27, 1986, p. 1

184 Cory's relatives . . . with a mission": Jose "Peping" Cojuangco, Dec. 11, 1986

184 "She wants to . . . be polarized": Emigdio "Ding" Tanjuatco, Dec. 17, 1986

184 Peping discussed . . . time: Cojuangco, Dec. 11, 1986

184 But in New York . . . picking candidates: author's notes, New York, Sept. 22, 1986

184 Cory met with . . . went ahead: Cojuangco, Dec. 11, 1986

184 "Definitely . . . Cory candidates": "Cory doesn't need a party—Pimentel," *MC*, Sept. 30, 1986

184 "We still want her . . . involved": Yap, Dec. 29, 1986

184 "There is no question . . . deals: ibid.

185 Laban would . . . any other: "Cory doesn't need a party—Pimentel," p. 1

185 Lakas ng Bansa . . . October 8: The core group included Peping Cojuangco, Public Works Minister Orlando Mercado, Tarlac Governor Bren Guiao, Auditor Teofisto Guingona, Metropolitan Water System head Jose Yap, Minister of Reorganization Luis Villafuerte, National Resources Minister Ernesto Maceda, Political Affairs Minister Antonio Cuenco, Commission on Good Government deputy chief Raul Daza, Justice Minister Neptali Gonzales, Agriculture Minister Ramon Mitra, Agrarian Reform Minister Heherson Alverez, and Budget Minister Alberto Romulo.

185 At her press . . . we are now": author's notes

186 Political Affairs . . . the future": "New political group launched," *MB*, Nov. 9, 1986, p. 1

186 "They are not . . . things": Tanjuatco, Dec. 17, 1986

186 Yap said . . . notorious": Yap, Dec. 29, 1986

186 Unido was . . . Malvar: "Laban opens door to KBL politicians," *Malaya*, Nov. 20, 1986, p. 1

Chapter 16, The Hot Fall

188 She replied . . . would not: "Aquino warns US not to meddle," *BD*, Sept. 11, 1986, p. 21

188 "Johnny is on . . . Cayetano: Renato "Rene" Cayetano, Dec. 19, 1986

189 By then, Cory . . . their loyalties: Luis Villafuerte, Dec. 28, 1986

189 Villafuerte told Cory . . . part of the team": ibid.

190 He said later . . . joking: Juan Ponce Enrile, Dec. 23, 1986

190 "Are we on . . . ?": "60 Minutes," CBS-TV, Sept. 14, 1986. The program was broadcast in the Philippines over the U.S. Military's Far East Network."

190 "At that time . . . enjoy this": "We have to reach out," *Asiaweek*, Sept. 28, 1986, p. 14

190 Normally, she . . . buoyant: interview, presidential aide, not for attribution.

Her aides did not . . . as that": Solita "Winnie" Monsod, Dec. 17, 1986

191 "Cory, you hit . . . she replied: "Cory, you hit a home run," PT, p. 1

191 Enrile spoke . . . atrocities," he declared: "Enrile to Cory: 'Decide rebel problem now'," PT, Sept. 20, 1986, p. 2

192 "I am not . . . decisively": "Cease-fire before peace talks: Aquino," BD, Sept. 25, 1986, p. 25

192 "I have to issue . . . all the Filipinos": palace official, not for attribution.

193 He said it . . . Salvador: "No clear anti-reb plan, says Enrile," MT, Oct. 10, 1986, p. 1

193 "There was order . . . later: "No anti-insurgency policy yet—Enrile," PDI, Oct. 10, 1986, p. 1

193 Ramos's spokesman . . . rebel troops: "NDF invited to probe 'hamlets'," MC, Oct. 10, 1986, p. 1

193 "When I started . . . now," she said: author's notes, Oct. 10, 1986

194 "You can't imagine . . . no cash": ibid.

194 He charged that . . . new elections: "Enrile puzzle," New Day, Oct. 13, 1986, p. 2

194 "Why can't Enrile . . . advisors: Villafuerte, Dec. 28, 1986

195 "I'm expendable . . . the revolution": "Enrile challenges Aquino to fire him," MT, Oct. 14, 1986, p. 1

195 He said cabinet . . . discussed": "Enrile boycotts cabinet meeting," Malaya, Oct. 15, 1986, p. 1

195 Laurel announced . . . not approved: "Laurel offers to mediate," MC, Oct. 16, 1986, p. 1

195 He claimed . . . decisions: "Enrile, Aquino heading on a collision course?" BD, Oct. 17, 1986, p. 12

195 She . . . opposition to Communism: Jose "Apeng" Yap, Dec. 29, 1986

196 "I always believe . . . my actions": "Cory rejects Enrile's demand to fire eight," MC, Oct. 25, 1986, p. 1

196 Cory would tell them . . . his insecurity: Teodoro "Teddy" Locsin, Jan. 4, 1987

196 "Why is it . . . the country?": interview, presidential aide, not for attribution.

196 "In all my . . . that way": interview with journalist, not for attribution

196 "The head of . . . institutional church": interview, Bishop Antonio Fortich, Oct. 15, 1986

196 "Colonel . . . with you": Bishop Fortich, Oct. 15, 1986

197 The NPA said . . . battalions: "Promise of revolution thwarted," MC, Oct. 20, 1986, p. 10

197 "Monsignor . . . dialogue": Bishop Fortich, Oct. 15, 1986

197 "I don't think . . . people," she declared: author's notes, Oct. 16, 1986

198 Cory, the archbishop . . . press later that day: Locsin, Jan. 4, 1987

199 "Father Torre is one . . . run-around": interview, Archbishop Piamonte, Oct. 17, 1986

199 Later, at a meeting . . . laughter, then applause: author's notes, Oct. 17, 1986.

199 In a northern . . . against the insurgents: "Aquino urged to ignore calls for military action vs. rebels," MT, Oct. 18, 1986, p. 1

200 He criticized her . . . share power: "Cory won't fire me—Enrile," Peoples Journal, Oct. 21, 1986, p. 1

200 He said if she . . . to Malacañang": "Cory meet Iloilo rebs; Enrile alarmed," PDI, Oct. 18, 1986, p. 1

200 Back in Manila, Laurel . . . fail: "Peace talks will fail, says Laurel," PDI, Oct. 19, 1986, p. 1

200 That same day . . . political statements: Amando Doronila, "A strongman emerges," MC, Oct. 26, 1986, p. 9

200 In Manila, Laurel . . . retained," he said: "Cabinet acts to head off crisis," *MC*, Oct. 20, 1986, p. 1

200 He lobbed . . . would collapse: "Cory won't fire me—Enrile," p. 1

201 By abolishing . . . Marcos regime": "President told to step down," *PDI*, Oct. 21, 1986, p. 1

201 "It's not her style . . . as you think": interview, presidential aide, not for attribution.

201 Cory told the gathering . . . my people": "Critics of peace efforts warned," *MT*, Oct. 21, 1986, p. 1; and "President tells defense chief to recant controversial remarks," *PDI*, Oct. 21, 1986, p. 1

202 She told the group . . . to do it": "Aquino to disarm CHDFs in Mindanao," *PT*, Oct. 21, 1986, p. 1

202 Ramos visited Cory . . . with her: Malou Mangahas, "Peace talk tack," *MC*, Oct. 28, 1986, p. 6

202 Hoping to calm . . . with his people: Belinda Olivares-Cunanan, "Reconciliation, Cory-style," *PDI*, Oct. 23, 1986, p. 1; and Jose Concepcion, Dec. 24, 1986

203 "The NDF deceived . . . February revolution: "Ramos trying to mediate between Aquino, Enrile," *BD*, Oct. 22, 1986, p. 24

203 Cory started . . . : The account of the meeting is a compilation of material from Locsin, Jan. 4, 1987; Belinda Olivares-Cunanan, "Reconciliation, Cory-style," p. 1; Luis Beltran, "How Cory disarmed Johnny," *PDI*, Oct. 23, 1986, p. 4; Malou Mangahas, "Enrile did not want peace talk," *MC*, Oct. 26, 1986, p. 1

204 She told them there . . . will be like this": "Cory yields to two Enrile demands," *PDI*, Oct. 24, 1986, p. 5

205 He won agreement . . . the military: Doronila, "A strongman emerges," p. 9

205 Cory told the . . . "cease-talk": Concepcion, Dec. 24, 1986

205 One participant . . . and Enrile: Villafuerte, Dec. 28, 1986

205 Concepcion . . . Pimentel": Concepcion, Dec. 24, 1986

205 She revealed that . . . and graft: author's notes, Oct. 22, 1986

207 Bracing against . . . by talking": "Aquino-Enrile 'cease-talk' temporary, say govt officials," *PT*, Oct. 23, 1986, p. 6

207 "I support the chain . . . the center": Malou Mangahas, "Peace talk tack," p. 6

207 "What should . . . enigmatic grin: author's notes, Oct. 24, 1986

207 "I fight my own . . . fight": "Cory rejects Enrile's demand to fire eight,"

207 Four days after . . . as himself: "Enrile resumes attack on Cory," *MC*, Oct. 26, 1986, p. 1

208 "The President . . . shenanigans": Rommel Corro, "Nobody knows who's telling the truth," *PT*, Oct. 207 1986, p. 4

208 Press Secretary . . . United States": "Aquino said to have full Reagan Support," *BD*, Oct. 28, 1986, p. 28

208 Cayetano . . . Cory's government: Cayetano, Dec. 19, 1986

209 She told a nurses' . . . warfare": "Dialogue first before war, says Aquino," *MB*, Oct. 29, 1986, p. 1

209 "We preceded almost . . . could survive?" Enrile asked: "Cory owes presidency to AFP, says MND," *PT*, Oct. 31, 1986, p. 1

209 He classed . . . presidential election: "Laurel-Enrile deal on polls revealed," *Malaya*, Oct. 26, 1986, p. 1

209 A few days . . . plebiscite: "Laurel sets minimum terms for stability," *Malaya*, Oct. 30, 1986, p. 1

209 And he proposed . . . ratification": "Cory turns down Doy's election bid," *MC*, Oct. 31, 1986, p. 1

209 "I do not feel . . . Mr. Marcos": "Aquino denies deal with Enrile," *MC*, Nov. 1, 1986, p. 3

209 Ramos believed . . . cease-fire: interview, Ramos's spokesman Col. Honesto Isleta, Dec. 11, 1986

209 At a forum . . . in private: "Ramos backs Aquino power," *Malaya*, Nov. 1, 1986, p. 1

210 "It's hopeless . . . together": Locsin, Jan. 4, 1987

Chapter 17, God Save the Queen

211 "They were rumors . . . the government": interview with high-ranking military officer associated with the pro-Enrile faction, not for attribution.

212 "The leaders . . . power to them": "Collision Course," *Time*, Nov. 10, 1986, p. 12

212 "If I am asked . . . of the government": ibid.

212 At the start . . . deadline: "NDF calls for 100-day cease-fire," MC, Nov. 2, 1986, p. 1

212 The military representative: Major General Jose Magno

213 That evening Victor Corpus . . . : account of meeting from interview with Corpus; and Letty Jimenez-Magsanoc, "Cory acts to stop Enrile plot," *PDI*, Nov. 9, 1986, p. 1

214 The NPA announced . . . Aquino government: "NPA, NAFP together on the campaign trail," *MT*, Nov. 5, 1986, p. 5

215 Cory saw . . . no reaction: Teodoro "Teddy" Locsin, Jan. 4, 1987

215 But officials . . . it quits": Rene Saguisag, Dec. 13, 1986

215 "She's tough . . . Saguisag said: ibid.

215 "It was astonishing . . . her behavior: palace aide, not for attribution.

215 However, she began . . . against her: Locsin, Jan. 4, 1987

215 Ramos, in a . . . by the military: "Enrile assessment 'accurate'—Ramos," *PDI*, Nov. 6, 1986, p. 2

215 "We are working . . . clear of politics: "Ramos says NAFP places highest premium on unity," *Philippine Star*, Nov. 6, 1986, p. 1

216 However, Cory . . . Paredes gathering: Soriano and Concepcion said a high-ranking officer who had been there told her; Locsin denied that.

216 Her confidence . . . the discussion: Concepcion, who is close to Cardinal Sin, said in an interview with the author that Cory complained to the Cardinal that Ramos hadn't told her. Sin denied this to the author. Citation also in Letty Jimenez-Magsanoc, "Cory acts to stop Enrile plot," p. 1

216 Ramos would . . . Born March 18, 1928, a graduate of West Point, class of 1950, with a master's degree in civil engineering from the University of Illinois, Ramos was a physical fitness buff who liked to jog at dawn and match his troops at strenuous exercise. He studied psychological warfare at Fort Bragg, North Carolina, was a reconaissance platoon leader with the Philippine troops in the Korean War and operations officer for the First Philippine Civic Action Group, non-combat troops, in Vietnam.

216 That same day . . . destabilizing": Armed Forces of the Philippines press release, Nov. 6, 1986

216 They promised . . . of command: "Key AFP men to uphold 'chain of command'," *PDI*, Nov. 9, 1986, p. 1

216 Ramos confronted . . . would happen: Col. Honesto Isleta, Dec. 11, 1986

216 He also met with . . . recognized abroad: interview, Brigadier General Alexander Aguirre, AFP chief of operations, Dec. 26, 1986

217 "All right . . . of the minister": Isleta, Dec. 11, 1986

217 "There are just . . . Ramos commented: "Ramos warns coup plotters in AFP," *PDI*, Nov. 7, 1986, p. 1

217 In the midst . . . Council: Isleta, Dec. 11, 1986

217 John Singlaub . . . Iran: Singlaub said he knew nothing of any illegal arms transfers.

217 The first, Enrile's . . . plan absurd: Juan Ponce Enrile, Dec. 19, 1986

218 "Enrile wants . . . the cabinet": presidential aide, not for attribution.

218 Military intelligence . . . Olalia: Locsin, Jan. 4, 1987

218 with top military officials . . . Air Force Chief Brigadier General Antonio Sotelo, Constabulary chief Renato De Villa, Capital Security Command commander Brigadier General Ramon Montana, and Western Police Department Superintendent Alfredo Lim.

218 The military officials . . . of God": Concepcion, Dec. 24, 1986, and Cardinal Sin, Dec. 27, 1986

218 The military discussed . . . slaughtered: Concepcion, Dec. 24, 1986

218 Adding to . . . military supremacy: Letty-Jimenez-Magsanoc, "Cory acts to stop Enrile plot," p. 1; and Locsin, Jan. 4, 1987

218 Corpus met . . . support the coup: Corpus, Dec. 20, 1986

218 The RAM boys . . . Enrile": "Ramos warns coup plotters in AFP," p. 1

219 "I have strongly . . . movement," he said; "Laurel urges military solution to rebellion," *PT*, Nov. 17, 1986, p. 1

219 And he gave . . . records: "Laurel submits to Aquino list of OICs he wants out," *MT*, Nov. 17, 1986, p. 1

219 She told them . . . problems: "Cory acts to stop Enrile plot," p. 1

219 The same morning . . . for investigation: Corpus, Dec. 20, 1986; and "Corpus names plotters of P. Miranda bombing," *PT*, Nov. 8, 1986, p. 1

221 Cardinal Sin called . . . bloodshed": Cardinal Sin, Dec. 27, 1986 and "President, Enrile on 'good terms,' says Sin," *MC*, Nov. 10, 1986, p. 1

222 "Every time I . . . Right now, no": author's notes, Nov. 7, 1986

222 She also promised to look . . . of a deadline," she said: ibid.

223 "I've heard . . . detail," she told him: Locsin, Jan. 4, 1987; Letty Jimenez-Magsanoc, "Cory acts to stop Enrile plot," p. 1; Luis Villafuerte, Dec. 28, 1986; "No coup, Enrile assures Aquino," *Malaya*, Nov. 9, 1986, p. 1

223 This talk . . . futile: Locsin, Jan. 4, 1987

223 If that day . . . be approved: "Laurel accepts charter but . . . ," *Philippine Star*, Nov. 8, 1986, p. 2

223 Ramos, pressing . . . from Japan: Max Soliven, "Cory needs 'peace talks' with military," *Philippine Star*, Nov. 13, 1986, p. 4

224 Bandila . . . were necessary: Emanuel "Noel" Soriano, Dec. 22, 1986

224 "How can we . . . this country: "Enrile, Honasan rapped for arms importation," *PT*, Nov. 10, 1986, p. 1

224 Ramos also . . . the armed forces: Aguirre, Dec. 26, 1986

224 When Cory learned . . . He agreed: Concepcion, Dec. 24, 1986

224 "I will not . . . to the streets": speech at Philippine Convention Center, Nov. 9, 1986

Chapter 18, Coup Redux

226 "If I don't . . . presidency": Rene Saguisag, Dec. 13, 1980

227 Cory said publicly . . . in Japan: "Aquino's new start," *Asiaweek*, Dec. 7, 1986, p. 14

227 "They didn't . . . palace official: interview, palace official, not for attribution.

227 Shortly before . . . Manila airport: Luis Beltran, "'Coop-koos' fail to rattle Cory," *PDI*, Nov. 20, 1986, p. 4

227 She laughed . . . story: interview, palace official, not for attribution.

227 At the Monday morning . . . of the military": author's notes, Nov. 10, 1986

227 Before she boarded . . . to succeed": "People alerted on coup," *MB*, Nov. 11, 1986, p. 1

228 They found Enrile . . . stunned: Emanuel "Noel" Soriano, Dec. 22, 1986

228 He banned all . . . the plotters: "Troop movement in Metro banned," *Malaya*, Nov. 11, 1986, p. 1

228 An embarrassing . . . highly embarrassed: Interview, local journalist, not for attribution.

229 Following a series . . . let-up": "Ramos orders attacks on NPA," *MC*, Nov. 12, 1986, p. 1

229 "A coalition . . . unwritten" agreement, he said: "Laurel: Gov't born out of 'informal' agreement," *Malaya*, Nov. 11, 1986, p. 2

229 noted there was . . . elections. "No evidence that we won, says Laurel," *Malaya*, Nov. 12, 1986, p. 1

229 He said he had "no knowledge" . . . provide them: "Doy owns up arms shipment," *Malaya*, Nov. 12, 1986, p. 1

229 Palace officials . . . of a coup: Presidential press secretary Teodoro Benigno, quoted in "Plotters considered killing Cory: palace," *MC*, Nov. 25, 1986, p. 1

229 "He is not an . . . replacing him": "Aquino says Enrile stays," *PDI*, Nov. 14, 1986, p. 1

230 "Joker, am . . . roared: interview, deputy press secretary Benedicto "Ben" David, Dec. 15, 1986

230 Less amusing . . . off the plane: Luis Beltran, "'Coop-koos' fail to rattle Cory," *PDI*, Nov. 20, 1986, p. 4

230 . . . of a coup: On that same day, Wednesday, November 12, U.S. military officials, at a meeting of the Philippine-U.S. Mutual Defense Board, offered their Filipino counterparts helicopter gunships and strategic maps to help them prosecute the war if the cease-fire collapsed: cable CIR-17-87 from Philippine Ministry of Foreign Affairs

230 "Every resource . . . justice done": author's notes, Nov. 14, 1986

230 "Why don't . . . it?" she replied: interview, not for attribution.

231 "There is a possibility . . . what I've done": "Testing times for Cory Aquino," *Asiaweek*, Nov. 30, 1986, p. 9

231 On her TV program . . . fatalist": "President vows to end destabilization," *MC*, Nov. 20, 1986, p. 1

231 "We don't know . . . an uprising": Saguisag, Dec. 13, 1986

232 The U.S. Embassy . . . with him: interview, Mary Carlin, press officer, U.S. Embassy, Manila, Dec. 18, 1986

232 Acknowledging . . . up already": "How Ramos foiled 'coup attempt'," *PT*, Nov. 25, 1986, p. 1

233 Benigno told reporters . . . to strike now: "Arroyo powers to be clipped," *MC*, Nov. 22, 1986, p. 1

233 Cory's supporters . . . the signal: Emigdio "Ding" Tanjuatco, Dec. 17, 1986

233 Her strategy . . . the plebiscite: interview, palace official, not for attribution.

233 The regional commander . . . communism": "Soldiers stage rallies in south," *MC*, Nov. 23, 1986, p. 1

235 Cayetano later . . . are holed up": Renato Cayetano, Dec. 19, 1986

235 Six truckloads . . . a clash: Brig. Gen. Alexander Aguirre, Dec. 26, 1986

236 "Why are you . . . maximum force": Conversation reconstructed from following

reports: "Another long day's journey into history," *PDI*, Nov. 25, 1986, p. 5; David Veridiano, "The foiled coup try: how it was planned," *PDI*, Nov. 24, 1986, p. 1; "Aquino's new start," *Asiaweek*, Dec. 7, 1986, p. 14; and Max Soliven, "The inside story of longest night," *Philippine Star*, Dec. 6, 1986, p. 4

236 "My chief of . . . people below": Brig. Gen. Aguirre, Dec. 26, 1986

237 "If we did not . . . stability yet": Dec. 11, 1986

237 When Cory asked . . . humiliate him": Max Soliven, "The inside story of longest night," p. 4

237 He would later . . . civil war: "Enrile ouster averted civil war, Ramos says," *MC*, Dec. 5, 1986, p. 1

237 Cory announced . . . government: Malou Mangahas, "President makes a 'checkmate'," *MC*, Nov. 24, 1986, p. 1

238 His absence . . . the cabinet: Luis Villafuerte, Dec. 28, 1986

238 Cory had fired . . . nothing happened": Saguisag, Dec. 13, 1986

238 "Let's face it . . . don't hesitate": "Aquino's new start," *Asiaweek*, Dec. 7, 1986, p. 18

239 Cory was impressed . . . had ever had: Teodoro "Teddy" Locsin, Jan. 4, 1987

239 "Of late my . . . if they try": statement by president, Malacañang Press Center, Nov. 23, 1986

239 He later told . . . behind her": "Cory lets Enrile go; vows new beginning," *Malaya*, Nov. 24, 1986, p. 1

239 Like Ramos . . . class of 1943: He also studied at the infantry school at Fort Benning, Georgia, the General Staff College in Fort Leavenworth, Kentucky, and the Defense Resources Management Course of the University of Pittsburgh.

239 Cory's confidence . . . he became president: Rodney Tasker, "A soldier's soldier enters the political theater," *FEER*, Dec. 4, 1986, p. 21

240 "There are New . . . Magsaysay": "Ileto to fight rebels with united military," *MC*, Nov. 24, 1986, p. 1

240 "Maybe there are . . . own way": "No MND action against Enrile," *PT*, Nov. 25, 1986, p. 1

240 Ileto said later . . . properly utilized": "Ileto to disband RAM," *PT*, Nov. 26, 1986, p. 1

240 "We could have . . . a division": interview, not for attribution.

240 Cory announced his . . . like threats: Saguisag, Dec. 13, 1986

241 Reporter James . . . U.S. links": interview, James Clad, Jan. 3, 1987

241 Laurel, in the . . . its challengers: "Laurel attacks freedom charter," *MC*, Nov. 26, 1986, p. 1

241 She realized . . . later on: interview, palace official, not for attribution.

242 The negotiators . . . They were Ramon "Monching" Mitra, Teofisto "Tito" Guingona, and Maria Serena "Maris" Diokno for the government, and Antonio Maria "Tony" Zumel, Saturnino "Satur" Ocampo, and Carolina Malay-Ocampo (his wife) for the NDF.

327 "It has often . . . bedroom of history": speech to Asian Development Bank Women's Club, Nov. 30, 1986

Chapter 19, Victory

245 "Believe me when . . . our country": "Aquino appeals for patience," *New York Times*, Jan. 21, 1987, p. A9

245 KMP chairman . . . barricades": "Death in Manila," *Time*, Feb. 2, 1987, p. 34; James Clad, "Revolt and retribution," *FEER*, Feb. 5, 1987, p. 11

246 "The Aquino government . . . dictatorship" Seth Mydens, "Philippine army chief says troops overracted," *New York Times*, Jan. 24, 1987, p. A4

246 "In the period . . . sobriety": "Death in Manila," p. 34

246 "We want to . . . a democracy": "Toll is 18 in Manila Shooting; leftist chief eases criticism," *New York Times*, Jan. 26, 1987, p. A2

246 "In the past . . . were unjustified": Mydens, p. A4

246 "There is blood . . . her troops?" "Troops in Manila Kill 12 in crowd at leftist rally," *New York Times*, Jan. 24, 1987, p. A4; and Mydens, p. A4

248 "There is no hope . . . it is": Mydens, "Army dissidents reported foiled in Manila raids," *New York Times*, Jan. 28, 1987, p. 1

248 "The situation is . . . has come": Clad, p. 10; "Crisis for Aquino," *Asiaweek*, Feb. 8, 1987, p. 10-13; "Bungled coup, foiled return," *Time*, Feb. 9, 1987, p. 34

249 Cory had ordered . . . comply: "Bungled coup, foiled return," p. 34; "Cory gets tough," *Newsweek*, Feb. 9, 1987, p. 30; Mydens, "National Reconciliation remains an elusive goal for Aquino," *New York Times*, Feb. 1, 1987, Sec. 4

250 "Everybody is . . . process": "Crisis for Aquino," p. 14

250 "Now I am . . . coup: David Shipler, "U.S. foils Marcos plan to return for coup attempt," *New York Times*, Jan. 30, 1987, p. 1; and "National Reconciliation remains an elusive goal for Aquino," Sec. 4

250 Nevertheless, Cory . . . account": cable CIR-37-87 from Philippine Ministry of Foreign Affairs

250 A palace official . . . Marcos: quote from Joker Arroyo in "Crisis for Aquino," p. 9

251 "I let them . . . law and order": cable CIR-37-87 from Philippine Ministry of Foreign Affairs

251 "I have been . . . countrymen": Clayton Jones, "Filipino plebiscite: a testing ground," *Christian Science Monitor*, Feb. 2, 1987, p. 1

Index

Index

Index

Index